CHINA AND HONG KONG: THE ECONOMIC NEXUS

CHINA AND HONG KONG
The Economic Nexus

Editor: A.J. Youngson

HONG KONG
OXFORD UNIVERSITY PRESS
OXFORD NEW YORK MELBOURNE
1983

Oxford University Press

Oxford London Glasgow
New York Toronto Melbourne Auckland
Kuala Lumpur Singapore Hong Kong Tokyo
Delhi Bombay Calcutta Madras Karachi
Nairobi Dar es Salaam Cape Town

and associated companies in
Beirut Berlin Ibadan Mexico City Nicosia

First published in 1983

ISBN 0 19 581518 1

Printed by Ko's Art Printing Co.,
16-18 Westlands Road, Quarry Bay, Hong Kong.
Published by Oxford University Press,
Warwick House, Quarry Bay, Hong Kong.

Contributors

Joseph Chai
Lecturer in Economics at the University of Hong Kong.

L.C. Chau
Senior Lecturer in Economics at the University of Hong Kong.

Edward K.Y. Chen
Director of the Centre of Asian Studies at the University of Hong Kong.

Fu-Sen Chen
Senior Lecturer in Economics at the University of Hong Kong.

Tow Cheung
Lecturer in Economics at the University of Hong Kong.

Audrey Donnithorne
Professorial Fellow, Australian National University.

John C. Hsu
Lecturer in Economics at the University of Hong Kong.

Y.C. Jao
Reader in Economics at the University of Hong Kong.

A.J. Youngson
Professor Emeritus, Australian National University.

Contents

Tables

Introduction

A.J. YOUNGSON

Hong Kong is a part of China that happens, for the time being, to be administered by someone else. The island itself, which helps to form the finest natural harbour on the south coast of China, and one of the great natural harbours of the world, was obtained by the British in 1841 as a result of the First Opium War. Nineteen years later Britain acquired the Kowloon Peninsula on the other side of the harbour and, in 1898, an additional part of the mainland now known as the New Territories. This last was not ceded by China, however, but was leased to Britain for 99 years. Each of these successive acquisitions was, at the time, of no more than potential importance. All that is now Hong Kong was, when given up by China, little used, almost entirely barren and very thinly populated. British policy was to create a trading post which would facilitate trade with China and throughout the Orient, and to do this on free trade principles. No attempt was therefore made to isolate Hong Kong from China, and its population, which grew rapidly, continued to be overwhelmingly Chinese. Moreover, the British followed their usual practice of leaving local customs and local laws largely intact, except where these seriously conflicted with normal European practice. As a result of these policies Hong Kong remained and remains Chinese not only geographically, but also ethnically, culturally and often emotionally.

Separated from China only by the artifice of political arrangements, Hong Kong was entirely free to pursue its own economic policies (subject to British approval) for one hundred years. But in 1941 it was occupied by Japanese troops. And only four years after their departure in 1945 China emerged as a great, united, Communist power. How long would the new Chinese Government tolerate a capitalist economy on its doorstep, one moreover whose very existence depended on 'unequal treaties' the validity of which China has never recognized? The rise of China, the diminishing of Britain, and the deep disfavour into which colonialism fell after the Second World War combined to make the position of Hong Kong look extremely uncertain. And although the city state has survived and prospered greatly for over thirty years, concern about its legal and political future has recently become widespread and has begun to have some influence on current economic decisions.

The trouble about Hong Kong as an independent entity and a field for capitalist enterprise is easily stated; the lease on the New Territories runs out in 1997. Even if China were to resume control over only the land covered by the lease, an independent existence for the rest of Hong Kong would at once become impossible; the New Territories and the rest of Hong Kong are economically inseparable. It is therefore easily understandable that there has been a good deal of recent discussion about what Beijing will do, and when. The answer, of course, is that no one knows. But the opinion of most educated Chinese in Hong Kong — who are almost certainly the best judges in this matter — is that China will not do anything that will be contrary to her own economic advantage. There seem to be two good reasons for accepting this view. Firstly, the Chinese are a very practical people; they are not likely to pursue a non-utilitarian objective — in this case, getting rid of a relic of colonialism on their doorstep — regardless of cost. Secondly, China had an excellent opportunity to absorb Hong Kong in 1967, and she did not take it. When the Red Guards on the other side of the border were running amok, the local Communists organized violent anti-British riots in Hong Kong, and serious disturbances continued for months. But the Chinese Government made no move to intervene so as to 'restore order'. Support from Beijing was little more than verbal, and the organizers of the riots seem to have ended in disgrace. It did not suit China to have Hong Kong's trade disrupted for very long.

Nevertheless, although China may be in no hurry to take steps to change the situation, she is also disinclined, in characteristic fashion, to enter into hard and fast commitments that would in any way hamper her future freedom of action, even though such commitments are wanted to clarify Hong Kong's political future and reduce business uncertainty. The situation is thus one of delicate balance. The Hong Kong Government seeks to promote prosperity in Hong Kong, but is at the same time very careful not to offend China in any way; while China makes no promises, but acts so as to provide as much reassurance about Hong Kong's future as appears to be needed to secure the continuation of enterprise and investment in Hong Kong at a satisfactory rate. How long this kind of balancing act can continue is anybody's guess. The prospect of 1997 is already a deterrent to investment in Hong Kong, especially foreign investment; although how much of a deterrent it is hard to estimate. Voices are to be heard saying that all long-term investment is being discouraged because no one knows how or whether returns on the capital invested will be secured after 1997 — or even after some earlier date if China changes the rules. This is certainly a serious problem, although its seriousness can be exaggerated. Investment in property is most liable to be affected. But this is only part of the story. A great deal of investment in Hong Kong — probably most industrial investment — is undertaken in the expectation of the capital being recovered in three to five years. Investments with a longer life are most often in the field of social overhead capital, undertaken by government, and in such cases the problem of guaranteeing returns could probably be the subject of reasonable negotiation. The fact is that both government and business in Hong Kong have to live with uncertainties and imponderables some of which are of a different kind from those usually found elsewhere; although the Hong Kong mixture is not necessarily, to those who are used to it, a great deal more disturbing.

Living with China has affected Hong Kong in another way, and has created problems over a much longer span of time. For centuries it has been a Chinese practice to escape from brigandage, starvation or war by taking refuge in another province or another city. Prior to 1941, the people of China consistently treated Hong Kong, in this respect, just as they treated Mukden (Shenyang) or Shanghai or any other place. It was available to them if they wanted to go there, for safety or other advantage; and from time to time many did. But in the late 1930's, when the Japanese invaded China, a mass exodus began, and approximately 750,000 people moved into Hong Kong between 1937 and 1939. By 1945, as a result of the Japanese occupation, the movement had been reversed, and the population had declined sharply to about 600,000; but civil war in China now produced the same response as war with Japan had done, and by the end of 1950 the population of Hong Kong had soared upwards again and had reached not much less than 2.5 million. Such massive influxes of people have not taken place a third time (although it is said that in 1962 100,000 immigrants crossed the border in six weeks), but movement into Hong Kong has been persistent, in some years on a large scale, and it has considerably affected the Hong Kong economy as well as tying Hong Kong to China by innumerable personal connections.

It is not possible to be sure about numbers, because since late in 1974 there have been two flows of immigrants, the legal and the illegal. Legal immigrants are those who have been given exit permits by the Chinese authorities. The understanding is that these are limited to 55,000 per annum, but actual numbers have fluctuated widely. In 1973, 56,000 legal immigrants arrived in Hong Kong, but by 1976 the number had fallen to 18,000. In the last years of the decade it increased again when many people were given permits which had been refused when the Gang of Four were in power. In general, the Hong Kong Government has sought to limit the flow of legal immigrants well below the limit of 55,000 per annum, but what is actually done is at the discretion of the Chinese authorities. Illegal immigrants are another matter. It was reckoned in 1974 that more than 27,000 illegal immigrants had entered Hong Kong in that year; and the government, alarmed about the effect of such numbers on the demand for housing, education, transport and other services, introduced a policy of returning to China all illegal immigrants captured anywhere before reaching Hong Kong Island itself. For a few years this policy reduced to less than 10,000 per annum the number of illegals who evaded capture and remained in Hong Kong. But in 1978 the figure suddenly rose (according to official sources) to just under 30,000, in 1979 to 197,600, and in the first ten months of 1980 stood at about 150,000. After discussions between the Governor of Hong Kong and the Chinese authorities a new policy was then introduced; all future illegal immigrants were to be repatriated to China, wherever and whenever they were found.

This series of developments is instructive in several ways. As far as the economy is concerned, the numbers were large enough to be significant. For the five years 1976 to 1981 the natural increase of population was about 270,000; immigrants from China, legal and illegal, added about 480,000 to this figure, or over 10 per cent of the total population at the beginning of 1976. It is little wonder that the government was concerned about the impact on the housing situation and the school programme. These immigrants also affected the labour market; they helped to keep wages down and labour ill-organized, and presumably also helped to retard the introduction of more capital-intensive processes to make higher-quality goods. But in seeking to restrain the inflow, the Hong Kong Government was in no position to act as if Hong Kong was an independent state. To close the frontier was unthinkable; migration across it had always taken place. The most that could be hoped for was Chinese agreement to strengthen their own forces so as to intercept more would-be emigrants. And to seek this agreement it was felt necessary for the Governor himself to go to Guangzhou and talk with high-ranking Chinese officials. In the event, the Chinese proved complaisant. Indeed, they seem to have welcomed the idea of more restraint, and to have suggested that the existing policy amounted to welcoming illegal immigrants into Hong Kong. Less emigration would suit China; it was reported that the workforce in some communes in Guangdong had recently fallen by 70 per cent.

Thus 1980 saw a major innovation in policy. For the first time ever, both China and Hong Kong are trying strictly to limit movement across the frontier to those, supposedly not more than 55,000 per annum, who are given Chinese exit permits. China has thus allowed Hong Kong to become a little more separate. But the frontier is not closed to migration. Friends and relatives from China are still joining friends and relatives in Hong Kong. Moreover, it is still true — and under present arrangements will continue to be true for some years to come — that a very large proportion of the population of Hong Kong was born in China. In 1971 the figure was 56 per cent; by 1981 it had been greatly reduced by the natural increase of population within Hong Kong, but was nevertheless only a fraction under 40 per cent. Probably few people in Hong Kong do not have relatives whom they know or know about in China. Hence arises the exodus at festival times of families going to visit in Guangdong or further afield, taking with them as gifts television sets, transistor radios, and all other manner of consumer goods available in Hong Kong. At Chinese New

Year, 1982, approximately half a million people crossed the border into China.

This strong human connection is matched by economic ties. Hong Kong has always been economically linked with China, but the form and the strength of the economic connection have varied a great deal since 1949. Historically, Hong Kong has acted as an entrepôt economy, facilitating trade in the Pacific region and especially trade between China on the one hand and Europe and America on the other. This role has required Hong Kong to develop a network of services such as are provided by refuelling points, ship-repairing yards, storage facilities, merchant houses, insurance companies and banks. War in China, and after 1941 general war in the Pacific, brought Hong Kong's economy to a virtual standstill. When the war was over Hong Kong prepared to resume her traditional role. But this proved to be impossible. Civil war in China did not help; and in 1950 the Korean War broke out, causing the United States to impose an embargo on the import of goods from China, and the United Nations to impose an embargo on the export of strategic goods to China. With much of her trade cut off Hong Kong had to find a new future, and so she embarked on the business — not very extensive in Hong Kong before the late 1940's — of making and exporting manufactured goods.

It is as an exporter of her own manufactures that Hong Kong has become world-famous. Starting with plain cotton goods and simple garments, she has become one of the world's greatest exporters of fabrics and garments of all kinds; she is the world's biggest exporter of toys; and she has a sizeable share of the world market in such items as transistor radios, watches, watch bands, electronic components, scientific instruments, artificial flowers and printing. All this was built up in less than thirty years — a staggering achievement. The structure of Hong Kong's economy was thus radically altered, while at the same time her population increased and her standard of living rose. Less than two million thirty years ago, the population is now over five million; more than one-third that of Australia. There has been a sustained rise in the standard of living (conventionally measured) that is perhaps without parallel in recent history; and since 1961 gross domestic product per capita at constant prices has risen by almost 7 per cent per annum.

Remarkably rapid economic development and Hong Kong have thus become synonymous. And in another respect the Hong Kong economy presents a singular appearance. It is, to an unusually large extent, a free market economy. Its liberal characteristics are indeed obvious. There is virtually complete freedom of importation and exportation; there is almost no subsidization of any kind of manufacturing activity; there is no 'economic plan'. It is true the government spends a substantial part of the economy's income, that it subsidizes housing, education and transport, that some private banks settle interest rates with government support and that there are several public utilities which are government-sponsored monopolies. But over a large area private enterprise is free to sink or to swim as it chooses, and if it does the latter it is not asked to pay a great deal in the way of taxes.

This development, and these characteristics, mark Hong Kong off in a very striking way from China. In the old days, before 1941, Hong Kong was not all that different from China. She was wealthier, certainly, but not enormously so; she changed faster, but not much faster; she relied on private enterprise, but there was almost as much private enterprise in Shanghai or Tianjin. For the past thirty years, however, Hong Kong and China have followed entirely different paths, and they now occupy very different economic positions. And yet, through the thirty years of divergence, Hong Kong has retained and even developed her old links with China. She does not serve as rich and spacious a hinterland as Shanghai, situated at the mouth of the Chang Jiang; but the work of the port has for over a hundred years been essential to the prosperity of large areas of South China, and indeed to China as a whole. Although now a manufacturing centre of considerable importance, exporting her goods all over the world, Hong Kong is still, quite apart from that, the greatest trading port in the Far East. She imports goods from many countries, most notably from the United States, China and Japan, and exports them again, especially to the United States, China, Indonesia, Singapore, Taiwan and Japan. Storage and transshipment services are provided on a large scale, and goods reach and leave Hong Kong by sea, air, and along the Kowloon–Canton Railway. Also, partly in support of her entrepôt trade, Hong Kong provides a full array of financing, insurance and business services. Indeed, she has emerged during the 1970's as a major international financial centre. As well as financing domestic industry and the entrepôt trade, banks and non-bank financial intermediaries in Hong Kong engage in a very wide range of offshore banking operations, borrowing in the Euro-dollar and Asian-dollar markets as well as — in the case of non-Hong Kong-based banks — from head offices overseas, and lending to numerous foreign countries in Europe and Asia. A majority of the world's largest commercial banks have offices in Hong Kong, and it seems that there are more international financial institutions doing business in Hong Kong than in any other place except London and New York. It is thus inevitable that Hong Kong should act as a financial as well as a trading intermediary between the rest of the world and China.

And if China benefits from the business she does with and through Hong Kong, it can be said with even more confidence that Hong Kong depends on China. From China comes between 40 and 50 per cent of Hong Kong's food supply, a large fraction of her petroleum supply, and much of the yarn that is required for her important textile industry. Even for water Hong Kong is dependent upon China. A series of agreements has been signed, and at present between one-third and one-half of Hong Kong's water supply comes from across the border; shipping water from somewhere else would be an intolerable burden.

The goodwill of China and the state of the Chinese economy are therefore always matters of the utmost importance for Hong Kong; and when China embarked on new economic policies after the fall of the Gang of Four, Hong Kong was bound to be affected. In February 1978 China announced a 10-year plan of modernization. Within seven years the output of steel and coal was to be doubled, agricultural production was to be nearly doubled, and 120 major industrial complexes were to be completed. These were impossible targets, and a few months later the plan was shelved and a much more realistic readjustment programme was put in its place. This is still an ambitious and difficult scheme of modernization, but, as everyone knows, China is now a far more open and probably a faster growing economy than before 1978. There are many uncertainties about the course that development will take, and many questions that lack clear answers.

For example, how much emphasis will be placed on new plant and equipment in heavy industry — a form of investment that is very likely to increase imports immediately without adding for several years either to production or to exports? Will China be able to eliminate the need to import steel? Will the more than 80 per cent of the population who live on the land be able to raise output sufficiently to do away with the need to import grain? And if they do, what will be the requirements for fertilizers, and how will these requirements be met? How fast will personal incomes rise and what will they be spent on? Such questions have a great and obvious importance for Hong Kong. China has for centuries been one of the most self-contained economies in the world. 'Our Celestial Empire possesses all things in prolific abundance, and lacks no product within its own borders; there is therefore no need to import the manufactures of outside barbarians.' So said the Chinese Government in 1793, and this attitude or something like it has persisted almost to the present day. But an outward-looking China, anxious to acquire foreign technology, to import what is required for faster development, and to co-operate with foreigners and borrow from them when necessary, is a new phenomenon that must affect the economy and prospects of the world at large, and of Hong Kong in particular.

Some effects of the new policy are now apparent. Chinese exports and imports rose sharply in 1980 and again in 1981. Hong Kong's exports to China in 1980, at constant prices, were about 50 per cent greater than in 1979, and in 1981 they rose by another 50 per cent; re-exports (more than twice as important by value) rose by similar amounts. China has replaced the United States as the largest market for Hong Kong's re-exports, and is more than ever the largest source of goods re-exported from Hong Kong. The lines of trade in which the greatest increases have taken place include machinery of all kinds, telecommunications equipment, road vehicles, building materials and equipment, and some items of consumer goods; and, on the side of Chinese exports, coal, petroleum and textiles. This upsurge of trade has been facilitated by the new Chinese policy of allowing trade to be conducted by individual provinces and organizations, instead of being entirely channelled through foreign trade corporations at state level.

In addition to the growth of trade, there is a much more visible sign of the strengthening connection between China and Hong Kong. It seems as if Hong Kong is being extended — or perhaps it would be better to say, duplicated — just over the border. Shenzhen Municipality has been designated as a zone for agricultural, industrial and recreational development, and the Shenzhen Special Economic Zone has turned in two years from a quiet rural area into a busy city. Employment has been provided for over 11,000 people, and the gap in living standards between those on the Shenzhen and those on the Hong Kong side of the border has narrowed significantly. Set up in May 1980, the Shenzhen zone has attracted in less than a year over HK$2 billion of foreign investment. Industry accounts for two-thirds of the projects, agriculture for a quarter, and tourism, transportation, commerce and real estate for the rest. Most of these projects are medium-sized or small joint ventures in which foreign firms co-operate with Chinese interests, but in a few cases foreign or Hong Kong capital exclusively is involved. In addition, the Hong Kong company, China Light and Power, now supplies up to one million kilowatt hours of electricity per day to the whole of Guangdong Province, making electric current the second most important item by value which is exported from Hong Kong to China. These developments are to some extent the reciprocal of the supply of water from China to Hong Kong, and of recent Chinese investment in Hong Kong, especially in real estate projects relating to office premises and domestic accommodation.

Increased trade and increased investment across the border involve, inevitably, improvement in the means of communication. As far as passengers are concerned, rail services have been improved with the electrification of the Kowloon-Canton Railway as far as the border, chartered air services began in 1978, and a daily hovercraft service has connected Hong Kong with Huangpu since late in 1978. An increased volume of commercial cargo has led to joint plans for further road extensions and improvements in Kowloon and the New Territories, extending into Guangdong (with a kilometre-long bridge at Lok Ma Chau), and for the provision of better transport facilities connected to the existing container terminals in Hong Kong.

The network of connections is thus far more extensive and more complex than is usually stretched across any frontier. Hong Kong and

China are inseparable, strange as the relationship must in some ways be between a gigantic, poor, centralized, professedly egalitarian and predominantly rural economy and tiny, capitalist, free-wheeling and relatively rich Hong Kong. It is a curious play of contradictions and advantages, and it may not last. Indeed, in its present form it cannot last. But in the meantime, China is one of the reasons for Hong Kong's prosperity, and Hong Kong is very useful to China. And it should always be remembered that many people in Hong Kong wish to be useful to China. They are Chinese, and they sympathize with Chinese national aspirations. For this reason, many who are not Communists but who have special skills that are needed in China go there to work for a few years, as technical experts or teachers, or, while remaining in Hong Kong, go out of their way to help and to promote Chinese interests. It is a unique symbiotic relationship. The purpose of the following chapters is to clarify some of the more important aspects of a fast-changing situation.

1. Hong Kong's Role in Financing China's Modernization

Y.C. JAO

Introduction

Although Hong Kong has been under British administration for more than 140 years, its economic ties with China, reinforced by cultural, ethnic and geographical factors, have always been so strong that for a long time before the Second World War, the prevailing view was that Hong Kong was economically a part of China. In the late 1940's and early 1950's, as a result of momentous events (the Communist victory on the mainland, the Korean War, and the United States and United Nations embargoes), China and Hong Kong embarked on two very divergent paths of economic development: the former followed a 'command economy' model, while the latter opted for a strategy of export industrialism within a framework of largely unfettered free enterprise. Economic ties between the two, however, have survived the post-1949 changes, despite severe strains that arose during the traumatic years of the Cultural Revolution.

Very recently, economic relationships between China and Hong Kong have taken on an entirely new dimension, also largely as a result of political changes, but this time on a much happier note. With the passing of the Maoist era towards the end of 1976, China began to adopt a much more pragmatic, rational and outward-looking economic policy. This in turn has led to a much more benevolent attitude towards Hong Kong. China has become increasingly aware of the fact that Hong Kong is an extremely convenient and rewarding place to make use of for its modernization. On Hong Kong's side, since the 1970's the territory has rapidly emerged as a leading financial centre for the whole Pacific Basin. Its rate of economic growth — averaging over 9 per cent in real terms per annum for the years 1970-81 — is the envy of the world. By virtue of its growing affluence and financial stature, not to say other traditional ties, Hong Kong is destined to play an important role in financing China's modernization. At the same time, Hong Kong's own industrial development had, by the late 1970's, reached a stage where it was clearly impossible to continue indefinitely the hitherto highly successful strategy of developing almost exclusively labour-intensive light industries. Diversification into higher value-added, skill- or technology-intensive product lines has become a pressing necessity. The establishment in the late 1970's of Special Economic Zones (SEZs) in China's southern provinces, particularly in areas adjacent to Hong Kong, could not have come at a more appropriate time in that it helped to relieve one of the critical bottlenecks to Hong Kong's industrial growth, namely, land supply. Hong Kong's economy has also during the 1970's undergone significant structural changes, with the tertiary industries, especially the financial service sector, gaining substantially in their relative share of the gross domestic product (GDP) at the expense of the manufacturing sector. While this structural change reflects primarily the inner dynamics of economic forces, to some extent it is also influenced by China's reorientation of its economic and financial policies.[1]

A full treatment of the economics of interdependence between China and Hong Kong would require a whole book rather than a single chapter. Our task is however much more modest due to the constraints of space: it is confined to an analysis of the role of Hong Kong in financing China's modernization. Traditionally, this topic has been discussed in terms of the hard currency earnings which Hong Kong contributes to China. While the quantification of this financial contribution must remain a key element of our analysis, it is our contention that the traditional approach is too simplistic, and in any case has been rendered inappropriate by the concatenation of changing circumstances over the past decade. In particular, we do not wish to convey the one-sided impression that China is financially dependent on Hong Kong. Our thesis is that Hong Kong's role can only be properly appreciated in a context of mutual dependence and interaction.

From this perspective it is proposed to organize this chapter into the following sections. The first deals with Hong Kong as a source of trade surplus for China. The second section then discusses Hong Kong as a centre of banking facilities and financial services. This is followed by a related section on Hong Kong as a source of non-trade earnings and unrequited transfers. The fourth section is concerned with Hong Kong as a source of investment capital. The chapter then ends with some concluding remarks. It must be emphasized at the outset that the absence of reliable and systematic balance of payments data for both China and Hong Kong makes it impossible to quantify precisely every aspect of our analysis. Some estimates given in the following sections can at best be regarded as educated guesses. It is hoped that this chapter can serve as an initial framework, so that when statistical coverage and data on both sides improve, our presentation will be modified, improved or updated as the case may be.

Hong Kong as a Source of Trade Surplus

Although comprehensive and detailed official balance of payments data do not yet exist for either the People's Republic of China or Hong Kong, visible trade statistics are reasonably adequate and reliable.[2] Table 1.1 shows visible trade at current prices between Hong Kong and China from 1950 to 1981.[3]

As the table makes clear, except for 1950 and 1951, when Hong Kong was able to enjoy a temporary surplus, due mainly to Chinese stockpiling after the outbreak of the Korean War but before the full effects of the United States and United Nations embargoes were felt, the trade balance since 1952 has always been unfavourable to Hong Kong. Furthermore, Hong Kong's trade deficit (or China's trade surplus) has shown a tendency to accelerated growth, especially since the 1970's. By 1981 it had reached a staggering figure of HK$18,542 million (US$3,335 million). This widening gap can be cxplained by several factors. One is the divergent growth paths of Hong Kong's exports to and imports from China. Hong Kong's total exports to

Table 1.1 VISIBLE TRADE BETWEEN HONG KONG AND CHINA (million HK dollars)

Year	Hong Kong Exports to China			Hong Kong Imports from China			Hong Kong Trade Balance
	Domestic Exports	Re-exports	Total	Goods	Water	Total	
1950	–	–	1,260	782	–	782	+478
1951	–	–	1,604	863	–	863	+741
1952	–	–	520	830	–	830	–310
1953	–	–	540	857	–	857	–317
1954	–	–	391	692	–	692	–301
1955	–	–	182	898	–	898	–716
1956	–	–	136	1,038	–	1,038	–902
1957	–	–	123	1,131	–	1,131	–1,008
1958	–	–	156	1,397	–	1,397	–1,241
1959	9	105	114	1,034	–	1,034	–920
1960	13	107	120	1,185	–	1,185	–1,065
1961	8	91	99	1,028	1	1,029	–930
1962	8	77	85	1,213	2	1,215	–1,130
1963	8	62	70	1,487	1	1,488	–1,418
1964	13	47	60	1,970	1	1,971	–1,911
1965	18	54	72	2,322	10	2,322	–2,260
1966	15	54	69	2,769	14	2,783	–2,714
1967	6	42	48	2,282	17	2,299	–2,251
1968	9	36	45	2,429	17	2,446	–2,401
1969	7	30	37	2,700	17	2,717	–2,680
1970	30	34	64	2,830	16	2,846	–2,782
1971	19	43	62	3,330	18	3,348	–3,286
1972	21	82	103	3,847	21	3,868	–3,765
1973	49	222	271	5,634	22	5,656	–5,385
1974	99	197	296	5,991	22	6,013	–5,717
1975	28	137	165	6,805	25	6,830	–6,665
1976	24	123	147	7,761	23	7,784	–7,637
1977	31	175	206	8,082	33	8,115	–7,909
1978	81	214	225	10,550	47	10,597	–10,302
1979	603	1,315	1,918	15,130	71	15,201	–13,283
1980	1,605	4,642	6,247	21,863	85	21,948	–15,701
1981	2,924	8,044	10,968	29,339	111	29,510	–18,542

Sources: Census and Statistics Department, *Hong Kong Statistics 1947-67* and *Hong Kong Review of Overseas Trade*, 1970–8; figures on water imports are supplied by the Assistant Commissioner of Census and Statistics.

China (domestic exports and re-exports were not separately reported until 1959) reached their peak in 1951, but as the United States and United Nations embargoes came into full effect later in the year, these exports began a long downtrend from 1952 onward, and by 1969 they had dwindled to almost nothing. From 1970 onward, however, as China started to seek *rapprochement* with the West and Japan, Hong Kong's exports to China also reversed their previous downtrend and grew dramatically over the next decade. By 1981, domestic exports had increased by more than 300 times, while re-exports had increased by more than 70 times in value terms. However, as they started from a very low base, their dramatic growth, particularly in the post-Mao era, was still not sufficient to make a significant impact on the trade deficit. Imports, on the other hand, generally followed a steady uptrend, despite occasional setbacks, notably in 1959, 1961 and 1967, due mainly to the disruptions caused by the ill-fated Great Leap Forward and the Cultural Revolution. But from 1968 onward, there has been an uninterrupted growth in imports from China: indeed, during the last four years 1978–81, the annual growth rate accelerated significantly to over 40 per cent. It is true that a large part of this growth has been accounted for by price inflation since the 1970's.[4] However, much the same forces operated on the export side as well, but owing to the divergent growth paths referred to earlier, the trade gap kept on widening. Another reason may well be that, given the relatively high income elasticities of demand of Hong Kong residents for non-food imports from China, Hong Kong's rapidly rising real income per capita, coupled with its population growth, can be counted upon to generate a sustained rise in total imports, whereas Hong Kong's total exports to China are constrained by the much lower per capita income in China and the availability of foreign exchange.[5]

Note that in tabulating Hong Kong imports from China, we also allow for the purchase of water from the Pearl River as from 1961. Prior to 1980, this item was not reported in the merchandise trade between Hong Kong and China, so that adjustments are necessary to arrive at correct estimates of total imports from China. Initially the amount involved was trivial, but from the late 1970's onwards the value of water imports increased sharply, and is likely to grow more rapidly in future, as a combined result of greater consumption and higher prices under a new agreement reached in 1981.[6]

China's cumulative trade surplus with Hong Kong, converted into US dollars, is shown in Table 1.2. Three major periods — the 1950's, 1960's, and 1970's — and one sub-period, the post-Mao era 1977–81, are distinguished. The surplus of the 1960's was 314 per cent higher than in the 1950's, while that in the 1970's was in turn 315 per cent more than in the 1960's. In the post-Mao years 1977–81, the trade surplus was three times as high as the combined total of the 1950's and 1960's, and nearly equal to the total of the 1970's. In sum, since 1950, China has earned a grand total of some US$23.8 billion from Hong Kong in the form of trade surplus alone.

A surplus of this magnitude, even allowing for inflation, is undoubtedly of vital importance to a poor and developing country like China. Before we accept the sum at its face value, however, we need to examine one query which has sometimes been raised. As a significant and growing proportion of Hong Kong's imports from China is re-exported to third countries, one wonders whether it is correct to treat all such imports as China's surplus specifically with Hong Kong. This question can perhaps be more conveniently discussed in the context of the entrepôt trade between Hong Kong and China.

Table 1.2 CHINA'S CUMULATIVE TRADE SURPLUS AGAINST HONG KONG (million US dollars)*

Period	Amount
1950–9	772.83
1960–9	3,202.83
1970–9	13,319.95
1977–81	13,032.80
Total (1950–81)	23,783.21

* Converted into US dollars at the free market monthly average TT exchange rate.

Sources: Exchange rate quotations from Census and Statistics Department, *Hong Kong Statistics 1947-1967; Far Eastern Economic Review,* 1950–3, 1968–73; and *Hong Kong Monthly Digest of Statistics*, 1974–81.

In Table 1.3, Column 1 shows Hong Kong's re-exports to China. The time series starts from 1959, the first year for which Hong Kong's domestic exports and re-exports were separately reported. As can be readily seen, these re-exports declined steadily from 1959 to 1969, and it was not until the early 1970's that they began to recover, reaching their first peak in 1973, concomitantly with the improve-

Table 1.3 HONG KONG'S ENTREPÔT TRADE WITH CHINA

Year	(1) Re-exports to China (million HK dollars)	(2) As a Percentage of Hong Kong's Re-exports	(3) Re-exports from China (million HK dollars)	(4) As a Percentage of Imports from China	(5) As a Percentage of Hong Kong's Re-exports
1959	105	10.5	N.A.	N.A.	N.A.
1960	107	10.0	N.A.	N.A.	N.A.
1961	91	9.2	N.A.	N.A.	N.A.
1962	77	7.2	N.A.	N.A.	N.A.
1963	62	5.3	N.A.	N.A.	N.A.
1964	47	3.5	N.A.	N.A.	N.A.
1965	54	3.6	N.A.	N.A.	N.A.
1966	54	2.9	627	22.5	34.2
1967	42	2.0	613	26.7	29.5
1968	36	1.7	550	22.5	25.7
1969	30	1.1	724	26.6	27.0
1970	34	1.2	688	24.2	23.8
1971	43	1.3	759	22.7	22.2
1972	82	2.0	983	25.4	23.7
1973	222	3.4	1,589	28.1	24.4
1974	197	2.8	1,582	26.3	22.2
1975	137	2.0	1,743	25.5	25.0
1976	123	1.4	2,402	30.9	26.9
1977	175	1.8	2,492	30.7	25.4
1978	214	1.6	3,659	34.5	27.7
1979	1,315	6.6	5,663	37.3	28.3
1980	4,642	15.4	8,394	38.2	27.9
1981	8,044	19.3	12,834	43.5	30.7

Source: As for Table 1.1.

ment in China's external relations with the non-Communist world. In the next three years there was another setback, partly no doubt a result of the world-wide recession, but partly also a result of the pressures of domestic politics when the so-called 'Gang of Four' was in ascendancy. However, a dramatic recovery occurred again in the post-Mao era, so much so that the value of re-exports recorded in 1981 was more than 65 times as high as that in 1976. Column 2 shows such re-exports as percentages of Hong Kong's total re-exports. Much the same pattern of changes can be discerned: a consistent downtrend from 1959 to 1969, followed by a mild recovery in 1970–3, then another setback in 1974–6, and finally a sharp recovery from 1977.

Re-exports from China through Hong Kong (or equivalently, Hong Kong's re-exports of goods of China origin) are given in Column 3. Unfortunately, the earliest year for which data are available is 1966. In contrast to Hong Kong's re-exports to China, re-exports from China through Hong Kong from 1968 onwards have shown a fairly consistent uptrend, apparently not much affected by internal dissensions between 1973–6. Two inferences may reasonably be drawn from this observation. First, even when xenophobia was at its height, the Chinese authorities thought it wise to export as much as possible in order to build up foreign exchange reserves. Second, Hong Kong's facilities as an entrepôt — an excellent harbour, fully modernized container terminals, and an efficient international network of transport, communications and commercial ties — were so attractive to China that re-exports through Hong Kong survived even the most bitter period of domestic power struggles and policy debates. It is also pertinent to point out that the trend in China's re-exports through Hong Kong has been generally consistent with that in China's final exports to Hong Kong (or Hong Kong's retained imports from China). The relative importance of re-exports from China in Hong Kong's external trade is indicated in the last two columns of the table. Column 4 expresses re-exports from China as a proportion of Hong Kong's total imports from the same source. As can be readily seen, the trend has clearly been upward, rising over the years from 22.5 per cent in 1966 to 43.5 per cent in 1981. Expressed as a percentage of Hong Kong's total re-exports, shown in Column 5, re-exports of Chinese goods have been generally stable, varying within a relatively narrow range of between 22 per cent and 34 per cent.

Turning now to the question whether re-exports of goods of China origin should be regarded as China's trade surplus with Hong Kong, the correct answer depends on how the re-exports are effected. There are two possible mechanisms. One, which is perhaps the prevailing one, is for a Hong Kong merchant to act as an intermediary: the goods are exported from China to him first, and then in turn are re-exported by him to a third-country destination. Another possibility is for a Chinese state trading company to export the goods in question to a third country, using Hong Kong only as a transshipment/transit point. From my research carried out at the Census and Statistics Department and Trade Industry and Customs Department, I am satisfied that nearly all re-exports of Chinese goods through Hong Kong are done through the first channel. With regard to the second channel, transit cargoes are not reported in Hong Kong's trade returns anyway, while even transshipments are mostly handled by Hong Kong intermediaries. One reason is the inadequacy of China's port facilities.[7] Another reason is that unofficial trade, such as that with Taiwan, Indonesia and South Korea, is routed through Hong Kong. Finally, China also wishes to minimize exchange and other financial risks by making use of Hong Kong intermediaries.

One conclusion which can safely be drawn is that Hong Kong's trade deficit with China, as shown in Tables 1.1 and 1.2, overstates the adverse balance of payments effect, since a substantial part (averaging some 37 per cent in the past five years) of imports is re-exported and will eventually show up as Hong Kong's export earnings. The adverse balance is further reduced if Hong Kong's handling charges and profits from the entrepôt trade are allowed for. On the other hand, figures in Table 1.2 only slightly overstate China's visible trade net earnings from Hong Kong, for reasons already stated. Present data do not permit us to quantify this overstatement, but it can be presumed to be negligible. For a first approximation, therefore, we will accept the figures in Table 1.2 as indicative of the importance of Hong Kong as a source of trade surplus for China.

This importance can be further analyzed, as is done in Table 1.4. Column 1 gives China's overall trade balance in 1950–80. Twelve out of thirty-one were deficit years. Except for 1974, 1976 and 1979,

Table 1.4 CHINA'S OVERALL TRADE BALANCE

Year	(1) Overall Trade Balance (million US dollars)	(2) Trade Balance Excluding Hong Kong (million US dollars)	(3) Exports to Hong Kong as a Percentage of Total Exports	(4) Imports from Hong Kong as a Percentage of Total Imports
1950	30	105	19.9	33.6
1951	−340	−224	17.3	22.3
1952	−140	−188	14.7	7.9
1953	−215	−268	13.7	7.1
1954	−230	−282	11.2	5.2
1955	−285	−407	11.2	1.9
1956	150	0	10.5	1.5
1957	175	9	11.5	1.4
1958	115	−98	12.4	1.5
1959	170	10	8.1	1.0
1960	−70	−256	10.6	1.0
1961	35	−127	11.7	1.2
1962	370	172	14.0	1.3
1963	375	128	16.5	1.0
1964	280	−53	19.6	0.7
1965	190	−203	19.9	0.7
1966	175	−295	21.8	0.6
1967	5	−381	20.1	0.4
1968	135	−256	20.3	0.4
1969	225	−211	21.5	0.3
1970	−150	−608	22.4	0.5
1971	190	−362	22.5	0.5
1972	300	−370	21.9	0.6
1973	−150	−1,194	21.6	1.0
1974	−760	−1,897	17.9	0.8
1975	−215	−1,564	19.3	0.5
1976	1,255	−320	22.0	0.5
1977	855	−842	21.9	0.6
1978	−196	−2,393	22.3	0.5
1979	−595	−3,246	22.0	2.7
1980	366	−2,787	22.3	6.5

Sources: Batsavage and Davie (1978); CIA, *China: International Trade*, various years; *Zhongguo Jingji Nianjian*, 1981; and others as for Table 1.1

however, both deficits and surpluses were relatively small, suggesting that the Chinese generally followed a conservative foreign trade policy by using exports to finance imports, and if possible, to achieve a small trade surplus. Column 2 then shows what would have happened to China's overall trade balance had Hong Kong been excluded. Except for 1950–1, China's overall trade balance would have seriously deteriorated, resulting in substantial deficits in no less than 24 years, even allowing for the fact that part of China's exports could have been diverted to other markets. Broadly speaking, China can be said to be following a policy of using its trade surplus with Hong Kong to finance its deficits with other countries. Column 3 describes China's exports to Hong Kong as a proportion of its total exports. During 1950–9, the proportion fell from 19.9 per cent to 8.1 per cent. This was of course the period when China was compelled to switch its trade to the Soviet bloc because of the embargoes. Following the Sino-Soviet rift in 1960–1, Hong Kong's share recovered steadily, and by the 1970's, Hong Kong had become the single largest export market for China, its share averaging about 22 per cent. Column 4 shows imports from Hong Kong as a proportion of China's total imports. From a record high of 33.6 per cent in 1950, when Hong Kong served as an entrepôt for China, the proportion fell precipitately in the next few years, again as a result of the embargoes, and by 1969 it had all but disappeared. Although imports from Hong Kong subsequently picked up, Hong Kong's relative share still remained negligible, and it was not until after 1979 that it showed any significant increase. The reason is to be found in the fact that, despite the recent liberalization in China's import policy, the predominant part of China's imports still consists of industrial plant and equipment, advanced technology, food grains, raw materials and fertilizers — all goods which suppliers supply direct to China. As far as China is concerned, then, Hong Kong is far more important as an export market and outlet than as a supplier.

The commodity composition of Sino-Hong Kong trade can only be briefly mentioned here, as our focus is on China's trade surplus with Hong Kong.[8] As can be expected, China's exports to Hong Kong consist mainly of (averaging over 60 per cent) resource-intensive goods like foodstuffs, raw materials and fuels, and labour-intensive consumer products (averaging over 20 per cent). Hong Kong's domestic exports to China, on the other hand, consist largely of industrial raw materials or semi-processed products, and skill- or technology-intensive products like telecommunications apparatus and equipment, photographic and optical goods, watches and clocks, and other labour-intensive consumer goods; while re-exports are composed mainly of industrial raw materials/semi-processed products, telecommunications apparatus and equipment, transport vehicles, crude animal and vegetable materials, and electrical machinery and appliances. Sales of electricity to China have expanded rapidly since 1979. The presence of raw materials/semi-processed products and consumer goods on both sides of the two-way trade suggests that there is a great deal of intra-industry trade going on, a phenomenon that deserves greater attention and further research.

Apart from geographic and ethnic considerations, the absence of tariffs and exchange control makes Hong Kong an especially attractive export market for China. One can expect China to continue its present policy of achieving a sizeable trade surplus with Hong Kong. However, since 1968 China has had to concede its position as Hong Kong's top supplier to Japan, mainly because in Hong Kong as elsewhere, Engel's Law operates so that a rise in income is accompanied by a less than proportionate increase in food consumption. A recent empirical study (Hsueh and Woo, 1981) confirms that Hong Kong's income elasticity of demand for food imports from China is quite low. The same study therefore recommends that China should devote more efforts to expanding the exports of non-food items if it is to increase, or at least maintain, its market share in Hong Kong.

Finally, it should also be stressed that while China earns valuable foreign exchange from its trade surplus with Hong Kong, Hong Kong also benefits a great deal from trade with China. It has been estimated that during 1961–73, if Hong Kong had not imported foodstuffs from China, its cost of living would have risen by at least 15 per cent for the same consumption level. Since 1973, as China began to adopt a more outward-oriented policy, prices of imports from China have risen sharply, but Chinese foodstuffs and consumer goods have continued to maintain their competitive edge against similar goods from other sources.[9] Thus it is not an exaggeration to say that

China's export-pricing policy has indirectly subsidized Hong Kong's post-war industrialization.

Hong Kong as a Financial Centre

Since about 1969, Hong Kong has been emerging rapidly as a major financial centre for the Asian-Pacific region. This is shown not only by the influx of a large number of foreign and multinational financial institutions, but also, and more importantly, by the growing external orientation of the territory's banking operations and financial activities. This remarkable development, which can be viewed as the advanced stage of Hong Kong's post-war industrial revolution, has been analyzed by this writer elsewhere.[10] In this section, we shall focus our attention on the significance of Hong Kong as a financial centre for China's modernization.

Hong Kong's evolution into a financial centre took place during a period when China's foreign and economic policies underwent a fundamental reappraisal and reorientation. This was not just a result of random historical coincidence: the two apparently independent developments were in fact interrelated. As is well known, Hong Kong possesses all the necessary ingredients for a successful financial centre, such as a free exchange market, a liberal and non-interventionist government, a central geographical location in the Pacific Basin, a proven record of economic growth, and a good network of transportation and communications. However, all these attributes had been in existence for some time, and the question still remains why Hong Kong's rise as a regional financial centre began *circa* 1969–70 and not earlier. A full explanation can only be made if the China dimension is taken into account. Jolted by its border clashes with the Soviet Union, China was groping in 1969 towards a *rapprochement* with the West and Japan. The so-called 'ping-pong diplomacy', initiated in 1971, followed by the historic visit of Richard Nixon to China in 1972, had an immediate stabilizing effect on Hong Kong and the whole Pacific Basin. Thus, even though the Vietnam War was still going on, it became clear to the multinational financial institutions that the region as a whole, including China, was poised for a new era of economic development in a relatively peaceful environment. In such a setting, the choice of Hong Kong as a regional base became irresistible to both financial and non-financial entities. An influx of financial institutions into Hong Kong, initially led by foreign merchant banks, began in 1970, and was accelerated in the late 1970's by favourable political changes inside China after Mao's death.[11] For its part, China under the post-Mao leadership, undoubtedly impressed by Hong Kong's economic success, began to modify significantly its previous obsession with 'self-reliance', and to adopt a much more open-minded and outward-looking attitude towards international trade and finance. Specifically, such measures as the establishment of 'Special Economic Zones' near Hong Kong, the acceptance of foreign credit, and the permission of foreign equity or joint-venture investment inside China, can arguably be interpreted as being at least partly inspired by the Hong Kong 'open economy' model. Moreover, Hong Kong's sophisticated banking facilities and financial services are not only always at China's disposal: they also provide an exemplary model of reform for China's antiquated domestic financial system. In short, Hong Kong's rise as a financial centre and China's policy changes seem to have generated a 'virtuous circle' highly beneficial to both sides.

Of immediate relevance is perhaps the change in China's stance towards international finance. In the 1960's, and especially during the Cultural Revolution, China's financial policy in general was rigidly based on self-reliance, epitomized by the puritanical guideline 'no foreign loans, no foreign investments, and no foreign aid.' In the early days of the Communist regime, China did borrow substantially from the Soviet Union to finance its intervention in the Korean War and the First Five-Year Plan. Subsequently, as a result of the Sino-Soviet rift, China decided to repay its debt to the Soviet Union ahead of schedule in the early 1960's, despite the severe difficulties caused by the Great Leap Forward (1958–60), the natural disasters (1959–61), and the abrupt cessation of Soviet aid in 1960.[12] By 1968, even domestic debts had been repaid on schedule, with no new national bonds being issued. China, therefore, rather prided itself on the fact that it had become 'a socialist country with no domestic or foreign debt.'[13]

In the early 1970's, following the improvement in China's relations with the non-Communist world, a slight liberalization of China's stance towards foreign credit became discernible, as China began to accept and accumulate short- and medium-term trade credit to finance imports of food grains and whole industrial plants. By 1977, the outstanding amount of these credits had reached US$1,315 million.[14] The Chinese, however, regarded these trade credits as a 'standard commercial practice for deferred payment in international trade' and not as a form of foreign debt. In any case, the amount involved was still relatively small.[15]

It was not until after the downfall of the Maoist 'Gang of Four', the second rehabilitation of Deng Xiaoping, and the reactivation of the 'Four Modernizations' programme in 1976–7, that a fundamental rethinking and reorientation on the whole question of foreign loans took place. It was recognized by the pragmatic post-Mao leadership that, given China's low level of income and limited export capability, its ambitious programme of modernization, dependent as it was on the import of whole plants and advanced technology, simply could not be achieved without substantial foreign financial assistance. The initial change in early 1978 was still cautious, and took the form of a 'mutual deposits' scheme whereby the Bank of China (now the Chinese bank which specializes in international trade and finance) and foreign banks would deposit funds with each other denominated in their respective national currencies. Since the foreign banks as a rule deposited more funds than the Bank of China did, the 'mutual deposits' scheme amounted to *de facto* inter-bank loans to China. Further liberalization in official policy came quickly, and from the end of 1978 onwards, China began to accept a series of loans from foreign private banks and governments. By the beginning of 1982, according to my estimate, China's foreign debt (medium- to long-term) had reached US$31.04 billion.[16]

Given this dramatic change in China's financial policy, it is interesting to discover what role Hong Kong plays in granting bank loans and other forms of credit to China. Virtually all the major banks involved in publicized loans to China have branches, representative offices, or subsidiaries in Hong Kong, but all these loans seem to have been negotiated between the head offices of the foreign banks and the Chinese Government or the Bank of China in Beijing. It can be safely assumed, however, that Hong Kong's facilities as a financial centre are too important to be ignored by all the parties concerned. For example, despite the more liberal policy towards foreign finance, at the end of 1980 there were only 23 foreign bank offices in China. In part this is the result of an acute shortage of office and residential accommodation in the major cities. Even those that are allowed in have had to operate out of a hotel room.[17] Most multinational banks that wish to enter the China market but are kept waiting have no alternative but to maintain an office in Hong Kong, with their executives commuting regularly between China and the British colony. Furthermore, China itself has a strong presence in the financial sector of Hong Kong in the form of 13 licensed banks and a score of finance companies and merchant banks. Face-to-face contacts between Chinese and foreign bankers can therefore be arranged daily as a matter of routine.

Prior to 1979, there were no published statistics at all about financial transactions between Hong Kong's financial institutions and their counterparts in China. Since the first quarter of 1979, the external liabilities and claims of licensed banks and deposit-taking companies (DTCs) by country of origin have been regularly compiled and released on a quarterly basis by the Banking Commissioner's Office at the request of the Bank of International Settlements in Basle. The information contained therein is most useful for ascertaining Hong Kong's role as a financial centre, as well as its financial transactions with individual countries, including China. Liabilities and claims of licensed banks and DTCs with respect to China are presented in Tables 1.5 and 1.6 respectively.

The tables show that gross financial transactions (liabilities to banks and claims on banks and non-banks in China) have shown a generally upward trend, and this is particularly true as regards the DTCs. These transactions may represent either inter-bank balances or inter-bank loans, though unfortunately no breakdown is available for this purpose. It will also be readily seen that both licensed commercial banks and DTCs have consistently maintained net claims on banks and non-banks in China, confirming Hong Kong's role as a source of

Table 1.5 HONG KONG LICENSED BANKS: EXTERNAL LIABILITIES AND CLAIMS AGAINST CHINA (million HK dollars)

Date	Liabilities to Banks	Claims on Banks	Claims on Non-banks	Net Liabilities (−) or Claims (+)
March 31, 1979	421	5,144	2	+4,725
June 30, 1979	348	5,569	10	+5,231
Sept. 30, 1979	393	5,623	36	+5,266
Dec. 31, 1979	205	5,797	109	+5,701
March 31, 1980	661	5,893	154	+5,386
June 30, 1980	1,160	5,647	189	+4,676
Sept. 30, 1980	1,279	5,551	345	+4,617
Dec. 31, 1980	773	6,631	399	+5,352
March 31, 1981	422	5,967	439	+5,984
June 30, 1981	1,779	5,556	514	+4,291
Sept. 30, 1981	2,838	5,612	569	+3,343
Dec. 31, 1981	4,419	6,367	619	+2,567

Source: Office of the Commissioner of Banking, *Quarterly Statement of External Liabilities and Claims.*

Table 1.6 HONG KONG DEPOSIT-TAKING COMPANIES: EXTERNAL LIABILITIES AND CLAIMS AGAINST CHINA (million HK dollars)

Date	Liabilities to Banks	Claims on Banks	Claims on Non-banks	Net Liabilities (−) or Claims (+)
March 31, 1979	–	96	–	+96
June 30, 1979	–	102	–	+102
Sept. 30, 1979	–	100	16	+116
Dec. 31, 1979	8	40	–	+32
March 31, 1980	1	190	1	+190
June 30, 1980	73	490	28	+445
Sept. 30, 1980	171	499	62	+390
Dec. 31, 1980	208	510	106	+445
March 31, 1981	246	602	231	+587
June 30, 1981	292	549	230	+487
Sept. 30, 1981	722	598	188	+64
Dec. 31, 1981	986	268	121	−597

Source: As for Table 1.5.

credit for China.[18] In Table 1.7, the total net claims of Hong Kong's financial institutions (licensed banks and DTCs) on China are converted into US dollars in order to facilitate international comparison. After reaching a peak in March 1981 at US$1.24 billion, the net claims dropped sharply to US$345.9 million at the end of 1981. The most plausible reason for this reversal in trend is the retrenchment consequent on the decision of China's leaders in late 1978 to devote three years (1979–81) to the readjustment and reform of the national economy. Normally, it takes time for a major policy change to be reflected in financial transactions, since prior contractual and financial commitments cannot be rescinded overnight. The cutbacks ordered in 1979 for capital investment projects therefore probably made their impact felt on the use of Hong Kong credit only after a time lag,

Table 1.7 TOTAL NET CLAIMS OF HONG KONG FINANCIAL INSTITUTIONS ON CHINA* (million US dollars)

Date	Total Net Claims of Licensed Banks and Deposit-taking Companies
March 31, 1979	964.2
June 30, 1979	1,044.9
Sept. 30, 1979	1,076.8
Dec. 31, 1979	1,145.9
March 31, 1980	1,110.8
June 30, 1980	1,040.4
Sept. 30, 1980	1,009.9
Dec. 31, 1980	1,126.9
March 31, 1981	1,240.0
June 30, 1981	865.4
Sept. 30, 1981	565.9
Dec. 31, 1981	345.9

* Converted into US dollars at the current market TT exchange rate.

Sources: As for Table 1.5; exchange quotations taken from *Hong Kong Monthly Digest of Statistics*, various issues.

notably after the first quarter of 1981. The second reason for the decline in net credits to China was the high level of interest rates prevailing from 1980 onwards in international financial markets. Although China already enjoyed very favourable terms from foreign commercial banks in that their lending rate was generally fixed at a mere 0.5 per cent over the London Inter-bank Offer Rate (LIBOR) — probably the lowest spread on any international loan granted by private sector banks — nevertheless LIBOR itself still floated upwards in line with the general level of interest rates, to a level that seemed exorbitant to China. Consequently, China in recent years has been more inclined to ask for 'soft loans' from international organizations such as the World Bank and International Monetary Fund. In any case, the drop in net claims of Hong Kong's financial institutions on China is consistent with reports that China has drawn sparingly from its credit lines arranged with foreign banks. Thus, Finance Minister Wang Bingqian disclosed, in his budget speech to the National People's Congress in September 1980, that the outstanding debt owed to foreign financial institutions amounted to US$3.4 billion, though it was known that a total credit of about US$28 billion had been lined up by that time. Despite the limited drawdowns, however, Hong Kong's net claims from June 30, 1979, to March 31, 1981, averaged about US$1.1 billion. It is also interesting to note that as at the end of the third quarter of 1980, China's net liabilities to Hong Kong accounted for about 30 per cent of the foreign debt quoted by Wang.

Hong Kong's financial system thus plays a not inconsiderable role in providing credit facilities to China. Once the present period of economic readjustment is over, and interest rates fall to a less prohibitive level, it is almost certain that China will make a much more aggressive use of external credit to speed up its modernization.[19] Given Hong Kong's growing stature and sophistication as a financial centre, there can also be little doubt that China will increasingly tap the territory's financial resources to its advantage.

Indeed, China already has an important stake in Hong Kong's financial sector. Table 1.8 shows the number of China's financial institutions in Hong Kong during 1969–81, a period characterized, as mentioned earlier, by Hong Kong's rise as a financial centre and China's reorientation in foreign and economic policies. As is clear

Table 1.8 CHINA'S FINANCIAL INSTITUTIONS IN HONG KONG

Year	Licensed Banks		Wholly-owned Deposit-taking Companies	Insurance Companies	Joint-venture Merchant Banks
	Main Offices	Branches			
1969	13	47	–	5	–
1970	13	55	–	5	–
1971	13	61	–	5	–
1972	13	65	–	5	–
1973	13	74	1	5	–
1974	13	94	1	5	–
1975	13	103	1	5	–
1976	13	113	1	5	–
1977	13	119	1	4	–
1978	13	128	1	4	–
1979	13	153	11	4	–
1980	13	172	13	5	2
1981	13	193	13	5	2

Sources: Banking Commissioner's Office and Registrar-General's Department.

from the table, the expansion of China's financial institutions in Hong Kong primarily took the form of more aggressive branching of licensed commercial banks, most of which had been established well before the founding of the People's Republic. While their number has remained unchanged at 13, their branches have more than trebled from 47 to 193. In terms of branch network, these Chinese state-controlled banks (CSCBs) had by the late 1970's overtaken the Chartered Bank as the second largest banking group in Hong Kong. At the end of 1981, the CSCBs stood next only to the Hong Kong Bank Group, which had 350 branches. The Chartered Bank had only 103 branches. In 1979–80 there was a rush by the CSCBs to form deposit-taking companies and joint-venture merchant banks, adding breadth and depth to China's financial presence in Hong Kong.

The 13 CSCBs are led by the Bank of China, whose head office is in Beijing. The bank can trace its origin to the Da Qing Bank under the

Qing Dynasty. When the Nationalists came to power in 1928, the bank was reorganized into a specialist bank of international exchange. This tradition was preserved under Communist rule, though until very recently it was administratively the foreign department of the People's Bank of China, specializing in international trade and foreign exchange. In 1979, however, the Bank of China was upgraded to an independent bank directly responsible to the State Council.[20] In the following year, its capital was raised from Rmb 400 million to Rmb 1,000 million. In addition to Hong Kong, the Bank of China also maintains branches or offices in Singapore, London, Manchester, Luxembourg, Tokyo, New York and Paris, but the Hong Kong branch remains the most important in the bank's international network.

Of the other 12 CSCBs, two (the Bank of Communications and the Kwangtung Provincial Bank) were government-owned banks even during the Nationalist era; six (China and South Sea Bank, China State Bank, Kincheng Banking Corporation, National Commercial Bank, Sin Hua Trust, Savings and Commercial Bank, and Yien Yieh Commercial Bank) were private banks taken over by the Communist government in 1949–52.[21] The remaining four (Chiyu Banking Corporation, Hua Chiao Commercial Bank, Nanyang Commercial Bank and Po Sang Bank) are incorporated under the Hong Kong Banking Ordinance, with Hong Kong or overseas Chinese residents holding minority equity shares.

Following the Bank of China, eight other China-incorporated banks also strengthened their capitalization in 1980: the Bank of Communications from Rmb 100 million to Rmb 300 million; the Kwangtung Provincial Bank, Sin Hua Trust, Savings and Commercial Bank, and Kincheng Banking Corporation from Rmb 80 million to Rmb 200 million each; and China and South Sea Bank, China State Bank, National Commercial Bank, and Yien Yieh Commercial Bank from Rmb 50 million to Rmb 150 million each. Then in 1981, the board of directors and management of the eight banks were reorganized, and all their head offices, hitherto scattered over Beijing, Shanghai, and Guangzhou, were transferred to Beijing.[22]

All these injections of capital and reorganizations of personnel took place against the background of increasing involvement by the CSCBs in various trade and financial activities in Hong Kong, and demonstrated beyond doubt the Chinese Government's appreciation of the importance of Hong Kong as a centre of international trade and finance.

Prior to 1970, the CSCBs generally confined themselves to China-related banking and fiscal business such as financing China's trade with Hong Kong and other countries, dealing in foreign exchange, handling remittances from Hong Kong residents and overseas Chinese, offering deposit facilities denominated in China's currency, *Renminbi* (Rmb), assisting and liaising with foreign businessmen and bankers wishing to do business with China, and acting as the Chinese Government's fiscal agents. Although accepting Hong Kong dollar deposits was also an important part of their business, only a small part of these funds was recycled to finance Hong Kong business activities unconnected with China.[23] Because of the huge trade surplus with Hong Kong, and the absence of any exchange control in the territory, one priority task of the state-controlled banks, especially the Bank of China, was, and still is, to convert such trade earnings into hard currencies and gold to build up China's foreign reserves. Before 1967, China preferred to use sterling both as a trading currency and as a reserve asset; but after sterling's devaluation in that year and the improvement of relations with the United States, China began to diversify into other non-sterling currencies, including the United States dollar, and into gold, though the extent of such diversification has been shrouded in mystery.[24] In 1981, China for the first time published its foreign exchange and gold reserves starting from the end of 1979, which are presented in Appendix 1. As can readily be seen, although the physical holdings of gold are given, there is no breakdown as to the currency composition of the foreign exchange reserves. Rmb remittances and deposits, and China travel financing are monopolized by the state-controlled banks as only they are authorized to deal in the Chinese currency.

Starting from about 1970, the CSCBs began to adopt a much more outward-looking strategy, as China's relations with Hong Kong and the non-Communist world steadily improved. Steps were taken to expand their branch network in order to attract Hong Kong dollar deposits, and to grant loans more liberally to Hong Kong-based industrial and commercial firms not connected with China. Hong Kong real properties and securities were readily accepted as collateral for loans. In the very recent post-Mao period, the CSCBs have become even more aggressive in expanding their operations in Hong Kong. It was reported that in 1977 Beijing actively encouraged, or even prodded, the 13 state-run banks to compete more actively with their local and foreign counterparts in Hong Kong by widening the range of their financial services. In 1979, a conference of the managers of the Bank of China's overseas branches resolved to strengthen its international banking business and to adopt modern business management techniques. In conformity with these policy guidelines, the CSCBs' high profile has become increasingly visible through their stepped-up activities in Hong Kong, too numerous to be recounted here.[25] Some of the salient features may, however, be briefly summarized:

(a) *Acquisition of real properties for use as bank premises and staff quarters*: From 1977 to 1981, the CSCBs spent over HK$500 million on new premises, as a result of which the total number of branches of the CSCBs had reached 193 by the end of 1981, second only to the Hong Kong Bank Group as the largest banking group in terms of retail branching network, holding about 23 per cent of total bank deposits in Hong Kong.

(b) *Computerization of banking business*: An IBM computer system was installed in 1979 and became operative in June 1980, through which a savings deposit holder may obtain services from any of the CSCBs' 193 branches throughout Hong Kong, Kowloon and the New Territories. The effect of this technological innovation was startling: it has been reported that in one month alone, the number of savings accounts increased by 14,000 and the amount of savings deposits by HK$810 million.[26] An official report claims that, at the end of 1980, the Bank of China's overseas deposits exceeded US$5 billion, representing a growth of 39 per cent over the previous year. No breakdown of the total deposits was given, but the growth rate of the Bank of China in Hong Kong and Macau was said to be even higher.[27] The computerization was to be extended, according to press reports, to demand and time deposits, and other banking activities. Other technological innovations to attract retail deposits, such as automatic teller machines (ATMs), are also being considered.[28]

(c) *Expansion of lending services*: Apart from increasing loans and advances to Hong Kong firms which may or may not be engaged in China-related business, one notable recent development is the CSCBs' readiness to participate in projects sponsored by the Hong Kong Government. Thus in 1978, the Bank of China and National Commercial Bank backed two companies involved in a joint-venture real estate development with the Hong Kong Mass Transit Railway Corporation, and in 1980 the same two banks joined 14 other financial institutions in providing mortgage finance to buyers of flats under the Home Ownership Scheme. Other innovations include lease and hire-purchase finance for capital goods and consumer durables, and credit card services.

(d) *Participation in syndicated loans*: The Bank of China began its debut in Hong Kong's international syndicated loan market in 1979 when it joined hands with a number of multinational banks in a US$42 million loan to a subsidiary of Sun Hung Kai Securities, the largest brokerage house in Hong Kong. Since then, the CSCBs have figured frequently in the territory's 'tombstone' advertisements of syndicated loans. Among the largest were a HK$600 million loan to China Cement Co., and a HK$1,500 million loan to Midstar Ltd./Byfair Ltd. These activities took place soon after the 1979 directive by the Chinese Government that the Bank of China and its associates in Hong Kong should expand their international banking business.

(e) *Establishment of finance companies and joint-venture merchant banks*: As noted briefly earlier, in 1979–80 there was a rush to establish wholly- or partly-owned DTCs. By the end of 1980 each CSCB had a DTC subsidiary of its own, as may be seen from Table 1.9. In 1980, the Bank of China and Kincheng Banking Corporation entered into a partnership with the Bank of Tokyo to form a merchant bank called Kincheng Tokyo Finance Ltd., the two Chinese banks contributing 15 per cent and 35 per cent respectively, while the Japanese bank provided the remaining 50 per cent of the capital. In another joint venture, the Bank of

Table 1.9 CHINESE STATE-CONTROLLED BANKS AND THEIR DEPOSIT-TAKING COMPANY SUBSIDIARIES

Names of Banks	Deposit-taking Company Subsidiaries/Affiliates
Bank of China	China Development Finance Co., (HK) Ltd. CCIC Finance Ltd. Kincheng Tokyo Finance Co., Ltd.
Bank of Communications	Chiao Tung Finance Co., Ltd.
Sin Hua Trust, Savings and Commercial Bank	Sin Hua Finance Co., Ltd.
Kincheng Banking Corporation	Kincheng Finance (HK) Ltd./ Kincheng Tokyo Finance Co.
Kwangtung Provincial Bank	Five Rams Finance Co., Ltd.
Nanyang Commercial Bank	Nanyang Finance Co., Ltd.
China and South Sea Bank	Chung Nan Finance Co., Ltd.
National Commercial Bank	Che Hsing Finance Co., Ltd.
China State Bank	The China State Finance Co., Ltd.
Yien Yieh Commercial Bank	The Yien Yieh Finance Co., Ltd.
Po Sang Bank	Po Fung Finance Co., Ltd.
Hua Chiao Commercial Bank	Chiao Yue Finance Co., Ltd.
Chiyu Bank Corporation	Chiyu Finance Co., Ltd.

Sources: Annual reports (1980) of CSCBs.

China, China Resources Co. (China's leading state trading corporation in Hong Kong), the First National Bank of Chicago, and the Industrial Bank of Japan teamed up to form CCIC Finance Ltd., of which each of the three banks owns 30 per cent and China Resources Co. owns 10 per cent. Like other commercial banks in Hong Kong, the CSCBs use their DTCs primarily as a device to circumvent the interest rate cartel in order to garner Hong Kong dollar deposits of HK$50,000 or more from the public and to engage in wholesale banking business. The joint-venture merchant banks, on the other hand, provide a useful vehicle for gaining experience in international banking business, and for the promotion, among other things, of foreign investment in China.

(*f*) *Inauguration of modern staff-training programmes*: Realizing that operational efficiency cannot be raised without upgrading the quality of their staff, the Bank of China and its associates in Hong Kong inaugurated a modern training programme in 1980. Hitherto, the CSCBs' staff-training programmes had been heavily ideological in orientation, but the new programme launched in 1980 was basically modelled on similar programmes in other major Western banks, with strong emphasis on vocational or market-oriented subjects such as bank management, business administration, law, economics and data-processing. Teaching staff from the two universities in Hong Kong were invited as guest lecturers on the programme.[29] Some senior officers of the CSCBs were reported to have been seconded to some foreign banks for specified periods in order to learn more about modern bank management and international business.

The expansion and internationalization of the CSCBs in Hong Kong is a good illustration of the interacting effects between Hong Kong's dynamic development and China's stabilization and modernization. On the one hand, the open and cosmopolitan environment in Hong Kong compels the CSCBs to undertake a series of organizational, managerial and technological innovations if for no other purpose than to maintain their market share. Even though they enjoy a monopolistic advantage in certain areas, notably remittances to China, Rmb deposits, and branch banking inside the Special Economic Zones,[30] in other areas they have to compete fiercely with hundreds of major financial institutions from all over the world. The competition thus engendered not only provides a healthy impetus to greater efficiency in the CSCBs, but, through them, it also indirectly facilitates banking reform inside China. As is well known, during the current readjustment period, one of the major tasks is *jingji tizhi gaige* (reform of the economic system), of which banking reform is an important integral part. Details of the banking reform cannot be discussed here; suffice it to say that the main objectives are to transform China's present banks from being mere Treasury agents into real financial intermediaries, and to allow interest rates to perform their real function as 'levers' in the economic system.[31] While it would be presumptuous to suggest that the Hong Kong banking system can serve as a paradigm for China, it remains true that much useful information and many valuable innovations can be transmitted via the CSCBs in Hong Kong to banks and other financial institutions in China for their reference and consideration. On the other side of the coin, Hong Kong's rise as a financial centre could never have occurred so rapidly without the reorientation, noted earlier, of China's foreign and economic policies, which carries with it an increasingly positive attitude towards Hong Kong. Indeed, Hong Kong's special ties with China are an advantage unlikely to be matched by any other rival financial centre, such as Singapore. And, of course, the expansion, modernization and internationalization of CSCBs in Hong Kong also enhances the territory's stature as a 'money metropolis'.

Hong Kong as a Source of Non-trade Income

China's non-trade earnings from Hong Kong consist of three major components: remittances and other unrequited transfers, tourist expenditure and investment profits. China, however, has never published any official statistics on these earnings, and until the Chinese Government changes its policy on this matter, the precise magnitude of China's invisible earnings from Hong Kong must continue to be a subject of private conjecture and estimates.

Remittances and Other Unrequited Transfers

Remittances and other unrequited transfers from overseas Chinese (including Chinese residents of Hong Kong) have been estimated by various scholars such as Y.L. Wu (1963), C.H. Wu (1967), Donnithorne (1967), and Mah (1972), and foreign government agencies such as the United States Central Intelligence Agency (CIA, 1968), and the

Japan External Trade Organization (JETRO, 1979). Of these estimates, Mah's study, which covers the period 1950–67, is the most thorough and complete, and includes not only currency remittances but also food parcels and taxes thereon. JETRO's study covers the more recent period 1970–8 and also includes a projection for 1979–82. It does not, however, distinguish between remittances in money and in kind.

Furthermore, these estimates are aggregates that do not contain information about Hong Kong residents' remittances and gifts to China. Although Hong Kong Chinese constitute only about 23 per cent of all ethnic Chinese living outside China and Taiwan, there are good reasons to believe that they are responsible for the predominant part of total remittances to China. First, they are culturally and geographically much closer to, and tend to care more for, their relatives on the mainland. Second, overseas Chinese, particularly those living in the United States and South-East Asia, were either not allowed to remit money at all, or were allowed to remit only small amounts of money to China before the 1970's.[32] But there have never been any restrictions on residents or the CSCBs in Hong Kong in respect of their financial transactions. In any case, for a considerable period, the CSCBs in Hong Kong served as the only channel through which overseas remittances were transferred to China, particularly for those countries with which China had no diplomatic relations or where there was no Bank of China office.

In the late 1970's, as a combined result of agricultural recovery, a more liberal economic policy, and rising expectations of the population in China, the food parcels of the early 1960's were replaced by consumer durables such as watches, transistor radios, hi-fi stereos, television sets, pocket calculators and other household appliances as the standard gifts by Hong Kong residents to their relatives and friends on the mainland. In response to China's call for assistance in its modernization programme, many wealthy Hong Kong residents are also reported to have made donations to schools, universities and hospitals in China. No systematic data on these gifts and donations have yet been compiled, but a recent Labour Force Survey conducted by the Census and Statistics Department of Hong Kong contains questions about the respondents' gifts to China. Although the results are fragmentary, relating as they do to only three-quarters of the years 1979–80, it can be reasonably inferred by suitable extrapolation that such unrequited transfers amounted to 0.84 per cent and 0.8 per cent respectively of Hong Kong's gross domestic product at current prices in 1979 and 1980.[33]

Table 1.10 HONG KONG'S REMITTANCES AND OTHER UNREQUITED TRANSFERS TO CHINA

Year	(1) Money Remittances (million US dollars)	(2) Gifts and Donations (million US dollars)	(3) Total (million US dollars)	(4) Percentage of Hong Kong GDP
1950	84.7	–	84.7	17.1
1951	94.6	–	94.6	18.8
1952	96.1	–	96.1	20.8
1953	70.7	–	70.7	13.6
1954	64.4	–	64.4	11.2
1955	59.6	–	59.6	9.5
1956	51.0	–	51.0	7.6
1957	35.7	–	35.7	5.0
1958	33.5	–	33.5	4.2
1959	24.4	1.1	25.5	2.8
1960	31.2	9.1	40.3	3.9
1961	27.9	32.7	60.6	5.8
1962	27.9	33.8	61.7	5.1
1963	37.2	22.0	59.2	4.3
1964	46.5	14.3	60.8	3.9
1965	62.3	–	62.3	3.4
1966	55.8	–	55.8	2.9
1967	27.9	–	27.9	1.3
1968	40.0	–	40.0	1.8
1969	41.0	–	41.0	1.6
1970	124.6	–	124.6	4.0
1971	140.4	–	140.4	3.8

Year	(1) Money Remittances (million US dollars)	(2) Gifts and Donations (million US dollars)	(3) Total (million US dollars)	(4) Percentage of Hong Kong GDP
1972	168.3	–	168.3	3.7
1973	176.6	–	176.6	2.7
1974	194.0	–	194.0	2.5
1975	213.2	–	213.2	2.6
1976	234.9	–	234.9	2.2
1977	305.4	89.5	394.9	3.1
1978	366.3	111.0	477.3	3.2
1979	419.2	143.7	562.9	3.3
1980	503.0	170.7	673.7	3.2

Sources: Underlying data from Mah (1972), JETRO (1979), and Census and Statistics Department, Hong Kong Government (unpublished).

From these various sources it is possible to compile a time series, however crude and tentative, of remittances and unrequited transfers from Hong Kong residents to China during 1950–80. In this estimation I have proceeded as follows: (a) it is assumed that the time series of Mah and JETRO (which also incorporates a separate estimate by the Japan Economic Research Institute for 1968–9) are reasonably reliable; (b) it is assumed that from 1950 to 1972, 93 per cent of total overseas remittances to China came from Hong Kong residents, but this proportion fell to 87 per cent during 1973–8 and further to 83 per cent from 1979 onwards, following the steady improvement of relations between China and the non-Communist countries in North America, Europe and Asia;[34] (c) these percentages are then applied to the Mah and JETRO time series for the money remittances; (d) it is assumed that for the four years 1977 to 1980, gifts in kind and other donations to China from Hong Kong residents amounted to 0.7 per cent, 0.75 per cent, 0.84 per cent, and 0.8 per cent respectively of Hong Kong's GDP; and (e) all unrequited transfers other than money remittances (food parcels, consumer durables and donations) are given

100 per cent weighting separately. The results of this statistical reconstruction are presented in Table 1.10. Needless to say, given the paucity of data, the table should be taken as no more than an indication of the possible order of magnitude.[35]

The first three columns of Table 1.10 do not require further comment, but some explanatory remarks may be necessary for Column 4, which measures the 'financial burden' on Hong Kong residents by the ratio of total remittances and other unrequited transfers to GDP. The ratio was very high in the early 1950's, reaching a peak of nearly 21 per cent in 1952. The main reason was that a high level of remittances was required to support the Chinese economy, which was then under severe strain due to the aftermath of the civil war and the Korean War. Moreover, the Communist *Wu-fan* campaign against the 'national bourgeoisie' in 1951–2 also forced many Hong Kong residents to remit foreign exchange to save their relatives in China. Subsequently, the ratio declined sharply, reaching a low of 2.8 per cent in 1959. In the early 1960's, the ratio rose again, caused by the large amount of food parcels sent to China following the failure of the Great Leap Forward movement and three consecutive years of natural disasters and poor harvests. During the height of the Cultural Revolution (1966–9) and the ascendancy of the 'Gang of Four' (1973–6), when overseas remittances were regarded with disfavour by the authorities, the ratio again fell to a very low level. The post-Mao period since 1977 has seen a resurgence of gifts and donations, along with money remittances, to China, but Hong Kong's growing affluence was such that, despite the sharp increase in unilateral transfers, the 'financial burden' indicator remained relatively low and highly stable (at about 3.2 per cent) in 1977–80.

Tourist and Travel Expenditure

For cultural, ethnic and geographical reasons, China should be the top tourist attraction for Hong Kong residents. In the past, self-imposed isolation during the Maoist era and internal disturbances discouraged the growth of the tourist industry. In the late 1970's, realizing the importance of tourism for generating foreign exchange and employment, China began to devote serious efforts to the development of the industry.

A substantial number of Hong Kong residents visit China regularly for a variety of business and personal reasons. Traffic across the border is especially busy during the Lunar New Year holidays and the bi-annual trade fair held in Guangzhou. Expenditure by Hong Kong residents during their sojourn on the mainland constitutes another important source of foreign exchange income for China.

In the absence of official statistics, rough estimates of such expenditure can be made by assuming different levels of per capita spending for different periods.[36] For our purpose, it is assumed, in the light of existing fragmentary evidence, that spending per visitor in China (excluding gifts, which are separately reported in Table 1.10) was US$90 in 1961–7, US$120 in 1968–9, US$170 in 1970–5, US$200 in 1976–7, and US$250 in 1978–80. These are then applied to the known visitors from Hong Kong (defined as holders of a Hong Kong Re-entry Permit or Hong Kong British passport). The results are presented in Table 1.11.

Table 1.11 EXPENDITURE BY HONG KONG VISITORS TO CHINA (million US dollars)

Year*	Expenditure in China
1961–2	35.1
1962–3	32.0
1963–4	27.9
1964–5	37.6
1965–6	39.2
1966–7	24.0
1967–8	22.8
1968–9	35.4
1969–70	47.9
1970–1	54.1
1971–2	98.1
1972–3	114.3
1973–4	153.2

Year*	Expenditure in China
1974–5	133.4
1975–6	118.3
1976–7	175.1
1977–8	223.5
1978–9	367.5
1979–80	819.4
1980–1	951.8

* April 1 to March 31, in accordance with Immigration Department records.

Source: For the number of Hong Kong visitors, Immigration Department, Hong Kong Government.

Travel and tourism is one area where China's internal policy changes can produce dramatic effects. In the 1960's, the average annual number of Hong Kong visitors was about 347,000. Indeed, in 1967–8, at the height of the Cultural Revolution, when Hong Kong itself was hit by the spillover of violent disturbances, the number dropped to only 253,198. The more normal period of 1970–6 saw a rapid increase in the average number of visitors to about 690,000. However, it was not until the advent of the post-Mao era that an explosive growth took place. In 1977, the number of Hong Kong visitors for the first time crossed the one million mark. By 1980, the number had more than trebled to 3.8 million. This astonishing growth, together with the rising affluence of Hong Kong people, was enough to generate a staggering foreign exchange income of some US$951.8 million in 1980, nearly 18 times as high as it was merely a decade ago.

Investment Income

Apart from its substantial stake in the financial sector, already discussed in a previous section, China also has extensive investments in other sectors of the Hong Kong economy. According to a pro-Beijing paper, there were more than 50 offices or branches representing China's state-run trading and investment corporations in Hong Kong at the end of 1981.[37] A left-wing economic yearbook for 1981 lists some 1,136 sub-agents or wholesalers and 101 department stores specializing in Chinese products.[38] These are marketing outlets mostly owned by private Hong Kong businessmen but indirectly controlled by China. The same source does not however give any information on companies in other areas of activity either wholly or partly owned by China. However, China is known to have invested substantially, through 40 or more companies, in warehouses, cold storage, transport, travel services, real estate, manufacturing, cinemas, film studios, petrol stations, and publishing.[39]

Estimates of China's total investments in Hong Kong are again a matter of guesswork. The latest one is by the Chairman of the Hong Kong General Chamber of Commerce, Mr David Newbigging, who gave a figure of US$3–5 billion as the total value of such investments for 1981.[40] However, no breakdown or explanation has been provided.

The involvement of China's financial institutions in Hong Kong can in principle be measured by their total net worth as shown in their financial statements. The financial standing of the 13 CSCBs at the end of 1980 is shown in Appendix 2. It must be emphasized, however, that the total net worth of the CSCBs is not equal to the sum of the net worth of individual banks in Hong Kong for two reasons. First, the balance sheet of the Bank of China is a consolidated account covering its global operations, even though the Hong Kong branch may be the most important constituent part of the whole. Second, the Bank of China owns a substantial proportion of the shareholdings of the other 12 banks, though the exact amount is not known. Simple aggregation would therefore result in double-counting and over-estimation. After suitable adjustments, the total net worth of China's financial institutions (including licensed banks, DTCs, insurance companies and joint-venture merchant banks) at the end of 1980 was probably in the region of US$1,556 million.[41]

We are unable to use the same method to quantify China's equity interests in the non-financial sector, as the balance sheets of non-financial firms are not readily available. The problem is complicated by the prevailing practice of using Hong Kong residents as 'fronts' to disguise the real ownership. However, from fragmentary and admittedly incomplete information from various sources (for example,

Company Registry records), the total net worth of China-owned non-financial establishments is conservatively estimated at about US$400 million in 1980. Together with its interests in the financial sector, China's total equity investment in Hong Kong in the same year would thus amount to about US$1,956 million.

Note that we are using net worth as a measuring rod. The China-controlled non-financial entities can, however, borrow quite freely in Hong Kong, and for our purpose we assume that they only borrow from the CSCBs and their DTCs. The CSCBs, in turn, borrow heavily from the Hong Kong public in the form of customers' deposits. Because of this financial leverage, the net equity investment of US$1,956 million can support, on some plausible assumptions, assets totalling some US$6,639 million, after netting out financial transactions between the CSCBs and the non-financial firms. The logic of this inference is explained by a T-account exercise in Appendix 3.

China's entry into the Hong Kong property market has been a very recent phenomenon. In the early 1970's, some CSCBs formed small subsidiary property firms as vehicles for the investment of idle funds.[42] This modest involvement in the real estate sector accelerated dramatically after 1976–7. There are two motives for this development. One is the obvious need for various financial and non-financial enterprises to acquire more premises in order to expand their operations. The other is the simple desire to make more money on Hong Kong's highly lucrative real estate market, often in partnership with major local property companies. Perhaps the most sensational project so far is the development of a 1,200-acre site at Tin Shui Wai, New Territories, by a consortium called Mighty City, in which China Resources, China's top trade organization in Hong Kong, has a 51 per cent controlling interest. The plan is to develop a new town for half a million people, at a cost of some HK$8 billion (1980 prices).[43] A mixture of the two motives, of course, is also possible. Thus, according to a left-wing press report, China Resources intends to retain only 26 floors of its new 53-floor building on the Wan Chai waterfront, due for completion in 1983, for the use of various official Chinese organizations, leaving the rest for lease to other firms.[44] The exact amount which China has invested in Hong Kong properties is not known, but a senior manager of Wardley, the merchant-banking arm of the Hongkong and Shanghai Banking Corporation, is reported to have estimated that from 1977 to 1980, China had acquired real estate worth at least HK$3 billion, but probably as much as HK$10 billion.[45]

An even more recent development is China's involvement in the manufacturing and public utilities sectors. Prior to 1976, China had only two firms in Hong Kong producing cigarettes and monosodium glutamate. Since then, China-controlled companies have set up a machine tool and heavy machinery plant, a shipyard, a cement plant (a joint venture with American and local interests), and a watch-casing plant (a joint venture with a Japanese company). In September 1981, a leading China-product company took over a flagging local textile firm for a cash price of HK$47.79 million. A triangular deal, worth some US$1.77 billion, whereby Britain would sell power generation equipment and services to Hong Kong, while China would provide coal to power stations operated by China Light and Power Co. Ltd., a Hong Kong firm, and import electricity from it for Guangdong Province, was concluded in 1978. There is also a plan to build a wharf in Hong Kong costing some US$80 million to facilitate entrepôt trade with Guangdong.[46]

Of the various components of China's total investment income from Hong Kong, only bank profits can be roughly estimated from the financial statements of the CSCBs. Table 1.12 presents the unadjusted and adjusted net profits of the CSCBs. The unadjusted profits are those aggregated from the balance sheet figures of each individual bank.[47] These exaggerate the true profits derived from Hong Kong for the same accounting reasons already mentioned earlier in respect of net worth. To adjust for these distorting factors, we make certain assumptions, which it is hoped are not unduly arbitrary. For the years 1975–8, we assume that 70 per cent of the Bank of China's profits, and half of the others' profits, are attributable to Hong Kong. For the year 1979, the proportion of the Bank of China is reduced to 60 per cent. For 1980, the respective proportions of the Bank of China and other banks are further reduced to 50 per cent and 40 per cent. The reasons for these reductions are that the Bank of China has in recent years aggressively expanded its global operations, and has also increased its shareholdings in other CSCBs. The adjusted profits, shown in the table, indicate that the CSCBs as a group were able to achieve an average annual growth rate of profits of over 40 per cent, a rate generally in keeping with those of other banks, and certainly consistent with the banking and overall economic boom in Hong Kong during that period.

Table 1.12 NET PROFITS OF CHINESE STATE-CONTROLLED BANKS IN HONG KONG

Year	Unadjusted Global Profits (million US dollars)	Adjusted Profits Attributable to Hong Kong (million US dollars)
1975	59.7	37.1
1976	86.6 (+41.5%)	52.6 (+41.8%)
1977	116.6 (+34.6%)	71.7 (+36.3%)
1978	162.8 (+39.6%)	100.9 (+40.7%)
1979	261.2 (+60.4%)	145.7 (+44.4%)
1980	498.6 (+90.9%)	229.8 (+57.7%)

Note: Numbers in brackets indicate annual growth rates.

Sources: Underlying data from Wilson (1980), Goodstadt (1980), and *China Trade Report*, December 1981.

No similar exercise can be done for non-banking profits, since it is impossible to obtain balance sheet information from all the China-owned enterprises in Hong Kong. Only a crude and aggregative estimate can be made, again on somewhat arbitrary though not unreasonable assumptions. The most often cited figure is that China derived an investment income of about US$300 million in 1976 from Hong Kong.[48] We take this as a benchmark figure and, given the banking profits, the non-banking profits are derived for 1976. We then assume that the non-banking profits grew at the same rate as the nominal GDP in 1976–80. To allow for the scale effect of increased investment after 1977, we add another 10 per cent to the GDP growth rate. However, since the CSCBs themselves own some equity interests in non-financial enterprises, we therefore deduct 5 per cent from the total growth rate to avoid double-counting. After making all these adjustments, the assumed growth rates of non-banking profits are 19.7 per cent for 1977, 21.6 per cent for 1978, 28.9 per cent for 1979, and 28.2 per cent for 1980. These are lower than those of banking profits, but not inconsistent with the economic reality during that period. The results are given in Table 1.13.

Table 1.13 CHINA'S TOTAL NET INVESTMENT EARNINGS FROM HONG KONG (million US dollars)

Year	Banking Profits	Non-banking Profits	Total
1976	52.6	247.4	300.0
1977	71.7	296.1	367.8
1978	100.9	360.1	461.0
1979	145.7	464.2	609.9
1980	229.8	595.1	824.9

Hong Kong as a Source of Investment Capital

In the early 1950's, a number of investment corporations were set up in various cities and provinces in China to accept capital subscriptions from overseas Chinese and 'Hong Kong and Macau compatriots', the proceeds from which were reinvested in industrial projects. Investors were guaranteed an annual 8 per cent dividend on their shareholdings. The exact amount of such investments by Hong Kong residents is not known, though it is believed to be small.[49] At any rate, these investment companies were suspended during the Cultural Revolution in May 1969, and were not re-established until about 1978.

Hong Kong residents did not begin to invest on any significant scale until after 1977. While China's abundant and cheap supply of land and labour acts as a powerful magnet, Hong Kong entrepreneurs are also influenced by a vague desire to help China's modernization, given that profit prospects are still highly uncertain. China, on its part, is extremely keen to attract Hong Kong capital and expertise.[50] Initially, Hong Kong investment inside China in 1977–9 primarily took the form of processing-on-consignment and compensation trade agreements, mostly in Shenzhen just across the border. The real impetus came in 1979–80, when China promulgated its joint-venture code, gave Guangdong and Fujian Provinces greater autonomy in matters of foreign trade and investment, and formally designated four cities as 'Special Economic Zones' (SEZs) — an idea borrowed from the successful experience of 'export-processing zones' in other developing countries, notably Taiwan. These four are Shenzhen, Zhuhai and Shantou in Guangdong Province, and Xiamen in Fujian Province. For obvious geographical reasons, Shenzhen is the most convenient and popular for Hong Kong investors and industrialists. Shenzhen itself is divided into several sections, of which the western section, Shekou, is earmarked for industrial development, and is managed by China Merchants Steam Navigation Co., a Hong Kong-based shipping unit under China's Ministry of Communications.

No official statistics on Hong Kong's investment in the SEZs have been prepared by either the Chinese or the Hong Kong Government. Hong Kong businessmen, of course, enjoy the advantages of geographical proximity and cultural affinity. But perhaps even more important is their renowned flexibility. They are known, for example, to be less fussy than their Western or Japanese counterparts about legal technicalities, and for this reason alone are more ready to enter into agreements with the Chinese authorities.

According to *Jingji Daobao*, a pro-Beijing periodical in Hong Kong, at the end of August 1981, the Shenzhen authorities had signed some 814 contracts with foreign investors, with a total pledged investment of HK$2,760 million (US$465 million). Of this total, Hong Kong investors accounted for no less than 91 per cent, with overseas Chinese and other foreign investors contributing the remaining 5.5 per cent and 3.5 per cent respectively.[51] A more up-to-date report has been published by a Western newspaper, *Asian Wall Street Journal*. For easy reference, the information is reproduced in Table 1.14.[52]

The table does not provide any breakdown as to the source of investment funds, but if we accept the 91 per cent figure reported by *Jingji Daobao*, then pledged investment from Hong Kong residents

Table 1.14 FOREIGN INVESTMENT IN SHENZHEN AS AT JANUARY 31, 1982

Category	Number of Contracts	Pledged Investment (million US dollars)
100 per cent equity investment	18	177
Equity joint venture	11	25
Co-operation joint venture	85	1,330
Processing and assembling	647	8.3
Compensation trade	6	13.4
Agriculture and fishery	233	16.8
Total	1,000	1,570.5

Source: *Asian Wall Street Journal*, February 5, 1982.

should amount to about US$1,429 million. The industrial zone at Shekou alone has attracted US$172 million in pledged investment, virtually all from Hong Kong businessmen or Hong Kong-based foreign companies, as geographically it is even closer to Hong Kong.[53] However, since Shekou is part of Shenzhen, investment there is presumably already included in Table 1.14.

Table 1.14 also does not provide information on the classification of investment by industry, and it is not clear whether three huge projects, signed at the end of 1981, are included. Two of these projects are financed by a Hong Kong company, Hopewell Holdings Ltd. One is the development of the Futian New Town in Shenzhen costing some HK$2 billion, for which China provides land and labour, and Hopewell provides capital funds. The other is the building of a 240-kilometre expressway network linking Shenzhen, Guangzhou and Macau. This joint venture, in which China provides land and labour, while Hopewell contributes funds and technology, is to cost HK$2.4 billion. The third project is the development of an industrial processing area and scientific and cultural facilities — including a university — in Shenzhen. Again, the Hong Kong partner, in this case Lian Cheng Enterprises, finances the whole project, which is to cost HK$2.5 billion.[54] These three projects alone require a capital investment totalling HK$6.9 billion (US$1.21 billion), all from Hong Kong Chinese.

The earlier report by *Jingji Daobao* does contain a breakdown of investment by industry. The relative proportions of total pledged investment as at the end of August 1981 were: manufacturing, 16.26 per cent, agriculture and fishing, 4.13 per cent, commerce, 7.87 per cent, tourism, 28.32 per cent, real estate, 39.45 per cent, transport and communications, 0.23 per cent, and others, 3.62 per cent. However, the three giant projects were definitely not included in this earlier estimate.

One favourite form of investment inside China is real estate, particularly residential buildings. China has good reasons to court capital and technology from Hong Kong in this area, partly to earn foreign exchange and partly to relieve the acute shortage of accommodation in Chinese cities. For their part, Hong Kong investors also have strong motivations for acquiring real properties in China, as long as there is a reasonable guarantee, which the present regime on the mainland appears willing to provide, against arbitrary expropriation. Most of the residential units have been purchased for the benefit of relatives in China, but Hong Kong investors may also buy them as retirement or holiday homes, temporary business premises, or even inflation hedges.[55] Furthermore, real estate development is an area in which Hong Kong entrepreneurs have very considerable expertise and experience. Property investment is not confined however to the SEZs, but is spreading to other major cities like Shanghai, Hangzhou, Fuzhou and Guangzhou. Table 1.15 gives an incomplete list of residential units built in China but marketed in Hong Kong as of May 31, 1981. Total investment by final buyers is estimated at about HK$1,038 million (US$185.4 million) of which HK$36.1 million (US$65 million) was in cities outside the SEZs. Most final buyers are Hong Kong residents, though overseas Chinese or even Taiwanese are also known to have bought such units from Hong Kong developers.

Another popular investment much favoured by both Hong Kong and overseas Chinese is the hotel industry. Hong Kong-based companies, both Chinese and foreign, are actively involved in the building, financing and management of hotels in major cities like Beijing, Nanjing, Guangzhou, and so on, in addition to their commitments in the SEZs. It is difficult to quantify exactly Hong Kong's involvement in the hotel industry outside the SEZs, because virtually all the projects are joint ventures, in which the partners' shares are often not disclosed. However, from press reports about individual projects, one can roughly estimate that Hong Kong's total investment in China's hotel industry as of mid-1981 should not be less than US$170 million.[56]

Information about Hong Kong's investment in other SEZs is very scanty. An official publication discloses that in 1980, 72 contracts with foreign businessmen had been concluded in Zhuhai and 103 in Xiamen, without any indication, however, as to the capital invested and its sources.[57] Hong Kong companies are said to be involved in a HK$150 million highway linking Guangzhou with Zhuhai, and a resort centre in the latter.[58] Generally speaking, these three SEZs are much less attractive than Shenzhen, not merely because of the geographical factor, but also because they were formed much later (particularly Shantou), and are still seriously lacking in infrastructural facilities.

Despite frequent suggestions and rumours in the past, China has not yet formally made use of Hong Kong's capital market. However, following its successful placement of yen bonds in Japan in early 1982, the China International Trust and Investment Corporation (CITIC) is reported to be considering the issue of bonds on European, American and Asian markets as well.[59] Since the late 1960's, a number of foreign companies have successfully issued securities on the Hong Kong capital market, and in principle there is no reason why Chinese enterprises cannot do so likewise.

In sum, since 1977, Hong Kong residents have pledged investment inside China amounting to nearly US$2 billion. China's recent introduction of a series of 'economic legislation' on taxation and employment, and regulations for the SEZs, is designed, among other things, to encourage a further inflow of capital funds from Hong Kong. Since Hong Kong's investment projects are predominantly in light industries, tourism, housing and infrastructure, they fit in with China's current priorities quite well, and they are unlikely to be affected by the retrenchment programme. Provided there is no sudden reversal in China's present pragmatic policy, prospects for the continued growth of Hong Kong investment in China should be reasonably good.

Table 1.15 PROPERTY DEVELOPMENT IN CHINA

Location	Development[1]	Date of Occupancy	Size (sq. ft.)
GUANGDONG PROVINCE			
Shenzhen	Green Bamboo Garden (first phase)	mid-1981	620–725
	Green Bamboo Garden (second phase)	early 1982	650–845
	Tung Wu Garden	mid-1981	650–666
	Starling Beach Resort	mid-1981	700–2,300
	Lowu Building	mid-1982	440–600
	Shenzhen International Commercial Building	late 1982	334–718
	Friendship Building	early 1983	432–557
	Astoria Building	N.A.	410–481
	Hai Feng Yuan	N.A.	516–1,200
	Golden Capital Court	late 1983	380–499
	Lake Centre Building	early 1983	586–715
Guangzhou	East Lake Villa	late 1981	706–1,157
	Hsiao Kang City	late 1981	534–661
	Chang Le Yuen	Sept. 1981	500–600
	White Cloud Garden	mid-1981	400–1,041
	Yi Cui Garden	early 1982	612–824
Wuzhou	Yuanyang Jiang New Village	Sept. 1981	538
Zhaoqing	Jianshe New Villa	mid-1981	790
Taishan	Overseas Chinese New Villa (first phase)	late 1980	588–1,548
Zhongshan	Qi Jiang Garden	late 1980	632–750

MARKETED IN HONG KONG

Unit Cost[2] (in HK dollars)	No. of Units Available	Developer
150,000–242,500	108	Cogi Estates Ltd.
131,500–208,000	N.A.	Cogi Estates Ltd.
148,000–180,000	216	Millie's Holdings
185,000–852,400	60	Chung Fat Co.
115,900–183,800	288	Whalsay Enterprises Ltd.
100,800–200,300	320	Chung Fat Tai Tung Property Co.
94,900–178,900	N.A.	Samlin Enterprises Co.
80,000	N.A.	Astoria (China) Development Ltd.
140,200–423,600	144	China Overseas Building Development Co. Ltd.
79,800–124,750	1,000	Haylee Estates Agency Co.
184,000–239,000	240	Bo Kiu Development Co.
146,000–274,700	290	Chrysoberyl River Development Ltd.
110,000–150,000	432	Guangzhou Hsiao Kang City Development (HK) Ltd.
95,000–119,800	96	Whalsay Enterprises Ltd.
118,200–280,000	250	Raycott Co. Ltd.
157,000–226,000	56	Quadrutec Development
69,960–74,160	80	Wah Tung Co.
70,000 up	N.A.	Hung Fook Land Investment Co.
81,000–194,610	120	Hang Fat Investment and Construction Ltd.
103,950–131,000	90	Silver River Investment Ltd.

Location	Development[1]	Date of Occupancy	Size (sq. ft.)
Weizhou	Wei Hua Garden	Apr. 1981	620–670
	Lian Teng Overseas Chinese New Villa	early 1981	365–515
Zhuhai	Silver Sea Garden	late 1982	876–1,700
	Pan Sea Villa	late 1982	525–1,500
Foshan	Kiu Yuen Sun Chuen	Nov. 1981	592–686
	Lan Yuen Sun Chuen	mid-1982	803–852
Pan Yu	Overseas Chinese New Villa	Dec. 1981	300 up
Shantou	Overseas Chinese New Villa	late 1980	536–1,000
SHANGHAI	Yuen Nan Overseas Chinese New Villa	mid-1981	735–962
ZHEJIANG PROVINCE			
Hangzhou	West Lake Overseas Chinese New Village	Sept. 1981	547–942
	Zhaohui Overseas Chinese New Village	Sept. 1981	606–757
FUJIAN PROVINCE			
Xiamen	Jimei Overseas Chinese New Village	late 1981	593–687
	Xiamen Overseas Chinese New Village	late 1981	390–950
Fuzhou	Overseas Chinese New Village	late 1980	650–750
JIANGSU PROVINCE			
Wuxi	Bai Hua Yuen Overseas Chinese Apartments	Aug. 1981	796

[1] Where official English names are not available, the name of the development is given in *pinyin*.

[2] The price given is the list price. Small discounts are available depending on payment methods.

Unit Cost[2] (in HK dollars)	No. of Units Available	Developer
120,000–141,500	108	Whalsay Enterprises Ltd.
43,500–58,800	48	Whalsay Enterprises Ltd.
193,500–700,000	416	Gold Fair Investment Ltd.
136,500–405,000	N.A.	Pan Sky Enterprises Co. Ltd.
94,000–128,000	210	Sun Su Tung Ltd.
162,000–192,000	126	Real Time Co. Ltd.
40,000 up	96	Merriment Development Co.
88,440–185,000	N.A.	Chung Fat Development Co.
145,000–245,500	200	Heysham Enterprises
94,500–195,000	72	Shing Kung Enterprises Co.
112,000–165,500	96	Coinway Investment Co. Ltd.
112,670–147,750	N.A.	Tung Fung Enterprises Co.
70,500–194,500	182	Chung Fat Development Co.
97,000–135,000	90	Beaconsland Development Co.
69,500–89,500	20	Shing Kung Development Co.

N.A.: not available.

Source: *China Trade Report*, June 1981.

Conclusion

In the previous sections we have analysed the various ways in which Hong Kong has helped to accumulate and mobilize capital funds for China's industrialization and modernization. In this concluding section, our aim is to make an overall assessment of Hong Kong's financial contributions and their importance to China.

One convenient and traditional starting point is to determine Hong Kong's percentage contribution to China's total foreign exchange earnings on current account. Due to the lack of data, we will confine our estimates to the recent period 1977–80 only. Although China has not so far published any official balance of payments statistics, a recent study by Yamada (1981) presented some figures for 1977–80 said to be derived from the Bank of China for submission to the International Monetary Fund. However tentative and sketchy these statistics are, they at least provide some basis for ascertaining Hong Kong's role in China's overall financial position.

Table 1.16 summarizes China's total net foreign exchange earnings

Table 1.16 CHINA'S NET FOREIGN EXCHANGE EARNINGS FROM HONG KONG (million US dollars)

	1977	1978	1979	1980
Trade surplus	1,741.4	2,259.5	3,034.1	4,407.2
Remittances and other unrequited transfers	394.9	477.3	562.9	673.7
Travel and tourism	223.5	367.5	819.4	951.8
Investment profits	367.8	461.0	609.9	824.9
Total	2,727.6	3,565.3	5,026.3	6,857.6
Percentage share in China's total current foreign exchange earnings (excluding loans and capital flows)	29.3	31.7	31.8	36.5

Sources: For various types of earnings from Hong Kong, see previous tables; for China's total current foreign exchange earnings, see Yamada (1981).

from Hong Kong for 1977–80. As may be readily seen, the estimated foreign earnings more than doubled from about US$2.7 billion in 1977 to about US$6.9 billion in 1980. Expressed as a percentage of China's total current foreign exchange earnings, visible and invisible, Hong Kong's relative share also increased steadily from 29.3 per cent to 36.5 per cent in that period, with an average of 32.3 per cent.

Hong Kong's importance as a source of foreign exchange can also be appreciated from another perspective. The official statistics on China's foreign reserves, given in Appendix 1, show that foreign exchange reserves amounted to US$2,154 million at the end of 1979 and US$2,262 million at the end of 1980. If the unchanged gold holdings at 12.8 million troy ounces, valued at the London year-end closing prices of US$524 and US$588 per ounce respectively, are added, China's total external reserves were US$8,861 million at the end of 1979 and US$9,788 million at the end of 1980. Since the figures in Table 1.16 are *net* earnings, they imply therefore that without the foreign exchange earnings obtained via Hong Kong, China would have lost about 57 per cent and 70 per cent of its total external reserves respectively in 1979 and 1980.

Hong Kong's role in financing China's modernization is not confined, however, to generating net foreign exchange earnings on the current account. As a financial centre in its own right, Hong Kong is providing both short- and long-term loans and other facilities to China. Although Hong Kong's net claims on China dropped sharply in 1980–1 due to China's retrenchment programme and the unprecedentedly high level of world interest rates, once economic readjustment is completed and interest rates fall to a more normal level, it is almost certain that China will make use of Hong Kong's financial system (including not only the banks and DTCs, but also the capital market) much more actively and aggressively, especially if the exploration and development of China's offshore oil fields in the South China Sea goes ahead as planned.

In addition, in the post-Mao era Hong Kong has emerged as a major source of equity capital. Since 1977, Hong Kong residents have pledged investments totalling some US$2 billion, more than that from any other country, and the amount is still growing. Most of the funds have gone to the SEZs in the southern coastal provinces of Guangdong and Fujian; in particular, Shenzhen is being almost entirely financed by Hong Kong Chinese entrepreneurs or Hong Kong-based foreign companies. In general, Hong Kong entrepreneurs are exceptionally responsive to incentives and, given the right investment climate, they will be more than willing to help their country of origin. Whether capital flow from Hong Kong to China can be sustained at a high rate and on a long-term basis depends crucially on internal political stability in China and the continuance of the present pragmatic, outward-looking economic policy.

Quantitative measures do not, however, exhaust Hong Kong's role in financing China's modernization. Although it is difficult, and perhaps impossible, to quantify the transfer of knowledge and technology from one financial system to another, the fact that a qualitative process of such transfer exists, and is vitally important to a developing country, can hardly be denied. Operating in a highly competitive and dynamic environment, the CSCBs have been compelled to initiate a series of organizational, managerial and technological innovations. The experience and lessons which they have accumulated will be a valuable input for the reform and modernization of China's domestic banking and financial structure.

While no one can dispute the vital role which Hong Kong performs in helping China to overcome the 'foreign exchange gap' and 'technological gap', it would be wrong to conclude that China is financially dependent on Hong Kong. Important as they are, China's annual earnings from Hong Kong still account for less than one per cent of its gross national product. The loss of such a revenue would represent a disastrous setback to China's modernization, but would not be necessarily fatal. It is also useful to be reminded of the fact that Hong Kong's industrialization in the 1950's and 1960's, and its rise as a financial centre in the 1970's, owed much to China's implicit support in the form of a stable supply of basic necessities at competitive prices, and of course, to the initiation of the modernization programme itself. Our analysis therefore confirms the importance of economic interdependence between China and Hong Kong. Fortunately, there is growing evidence that this homely truth is being appreciated, more explicitly than ever, by policy-makers at all levels in Beijing, London and Hong Kong.

Notes

[1] Thus, in the Budget Speech for 1981–2, the then Financial Secretary of Hong Kong, Sir Philip Haddon-Cave, declared: 'I envisage that the relative size of the contribution of the tertiary services will continue to increase, due, in no small measure, to the demands likely to arise from the expansion of China's international trade, a condition and a consequence of the four modernizations programme. The provision of such additional facilities as may be necessary to enable Hong Kong to cope with these demands will constitute a further diversification of our economy and should make it less vulnerable to downturns in specific trades,' *The 1981-2 Budget*, February 25, 1981, para. 263. In the *Report of the Advisory Committee on Diversification* (1979), the need to expand Hong Kong's infrastructure and service sectors to support China's modernization is also stressed. See Chapter V of the Report.

[2] Prior to 1981, few or no financial statistics were released by China. Partly as a result of China's admission into the International Monetary Fund and World Bank, and partly because of the more pragmatic policies of the post-Mao leadership, China began to publish regularly certain basic financial statistics such as bank deposits and loans, foreign exchange rates and reserves, and so on, in 1981, though a systematic balance of payments accounting is still lacking. In Hong Kong, official attempts to compile balance of payments data began only very recently, and so far only estimates of the current account balance have been made. See *The 1981-2 Budget*, Statistical Appendix, Table 4. Unofficial estimates of China's balance of payments have been made by the United States Central Intelligence Agency (CIA) and Japan External Trade Organization (JETRO).

[3] Although the People's Republic of China was officially proclaimed on October 1, 1949, Hong Kong trade statistics did not separate mainland China from Taiwan until 1950.

[4] With base year 1973 = 100, the unit value index of imports from China rose to 170, while the quantum index rose to 229 in 1980.

[5] For a recent study of income and price elasticities of Hong Kong's demand for imports from China, see Hsueh and Woo (1981).

[6] In November 1981, an agreement was signed whereby Guangdong Province would increase its supply of water to Hong Kong by 30 per cent from November 1981 to April 1982, and by 20 per cent from May 1982 to February 1983. The price of water was also increased by 66 per cent from Rmb 0.15 to Rmb 0.25 per

cubic metre. For the water import figures, I am indebted to Mr K.L. Ng, Assistant Commissioner of Census and Statistics, Hong Kong Government.

[7] When I visited China in November 1981 as a guest of the Chinese Academy of Social Sciences, I was informed by economists and officials in Shanghai that owing to port congestion in that city, export goods from interior provinces were often diverted to Hong Kong for transshipment to third countries. The main difficulty is the lack of deepwater berths and facilities for containers, and specialized bulk-handling equipment.

[8] For more detailed discussions on trade between China and Hong Kong, see Szczepanik (1961), Yeung (1970, 1974), Hsueh and Woo (1981), and Hang Seng Bank (1982). For recent studies of China's external trade in general, see Mah (1972), Hsiao (1977), Batsavage and Davie (1978), Kravalis (1978), and Hsueh and Shea (1981).

[9] See Woo (1977), pp. 65–89.

[10] See Jao (1979, 1981).

[11] Internal developments in Hong Kong, such as the relaxation of the moratorium on licences for full-service commercial banks in 1978, also helped. But China's policy reorientation was clearly of more fundamental and pervasive importance.

[12] For more details about China's handling of Soviet loans, see Hsia and Chin (1965), and Mah (1972), pp. 148–61.

[13] Quoted from Tsai (1969).

[14] See Central Intelligence Agency (1978), Table A-12, p. 22.

[15] Even so, the question of foreign trade credit became one of the issues in the bitter debate and power struggle between the moderates and the radicals in the Chinese Communist party between 1970–6.

[16] At the end of 1981, China had contracted foreign credit totalling some US$30 billion. See Yamada (1981). In early 1982, the China International Trust and Investment Corporation (CITIC) arranged a credit line of US$1 billion with more than 40 foreign banks, and placed a 10-billion yen (US$43 million) bond with Japanese financial institutions, making a total foreign debt position to date of some US$31.04 billion.

[17] *The Banker*, February 1981, pp. 15–16. For the latest number of foreign banks in China, see *Ta Kung Pao*, January 20, 1982.

[18] In Tables 1.5 and 1.6, the external liabilities and claims are reported against the

country of the branch making or accepting the deposits, and not against the country of its head office; for example, a claim on the London branch of a United States bank is reported against the United Kingdom, and not against the United States. In theory, items in both tables may pertain, for example, to a foreign financial institution's branch inside China. In practice, however, this quibble is purely academic, since only 23 foreign banks have so far been permitted to do business inside China, and of these only five operate branches on a limited service basis. Another query might be that part of the net claims against China could originate (although we do not know how much) from China-owned financial institutions in Hong Kong. This may well be the case, but on reflection this contention, even if true, does not affect our argument. For the China-owned financial institutions merely act as intermediaries by channelling funds from Hong Kong to China. Ultimately, it is the Hong Kong depositors who lend to China.

[19] According to Premier Zhao Ziyang in his speech to the National People's Congress in December 1981, the period of economic readjustment would last for at least another five years.

[20] In 1980, the Bank of China's articles of association were also amended to clear up its authority to borrow, a legal question that became important to foreign banks as China entered the international money market. See Cohen (1980).

[21] The Bank of Communications was taken over by the Ministry of Finance, while the Kwangtung Provincial Bank was absorbed by the People's Bank of China. The six private banks were reorganized into the so-called joint state-private banks and became in effect part of the People's Bank. See Miyashita (1966), Chapter 6; Hsiao (1971), pp. 24–8; and Jao (1971). In China itself, all these banks except the Bank of China have lost their identities, but in Hong Kong they are allowed to retain their original names.

[22] *Xinbao (Hong Kong Economic Journal)*, April 17, 1980; *Ta Kung Pao*, March 16, 1981; and *Ming Pao*, April 10, 1981. The increased capital funds for the eight banks came from the Ministry of Finance via the Bank of China. The paid-up capital of these banks was last increased in 1974.

[23] For a detailed description of the activities of the Chinese state-controlled banks in Hong Kong before 1972, see Nihon Boeki Shinkokai (1973).

[24] For further details, see Cheng (1975) and Weintraub (1977).

[25] See Liu (1978, 1979); *South China Morning Post Business News*, April 29, 1980; *Xinbao*, April 17, 1980, and December 7, 1981; Zhong (1981); 'Interview with Bu Min, President of the Bank of China', *Jingji Daobao* (*Economic Reporter*), January 7, 1981, pp. 4–5.

[26] *Ta Kung Pao*, March 6, 1981.

[27] *Ta Kung Pao*, March 6, 1981. In official statements, the 'Bank of China' includes not only the Bank of China proper, but also the 12 other CSCBs in Hong Kong. The CSCBs' branches in Hong Kong accounted for about 82 per cent of the Bank of China's overseas network of 207 branches at the end of 1980.

[28] *South China Morning Post Business News*, February 5, 1982.

[29] The present writer served as one of the guest lecturers in 1980.

[30] Up to January 1982, only the Bank of China and Nanyang Commercial Bank were allowed to open branches in Shenzhen. *Jingji Daobao*, January 18, 1982, p. 4.

[31] For a more detailed discussion of the proposed reform, see Liu (1980), Chapter 10; Chai (1981); Zhang (1981); and Huang *et al.* (1981), Chapter 19.

[32] See Mah (1972), pp. 170–5.

[33] According to unpublished data in the Labour Force Survey, Hong Kong residents' gifts to China amounted to HK$126 million in the first quarter of 1979, HK$205 million in the third quarter of 1979, and HK$218 million in the third quarter of 1980. I am indebted for this information to Mr K.L. Ng, Assistant Commissioner, and Ms Lily Fong, Statistician, of the Census and Statistics Department. Since these gifts were mostly consumer durables such as television sets, hi-fi stereos, and so on, imported from abroad, they are widely believed to be one of the factors responsible for the sharp deterioration in Hong Kong's trade deficit since 1977.

[34] Mah's study contains an estimate of remittances from Singapore and Malaya during 1950–60, which averaged less than 5 per cent of the total. See Mah (1972), p. 238, and also Wu and Wu (1980), Chapter 4.

[35] Actually, apart from food parcels and consumer durables, other goods such as medicines, pharmaceutical products and clothing (mainly used) have regularly been sent by Hong Kong residents to their relatives in China since 1949. For want of reliable information, they are not included in Table 1.10. Also, Mah's estimates of 'investment remittances' are excluded from Table 1.10.

[36] Similar assumptions have also been made by JETRO (1979), though for 1970–82 only. The assumed per capita spending figures are: US$200 for 1970–3, US$225 for 1974–6, and US$250 for 1977–82. According to another estimate, Hong Kong travellers to China spent about HK$2,000 (US$360) per person in 1981. *Xinbao*, December 26, 1981.

[37] *Ta Kung Pao*, January 14, 1982. Among the most important sole agents or

branches of official Chinese trading and investment companies are: China Resources Co., Tack Soon Hong Ltd., Ng Fung Hong, Hua Yuen Co., Chinese Arts and Crafts (HK) Ltd., China Resources Textiles Co. Ltd., China International Trust and Investment Corporation, Guangdong Trust and Investment Corporation, Guangdong Enterprises Ltd., and Fujian Economic Enterprises Ltd.

[38] *Xianggang Jingji Nianjian (Hong Kong Economic Yearbook)*, 1981, Part V, pp. 100–45.

[39] See Bonavia (1976), Strauss (1976), Lau (1981), and 'The Golden Age of Our Economic Relations', *Far Eastern Economic Review*, March 13, 1981, pp. 49–56.

[40] Quoted from the text of his speech to an American audience. *South China Morning Post*, December 9, 1981.

[41] For this estimate, it is assumed that 50 per cent of the Bank of China's net worth was held in Hong Kong, and that 40 per cent of the net worth of the 12 other CSCBs was independently held in Hong Kong. However, the capitalization of Hong Kong-incorporated DTCs and joint-venture merchant banks is given 100 per cent weighting. The net worth of insurance companies is estimated at about US$10 million from the records in the Insurance Registry of the Hong Kong Government.

[42] See Nihon Boeki Shinkokai (1973).

[43] *Far Eastern Economic Review*, September 12, 1980, pp. 48–50, and March 13, 1981, p. 56. The project was later scaled down and transformed into a joint venture between the Hong Kong Government and Mighty City, under which HK$2.258 billion was to be spent on a housing project for 135,000 people. *South China Morning Post*, July 30, 1982.

[44] *Ta Kung Pao*, February 4, 1982.

[45] *Far Eastern Economic Review*, March 13, 1981, p. 56.

[46] See *Far Eastern Economic Review*, October 1, 1976, p. 61, and October 6, 1978, pp. 59–60; *Asian Finance*, March 15, 1981; *Asian Wall Street Journal*, October 15, 1980; and *South China Morning Post*, September 21, 1981, and January 19, 1982.

[47] For the profits of the CSCBs in the late 1960's and early 1970's, see Nihon Boeki Shinkokai (1973), Statistical Appendix.

[48] See Bonavia (1976), and Chai (1981a).

[49] According to Mah (1972), investment by overseas Chinese in the Fujian Overseas Chinese Investment Corporation and the Guangdong Overseas Investment Corporation amounted to a cumulative total of US$41.4 million during 1953–9.

[50] See Goodstadt (1981), and Kurata (1981b).

[51] *Jingji Daobao*, November 11, 1981, p. 8.

[52] In equity joint ventures, foreigners take shares in existing Chinese enterprises, or a new venture is formed in which all Chinese and foreign parties hold shares. In co-operation joint ventures, foreigners usually provide funds, equipment and techniques. Shenzhen supplies land, labour, raw materials and some managerial staff. Each side is allotted a set ratio of products and profits. In compensation trade, investors provide capital in return for a share of the finished products.

[53] *Asian Wall Street Journal,* February 8, 1982.

[54] *China Trade Report,* December 1981 and January 1982.

[55] See Kurata (1971a).

[56] This is my estimate based on information in *China Trade Report*, March 1980 and August 1981.

[57] *Beijing Review*, December 1981, pp. 19–21.

[58] *China Trade Report*, October 1980.

[59] *South China Morning Post Business News*, February 11, 1982. The yen bonds carried an annual interest of 8.7 per cent and were sold to about 30 Japanese financial institutions through a private placement.

Appendix 1

CHINA'S FOREIGN EXCHANGE AND GOLD RESERVES

End of Year	Foreign Exchange (million US dollars)	Gold (million troy ounces)
1979	2,154	12.80
1980	2,262	12.80
1981	4,773	12.67

Source: *Zhongguo Jinrong (China's Banking and Finance)*, various issues.

Appendix 2

CHINESE STATE-CONTROLLED BANKS:

	Total Assets[1] (million)	Percentage Increase[2] over 1979
Bank of China	Rmb 76,020.0 US$ 49,800.2	40.2
Bank of Communications	Rmb 4,294.9 US$ 2,813.6	41.9
Sin Hua Trust, Savings and Commercial Bank	Rmb 2,450.7 US$ 1,605.4	42.8
Kincheng Banking Corporation	Rmb 2,110.5 US$ 1,382.6	44.0
Kwangtung Provincial Bank	Rmb 2,005.2 US$ 1,313.6	46.3
Nanyang Commercial Bank	HK$ 6,198.3 US$ 1,205.9	47.2
China and South Sea Bank	Rmb 1,719.6 US$ 1,126.5	41.2
China State Bank	Rmb 1,648.4 US$ 1,079.9	43.9
National Commercial Bank	Rmb 1,499.2 US$ 982.1	41.6
Yien Yieh Commercial Bank	Rmb 1,456.4 US$ 954.1	44.5
Hua Chiao Commercial Bank	HK$ 2,090.2 US$ 406.6	65.2
Po Sang Bank	HK$ 1,803.3 US$ 350.8	32.2
Chiyu Banking Corporation	HK$ 1,313.3 US$ 255.5	35.1

FINANCIAL STANDING AT THE END OF 1980

Liquid Assets[3] (million)	Percentage Increase[4] over 1979	Total Loans[5] (million)	Percentage Increase over 1979
Rmb 22,379.3 US$ 14,660.5	23.5	Rmb 25,777.4 US$ 17,818.8	76.8
Rmb 1,217.5 US$ 797.6	40.8	Rmb 2,027.2 US$ 1,328.0	34.3
Rmb 544.7 US$ 356.8	5.9	Rmb 1,365.8 US$ 894.7	58.3
Rmb 589.8 US$ 386.4	58.4	Rmb 1,127.0 US$ 738.3	37.6
Rmb 580.3 US$ 380.1	42.2	Rmb 1,042.9 US$ 683.2	47.8
HK$ 1,342.8 US$ 261.2	(12.0)	HK$ 2,940.6 US$ 572.1	82.3
Rmb 507.0 US$ 332.1	23.5	Rmb 749.6 US$ 491.1	44.6
Rmb 408.5 US$ 267.6	64.9	Rmb 730.3 US$ 478.4	52.4
Rmb 340.2 US$ 222.9	30.0	Rmb 833.2 US$ 545.8	45.4
Rmb 383.7 US$ 251.3	27.9	Rmb 710.4 US$ 465.4	40.8
HK$ 368.2 US$ 71.6	38.9	HK$ 761.2 US$ 148.1	46.0
HK$ 503.2 US$ 97.9	4.9	HK$ 697.6 US$ 135.7	67.3
HK$ 222.3 US$ 43.2	19.2	HK$ 497.7 US$ 96.8	46.2

	Total Deposits[6] (million)	Percentage Increase over 1979
Bank of China	Rmb 47,518.0 US$ 31,128.7	46.2
Bank of Communications	Rmb 2,332.4 US$ 1,704.8	13.3
Sin Hua Trust, Savings and Commercial Bank	Rmb 1,504.9 US$ 985.9	27.9
Kincheng Banking Corporation	Rmb 1,402.9 US$ 919.0	36.5
Kwangtung Provincial Bank	Rmb 1,299.8 US$ 851.5	39.0
Nanyang Commercial Bank	HK$ 3,160.5 US$ 614.9	22.7
China and South Sea Bank	Rmb 1,024.0 US$ 669.5	27.1
China State Bank	Rmb 843.6 US$ 552.6	36.2
National Commercial Bank	Rmb 912.6 US$ 597.9	26.9
Yien Yieh Commercial Bank	Rmb 826.5 US$ 541.4	25.2
Hua Chiao Commercial Bank	HK$ 745.8 US$ 145.1	37.0
Po Sang Bank	HK$ 861.7 US$ 167.6	13.4
Chiyu Banking Corporation	HK$ 458.9 US$ 89.3	29.7

[1] Balance sheet total.

[2] All percentage increases in local currency terms.

[3] Cash and balances with other banks/institutions.

[4] Decrease in parentheses.

Net Worth (million)	Percentage Increase over 1979	Net Earnings (million)	Percentage Increase over 1979
Rmb 2,555.1	84.3	Rmb 464.4	101.2
US$ 1,673.8		US$ 304.2	
Rmb 500.5	102.1	Rmb 46.4	70.8
US$ 327.9		US$ 30.4	
Rmb 334.6	87.2	Rmb 33.4	65.3
US$ 219.2		US$ 21.9	
Rmb 323.7	89.3	Rmb 32.1	72.1
US$ 212.0		US$ 21.0	
Rmb 310.4	97.6	Rmb 35.7	73.1
US$ 203.3		US$ 23.4	
HK$ 323.3	84.5	HK$ 56.1	106.0
US$ 62.9		US$ 10.9	
Rmb 246.1	103.9	Rmb 26.1	74.1
US$ 161.2		US$ 17.1	
Rmb 255.4	96.6	Rmb 25.2	66.7
US$ 167.3		US$ 16.5	
Rmb 247.0	101.5	Rmb 24.4	66.8
US$ 161.8		US$ 16.0	
Rmb 263.8	102.8	Rmb 32.2	85.0
US$ 172.8		US$ 21.1	
HK$ 95.2	65.6	HK$ 21.5	71.7
US$ 18.5		US$ 4.2	
HK$ 114.9	55.3	HK$ 40.8	158.7
US$ 22.3		US$ 7.9	
HK$ 66.0	35.0	HK$ 20.6	123.3
US$ 12.8		US$ 4.0	

[5] Loans and discounts, and bills receivable.

[6] Deposits of customers, bankers and agents.

Currency converted at US$1:Rmb 1.5265; US$1:HK$5.14.

Source: *China Trade Report*, December 1981.

Appendix 3

China's Equity Investment in Hong Kong: An Illustrative Exercise

From Appendix 2, it can be established that the CSCBs in 1980 maintained on average a deposit/net worth ratio of 11, a liquidity ratio (ratio of liquid assets to deposits) of 46 per cent, and a loans/deposits ratio of 60 per cent. These conservative ratios are consistent with the expected behaviour of the CSCBs in Hong Kong.

It seems reasonable to make two other assumptions. First, the CSCBs allocate 60 per cent of their loan portfolio to China-affiliated enterprises, and 40 per cent to non-China firms. Second, the Chinese non-financial firms keep 10 per cent of their bank borrowing in the form of liquid assets for transactions and precautionary purposes.

From the basic information of net worth as given in the text, one can derive a series of T-accounts with the aid of the given ratios and assumptions. Thus, in T-account A for the CSCBs and their associates, given the net worth of US$1,556 million and deposits/net worth ratio, the liabilities side of the balance sheet is derived. Similarly, given the liquidity ratio, the loans/deposits ratio, and the allocation ratio to Chinese enterprises, the assets side is completed. T-account B for the Chinese non-financial enterprises is constructed along the same lines, given their net worth, bank borrowing, and liquidity ratio. In both accounts, the residual item, other investments, is of course determined by the accounting identity. T-account C is a consolidated account of all Chinese financial and non-financial entities. It is clear that on consolidation, the item 'loans to Chinese enterprises' in T-account A and the item 'bank borrowing' in T-account B cancel out. The aggregate net worth is US$1,956 million, while the aggregate investment in non-liquid assets is US$6,639 million, as stated in the text. The leverage factor, or the net worth multiplier, is about 3.4, which is quite conservative and consistent with the general behavioural pattern of Chinese entities in Hong Kong.

(A) Chinese State-controlled Banks and Associates
(million US dollars)

Assets		*Liabilities*	
Liquid assets	8,159	Customers' deposits	17,738
Loans:		Net worth	1,556
Chinese enterprises	6,385		
non-Chinese firms	4,257		
Other investments	493		
	19,294		19,294

(B) Chinese Non-financial Enterprises
(million US dollars)

Assets		Liabilities	
Liquid assets	639	Bank borrowing	6,385
Other investments	6,146	Net worth	400
	6,785		6,785

(C) Consolidated Account
(million US dollars)

Assets		Liabilities	
Liquid Assets	8,798	Customers' deposits	17,738
Loans to non-Chinese firms	4,257	Net worth	1,956
Other investments	6,639		
	19,694		19,694

References

Batsavage, R.E., and Davie, J.L. (1978), 'China's International Trade and Finance', *China Economy Post-Mao* (Washington, U.S. Congress, Joint Economic Committee, U.S. Government Printing Office), pp. 707–41.

Beazer, W.F. (1978), *The Commercial Future of Hong Kong* (New York, Praeger).

Bonavia, D. (1976), 'The Communist Capitalists', *Far Eastern Economic Review*, July 30, pp. 44–5.

Central Intelligence Agency (1968), 'Communist China's Balance of Payments, 1950–65', *An Economic Profile of Mainland China* (Washington, U.S. Congress, Joint Economic Committee, U.S. Government Printing Office), pp. 621–60.

—— (1980), 'China: The Continuing Search for a Modernization Strategy' (Washington), Research Paper ER 80–10248.

Chai, C.H. (1981a), 'Xianggang Ruhe Zai Zijin Rongtong Shang Xiezhu Zhongguo Sihua Jianshe' (How Hong Kong Helps Finance China's Four Modernizations), *Jingji Daobao*, January 28, pp. 14–16.

—— (1981b), 'Money and Banking Reforms in China', mimeograph.

Chen, N.R. (1979), 'China's Balance of Payments: The Experience of Financing a Long-term Trade Deficit in 20th Century', in Chin-ming Hou and Tzong-shian Yu (eds.), *Conference on Modern Chinese Economic History* (Taipei, Academia Sinica).

Cheng, H. (1975), 'Peking Calls the Tune for Chinese Banks', *Asian Finance*, September, pp. 19–22.

Cohen, J.A. (1980), 'The Bank of China Clears Up its Legal Status', *Euromoney*, December, pp. 108–13.

Davies, D. (1963), 'China Earns from Hong Kong', *Far Eastern Economic Review*, June 20, pp. 689–95.

Donnithorne, A. (1967), *China's Economic System* (London, Allen and Unwin).

Eckstein, A. (1966), *Communist China's Economic Growth and Foreign Trade* (New York, McGraw-Hill).

Goodstadt, L. (1980), 'China's Banks in the Capitalist Garden', *Asian Banking*, December, pp. 40–6.

—— (1981), 'The Cantonese Piece in the Investment Jigsaw', *Asian Banking*, April, pp. 45–50.

Hang Seng Bank Research Department (1975), 'China's Support for the Hong Kong Economy', mimeograph.

—— (1982), 'Hong Kong–China Trade', *Hang Seng Economic Quarterly*, January, pp. 8–17.

Hsia, R., and Chin, S.K. (1965), 'Soviet Loans and Repayment', *The China Mainland Review*, June, pp. 1–12.

Hsiao, G.T. (1977), *The Foreign Trade of China* (Berkeley, University of California Press).

Hsiao, K.H. (1971), *Money and Monetary Policy in Communist China* (New York, Columbia University Press).

Hsueh, T.T., and Woo, T.O. (1981), 'Trade between Hong Kong and China: Issues and Prospects', mimeograph.

Hsueh, T.T., and Shea, K.L. (1981), 'Trade Stability, Balance and Trading Partners of the People's Republic of China', *The Developing Economies*, September, pp. 242–54.

Huang, Da, Chen Gong, Hou Mengchan, Zhou Shengye, and Han Yinjie (1981), *Shehuizhuyi Caizheng Jinrong Wenti* (Fiscal and Monetary Problems of Socialism), 2 vols. (Beijing, Chinese People's University Press).

Jao, Y.C. (1971), 'China: Overseer of a Colossus', *World Banking 1971-2*, pp. 32–4.

—— (1979), 'The Rise of Hong Kong as a Financial Centre', *Asian Survey*, July, pp. 674–94.

—— (1981), 'Hong Kong as a Regional Financial Centre: Evolution and Prospects', in C.K. Leung, J.W. Cushman, and Wang Gungwu (eds.), *Hong Kong: Dilemmas of Growth* (Canberra, Australian University Press), pp. 161–94.

Japan External Trade Organization (JETRO) (1979), *China: A Business Guide, the Japanese Perspective on China's Opening Economy* (Tokyo, Press International Ltd.).

Kravalis, H.H. (1978), 'An Analysis of China's Hard Currency Exports: Recent Trends, Present Problems, and Future Potential', *Chinese Economy Post-Mao* (Washington, U.S. Congress, Joint Economic Committee, U.S. Government Printing Office), pp. 789–811.

Kulkarni, V.G. (1981), 'A Honeymoon That Works', *Asian Finance,* March 15, pp. 37–9.

Kunze, B. (1972), *Die Wirtschaftsbeziehungen zwischen der Volksrepublik China und den westlichen Industriestaaten* (Hamburg, HWWA-Institut für Wirtschaftsforschung).

Kurata, P. (1981a), 'A Home in the Motherland', *Far Eastern Economic Review,* January 30, pp. 53–6.

—— (1981b), 'Lower Costs Lure China Traders', *Far Eastern Economic Review,* February 27, pp. 68–72.

Lau, Pui-king (1981), 'The Recent Development of Non-trade Economic Relations between China and Hong Kong', mimeograph.

Lin, Jixin (1979), 'Zhongguo Yinhang Jiqi Duiwai Yewu' (The Bank of China and its Foreign Operations), *Jingji Daobao,* October 31, pp. 4–6.

Liu, Hongru (1980), *Shehuizhuyi Huobi Yu Yinhang Wenti* (Monetary and Banking Problems of Socialism), (Beijing, China Finance and Economics Publishing House).

Liu, M. (1978a), 'Open Capitalism for Peking', *Far Eastern Economic Review,* July 21, pp. 49–51.

—— (1978b), 'China and the Capitalists', *Far Eastern Economic Review,* September 8, pp. 64–5.

—— (1979), 'China Comes in from the Cold', *Far Eastern Economic Review,* June 1, pp. 42–4.

Lupton, C. Macdougall (1972), 'Hong Kong's Role in Sino-Western Trade', in A.A. Stahnke (ed.), *China's Trade with the West* (New York, Praeger), Chapter 5.

Mah, Feng-hwa (1972), *The Foreign Trade of Mainland China* (Edinburgh, University of Edinburgh Press).

Miyashita, T. (1966), *The Currency and Financial System of Mainland China* (Tokyo, Institute of Asian Affairs).

Nihon Boeki Shinkokai (1973), *Honkon ni okeru Chugoku-dei ginko no katsudo to yakuwari* (The Activities and Operations of China-controlled Banks in Hong

Kong), (Tokyo, Japan External Trade Organization).

Rafferty, K. (1981), 'Compelling Reasons for Partnership', *Financial Times*, June 15.

Szczepanik, E.F. (1961), 'Hong Kong's Trade with Mainland China', *Hong Kong Economic Papers*, No. 1, pp. 65–74.

Strauss, P. (1976), 'Hong Kong; the Nth Degree of Ideology', *Far Eastern Economic Review*, October 1, pp. 60–1.

Tsai, Cheng (1969), 'China is now a Socialist Country without Internal or External Debts', *Peking Review*, May 23, pp. 15–17.

Weintraub, P. (1977), 'Judgement Day Coming Up', *Far Eastern Economic Review*, April 8, p. 80.

Wilson, D. (1980), 'How Banks Work in China', *The Banker*, January, pp. 19–27.

Woo, T.O. (1977), *Imports from China: Its Impact on Hong Kong's Manufactured Export Performance* (M. Phil. thesis, The Chinese University of Hong Kong).

Wu, C.H. (1967), *Dollars, Dependents and Dogma* (Stanford, Hoover Institution Press).

Wu, Y.L., *et al.* (1963), *The Economic Potential of Communist China*, (Menlo Park, California, Stanford Research Institute), Vol. 1.

Wu, Y.L., and Wu, C.H. (1980), *Economic Development in Southeast Asia: the Chinese Dimension* (Stanford, Hoover Institution Press).

Yamada, Y. (1981), 'China's Foreign Financial Position', *JETRO China Newsletter*, No. 35, pp. 2–12 and 32.

Yeung, P. (1970), 'Trade Ties between Hong Kong and Mainland China', *Asian Survey*, September, pp. 820–39.

—— (1974), 'Pattern of Trade between Mainland China and Hong Kong', *Hong Kong Economic Papers*, March, pp. 46–64.

Zhang, Enhua (1981), 'On Banking Reform', *Beijing Review*, July 29, pp. 24–7.

Zhong, Zhizhang (1981), 'Zhongguo Yinhang Zenyang Ba Waihui Yewu Zuohuo?' (How Does the Bank of China Activate its Foreign Exchange Business?), *Jingji Daobao,* January 1, pp. 74–5.

2. The Impact of China's Four Modernizations on Hong Kong's Economic Development

EDWARD K.Y. CHEN

This chapter focuses on the impact of China's four modernizations since 1977 on Hong Kong's general direction of economic development and the activities in the industrial sector. Elsewhere in this book, the changing patterns of Hong Kong–China trade and the impact of Hong Kong–China industrial co-operation on China's economy are discussed. Before we analyse this impact, let us first look at the 'new' economic policy of China since 1977. For two reasons, the following account of China's economic development since 1977 is given in some detail. First, such an account is not given elsewhere in this book; and second, some idea of China's economic development in the past few years is necessary for understanding the impact of China on recent changes in the structure of the Hong Kong economy.

China's Economic Development since 1977

The Great Leap Outward of 1977 and 1978

With the fall of the Gang of Four in October 1976, the new regime began to implement its new economic policy as early as 1977. This followed Zhou Enlai's call for the initiation of an essentially pragmatic modernization programme at the Fourth National People's Congress in January 1975. 1977–8 was the period of the 'Great Leap Outward' during which foreign technology and capital goods were imported without much constraint or discrimination. In 1977, of the US$7,100 million imports into China, 17 per cent consisted of foodstuffs, 65 per cent consisted of industrial supplies, and the remaining 18 per cent comprised capital goods.[1] The import of consumer goods was negligible; of the 65 per cent of industrial supplies imported, 22 per cent consisted of iron and steel and 12 per cent consisted of chemicals. Thus, although Hua Guofeng, in his report on the work of the government to the Fifth National People's Congress (February 26 to March 5, 1978), stressed that the whole nation should be mobilized and 'go in for agriculture in a big way' and that 'along with the strengthening of the basic industries there should be a vigorous development of light industry,' the basic line of development during 1977 and 1978 was heavily biased towards the building up of the basic or heavy industries. It was admitted that 'we must take steel as the key link.' Similarly, although the Chinese leaders advocated a policy of simultaneous development of large-, medium- and small-scale enterprises, the greatest emphasis was placed on the building of large-scale projects. In the 1978 State Plan, 120 large-scale projects were proposed, including 10 iron and steel complexes, 9 non-ferrous metal complexes, 8 coal mines, 10 oil and gas fields, 30 power stations, 6 new trunk railways and 5 key harbours.

In 1978, the output of iron and steel products increased by almost 40 per cent, cement by 20 per cent, chemical fertilizers by 30 per cent, metallurgy equipment by 27 per cent, electricity generation equipment by almost 60 per cent, tractors by 22 per cent and motor vehicles by 70 per cent. On the other hand, the output of textile products in 1978 increased by less than 10 per cent, bicycles by 16 per cent and radios by 7 per cent. The increase of production in television sets was almost 100 per cent but only because of the tiny scale of production in the previous year.

In 1977, China sent large numbers of technical missions and trade representatives to virtually all the major industrialized countries to look for capital goods and other industrial supplies. At the same time, overseas merchants were invited to China to introduce their products and services. The actual buying spree of the Chinese took place in 1978 during which imports increased by 56 per cent and exports by 26 per cent.[2] It was estimated that in 1978 the Chinese signed contracts for close to US$7 billion's worth of complete plants and showed active interest in the purchase of plants, equipment and related technology that amounted to US$40 billion or more.[3] In 1978, Chinese exports amounted to about US$10 billion, implying that at that rate it would take five years of China's total export effort to pay for the purchases of foreign goods and technology made in 1978. A large proportion of the purchases were in the fields of metallurgical, petrochemical and iron and steel plants. Given the disrupted economy after the Cultural Revolution, this sudden and huge importation of foreign capital goods and technology must surely have caused serious problems. It was difficult for China to absorb all these imports in a short period of time, and above all the imported capital goods and technology might not then have been appropriate. Moreover, financing such an unprecedented 'buying spree' was obviously not easy given the scarcity of China's export potential and foreign exchange reserves. Towards the end of 1978, Chinese leaders began to realize the seriousness of the problem. To tackle the difficulties of financing, a more flexible foreign trade system was adopted, and specifically, various compensation trade schemes were introduced. As a further step, joint ventures with foreign investors were proposed. But the problems in fact went beyond financing and concerned the basic line of economic development and the choice of technology. Owing to all these problems, China had no alternative but to readjust its plans and reform its economic system.

Economic Readjustment and Reforms since 1979

Economic readjustment and reforms began in early 1979, and were officially announced by Hua Guofeng in his report on the work of the government delivered at the second session of the Fifth National People's Congress on June 18, 1979. The essence of such readjustment and reforms can be summarized very well by the following statements of Ye Jianying.[4]

> In order to strike an overall balance, the national financial and material resources must be allotted in accordance with the principle of giving

priority to production of finished goods over capital construction and to tapping existing potential over starting new projects . . . We must resolutely curtail capital construction and concentrate on speeding up production in agriculture, light industry (including textiles), the fuel and power industries, transport and communications, and other weak lines in our economy.

Enterprises must be given greater power of decision in production, management, allocation of funds, control of materials, assignment of the labour force, distribution of income and other matters . . . The scope for decision-making in economic affairs in the localities will also be appropriately broadened under the unified central leadership.

First, economic readjustment deals with the proportion between accumulation and consumption. The objective is to reduce the average accumulation ratio of about 40 per cent during the early 1970's to 20–25 per cent. The way to do this is to cut down capital construction drastically. By 1981, accumulation accounted for 30 per cent of national output. Second, the importance of agriculture and light industry is placed above that of heavy industry. However, the success of promoting agriculture has been limited, as it has been in the past. The importance of agriculture (in terms of its share in total industrial and agricultural output) in 1980–1 was actually smaller than in 1979. On the other hand, the readjustment regarding the proportion

Table 2.1 PERCENTAGE OF ACCUMULATION AND CONSUMPTION IN NATIONAL INCOME

Year	Accumulation	Consumption
1977	32.3	67.7
1978	36.5	63.5
1979	34.6	65.4
1980	32.4	67.6
1981	30.0	70.0

Sources: Figures for 1977 are taken from *Renmin Ribao*, May 15, 1980; figures for 1978 and 1981 are taken from *Renmin Ribao*, December 14, 1981; and figures for 1979 and 1980 are taken from *Zhongquo Zingji Nianjian*, 1981, pp. III 2–8.

between light industry and heavy industry has progressed well since 1979. This is illustrated in Table 2.2 which shows the shares of agriculture, light industry and heavy industry in total output during 1949–81.

In the post-Mao readjustment, heavy industry is assigned only a supporting role. It is argued that the development of heavy industry is crucial to (a) supplying materials and parts to light industry, (b) supplying technology and machinery to light industry, (c) supplying chemical fertilizers, machinery and other means of production to agriculture, and (d) supplying durable consumer goods.[5] But concern was expressed by the government over the fact that the output of light industry increased by 13.6 per cent in 1981, while that of heavy industry went down by 4.5 per cent. Towards the end of 1981, measures were taken to ensure that this declining trend of heavy

Table 2.2 PERCENTAGE OF AGRICULTURAL AND INDUSTRIAL OUTPUT VALUE OUT OF TOTAL OUTPUT VALUE

Year	Agriculture	Light Industry	Heavy Industry
1949	70.0	22.1	7.9
1952	58.5	26.7	14.8
1953	58.5	26.7	14.8
1957	43.3	30.1	26.6
1965	29.7	35.5	34.8
1975	28.5	30.9	40.6
1978	25.6	31.8	42.6
1979	25.6	32.1	42.3
1980	24.6	35.4	40.0
1981	24.6	38.5	36.9

Sources: Figures for 1949, 1952, 1957, 1965, 1975 and 1979 are taken from *Zhongquo Jingji Nianjian 1981*, p. VI 4. The figure for 1953 is calculated from *Renmin Ribao*, November 1, 1979; the figure for 1979 is calculated from *Renmin Ribao*, May 1, 1980; the figure for 1980 is calculated from *Renmin Ribao*, April 30, 1981; and the figure for 1981 is calculated from the budget announced by Zhao Ziyang, *Renmin Ribao*, December 14, 1981.

industry was corrected. In fact the Chinese Government is more concerned with the restructuring of heavy industry rather than the fall in its share in total output.[6]

Economic management reform is new to China; it was not carried out in the previous readjustment period between 1961–5. The objective of economic management reform is to create a suitable organizational structure for the introduction of greater material incentives. The basic principle of economic management reform is to give greater autonomy to individuals and enterprises so that production is not only determined by administrative methods, but also by economic methods which work through the price mechanism.[7]

The following are the major changes in economic management reform.

Expansion of the Market Economy

Up to July 1980, 2,300 agricultural subsidiary product markets were opened in the various small and big cities all over China.[8] In 1979, there were 16,000 industrial enterprises which had established their own marketing channels and sold their own products amounting to Rmb 10.3 billion.[9] By the end of 1980, 600 production materials service companies and 60 production materials exchange markets were established. The value of transactions was Rmb 3.5 billion in 1979 and Rmb 4.1 billion in 1980.[10] In 1979, 35 per cent of the total amount of retailing commodities was exchanged through the free market. In 1980, about 30 per cent of the total amount of retailing commodities was produced on the basis of the needs of the market.[11] Shanghai has become the centre of these market activities; its connections spread all over China and to all kinds of commodities.[12] Under a system of commodity sales in free markets, black markets have developed in many cases because supply falls short of demand. Considerable confusion in production has also been produced because of the shortage of raw materials.

Decentralization of Financial Controls

Certain financial controls have been given to local authorities and to individual enterprises. The budgets of local authorities have been increased since 1979. In 1979, the total expenditure and revenue of local authorities were Rmb 63.4 billion and Rmb 75 billion respectively, resulting in a surplus of Rmb 11.6 billion. In 1980, the surplus went up to Rmb 21.2 billion.[13] On the other hand, during these two years, the central government had deficits of Rmb 17 billion and Rmb 12.7 billion respectively.[14] The expansion of enterprises' financial controls has also led to a decrease in the amount of enterprise profits remitted to the central government. The figure went down from Rmb 49.3 billion in 1979 to Rmb 43.5 billion in 1980, and to an estimated Rmb 34.7 billion in 1981. Expansion of financial controls by local authorities and enterprises has thus given greater material incentives to the various units of production, but has also created financial problems for the central government.

Enterprise Autonomy

In 1980, there were about 6,600 experimental enterprises which were given some degree of enterprise autonomy. These were large and relatively more productive enterprises; they accounted for roughly 60 per cent of the output value of all publicly-owned enterprises. In 1980, the output value and profits of these experimental units went up by 6.8 per cent and 11.8 per cent respectively.[15] Their performance was therefore not particularly outstanding considering the fact that they were already the more efficient enterprises. It seems that further measures must be taken to cope with the situation. Recently, Premier Zhao has proposed a separation of political administration from business administration, meaning that the upper administrative offices should surrender their control over business activities to the enterprises themselves.[16] Furthermore, to prepare the ground for enterprise autonomy, enterprises must be consolidated for the improvement of efficiency. The method of enterprise consolidation is the introduction of economic responsibility systems.

Specialization and Unification

By the end of 1980, there were 1,600 specialized companies with 168,000 participating enterprises. At the same time, there were also 1,700 economic unions.[17] Specialization and unification of enterprises are another form of enterprise consolidation. By so doing, inefficient enterprises are eliminated, inadequate enterprises are united, and co-ordination between enterprises is promoted. More importantly, enterprises cutting across different departments and localities can thus be set up.

In addition to all these, China has set up four Special Economic Zones (SEZs) which are more than the export-processing zones of other developing countries; they are actually testing grounds for new economic systems and strategies. The Shenzhen SEZ and the Zhuhai SEZ were formally approved in August 1980, and the Xiamen SEZ and the Shantou SEZ in October 1980. By far the greatest proportion of investment in these SEZs comes from Hong Kong. The industrial co-operation between Hong Kong and China in the SEZs and their impact on China's economy are dealt with in another chapter of this book. The impact of such co-operation on Hong Kong industry will however be analysed below.

China and Hong Kong's Direction of Economic Development

No one can deny the important role of China in Hong Kong's economic development. It has often been emphasized that the prosperity of Hong Kong's manufacturing depends on two aspects of the China connection. First, the ample supply and stable prices of food and raw materials have been important in maintaining a rapid growth of Hong Kong manufacturing in the face of international competition. Specifically, stable food prices have contributed to stable wage rates and therefore to low inflation rates and a competitive cost structure. Second, the sporadic influx of population from China has assisted in softening the tight labour market so that Hong Kong can rely on its export of labour-intensive products to generate export-led growth.

But in fact the impact of China on Hong Kong's economic development has been more fundamental than just assisting Hong Kong's manufacturing to grow. In the post-war years, political and economic changes in China have actually influenced the direction of Hong Kong's economic development and the structure of the Hong Kong economy. The rapid transformation of the Hong Kong economy from an entrepôt to an industrialized economy in the second half of the 1950's was the result of a decline of entrepôt trade and an inflow of resources to support industrialization and the export of light manufactured goods. These two factors, a decline of entrepôt trade and an inflow of resources, are the result of historical developments closely related to China rather than any conscious plans on the part of the Hong Kong Government.[18] The decline in entrepôt trade after 1951 can be attributed in turn to two factors. The first was the Communist takeover in China. Hong Kong's entrepôt trade to a large extent depended on the trade between China and the West. For political reasons, the Communist Government in China traded with Soviet Russia and the Eastern European countries rather than with the West and other parts of Asia. Under these circumstances, Hong Kong lost its traditional importance as an agent of China's foreign trade. The second factor was the outbreak of the Korean War in 1950 which led to the United Nations embargo in 1951. The embargo was imposed on the export of strategic goods to China. It was rigidly enforced by the Hong Kong Government. This resulted in a sharp fall in Hong Kong's trade with China.

It is of course obvious that Hong Kong could not have succeeded in its industrialization if it had not had the resources and the potential to industrialize at the time of the decline of entrepôt trade. In consequence of the civil war and the establishment of a Communist regime in China, a huge inflow of labour, capital and entrepreneurial skill into Hong Kong occurred during the period 1948–51. Those taking refuge in Hong Kong included (a) young and energetic people who were intelligent and willing to work hard, (b) people with much money capital, and (c) high-quality entrepreneurs who were mostly Shanghainese industrialists engaged in the textile industry. This huge inflow of human and capital resources from China formed the basis on which Hong Kong's industrialization took place.

Thus, without a change in the government in China in 1949 to a Communist regime, Hong Kong might not have transformed its economy in the 1950's. In the 1960's, Hong Kong underwent its first industrial revolution and set an example of export-led growth on the basis of producing light manufactured goods. Hong Kong was able during this period to establish successfully the textile, garment, plastics and electronics industries. Despite the fact that other countries such as Taiwan, South Korea and Singapore became Hong Kong's keen competitors in the international market for light manufactured goods, Hong Kong industries managed to survive very well thanks to the rapid process of product diversification undertaken by the highly adaptable and dynamic entrepreneurs of Hong Kong. For example, textiles have gone from cotton to synthetics and to denim and artificial silk; garments have gone from shirts to jeans, fashions and fur coats; electronics have gone from single-band radios to semi-conductors, electronic watches, integrated circuits and micro-computers; plastics have changed from flowers to household goods and toys. Throughout the 1960's and 1970's the industrial structure of Hong Kong at the three-digit level underwent very little change. Yet the rapid process of product diversification within the three-digit level has successfully maintained a high rate of industrial growth and therefore a high rate of overall economic growth.

Of course, during the 1970's and especially in the latter half of the 1970's, Hong Kong increasingly became an international financial centre. Financial services would have gained important ground in Hong Kong as early as the late 1960's and early 1970's had there not been a reluctance on the part of the government to abolish the withholding tax on foreign currency deposits in Hong Kong.[19] As a result of this reluctance, the Asian dollar market was established in Singapore instead of Hong Kong. Since 1976, when Hong Kong recovered before anybody else from the world recession, the Hong Kong economy has undergone changes in its economic structure. Specifically, the relative importance of financial services has increased while that of manufacturing has decreased. Tables 2.3 and 2.4 illustrate clearly this trend. The share of financing, insurance, real estate and business services in GDP increased from 15 per cent in 1970 to 22 per cent in 1980. Similarly, the share of this sector in total employment increased from 2.7 per cent in 1971 to 4.8 per cent in 1981. This process of economic diversification is closely related to China's modernization programmes and new economic policies after the fall of the Gang of Four.

When China opened its door and began its buying spree in 1977, the importance of Hong Kong's entrepôt trade was revived. China

Table 2.3 GROSS DOMESTIC PRODUCT BY INDUSTRIAL ORIGIN, 1970–80 (percentage)

ISIC Major Division	1970	1971	1972	1973	1974	1975	1976	1977	1978	1979	1980
1. Agriculture and fishing	2.0	1.8	1.6	1.6	1.5	1.4	1.4	1.3	1.3	1.0	1.1
2. Mining and quarrying	0.2	0.1	0.1	0.1	0.1	0.1	0.1	*	*	*	0.1
3. Manufacturing	30.9	28.1	26.9	26.5	25.8	26.9	28.3	27.2	26.9	27.6	26.7
4. Electricity, gas and water	2.0	1.8	1.7	1.6	1.8	1.8	1.7	1.5	1.5	1.3	1.9
5. Construction	4.2	4.9	5.3	5.5	6.1	5.7	5.4	5.9	7.0	7.3	6.7
6. Wholesale and retail trades, and restaurants and hotels	19.6	19.5	20.1	21.5	20.8	20.7	21.1	21.6	21.3	21.7	18.8
7. Transport, storage and communication	7.6	6.8	6.2	6.4	6.9	7.2	6.8	6.0	5.9	5.4	6.5
8. Financing, insurance, real estate and business services	14.9	17.5	20.5	19.2	17.6	17.0	17.9	19.6	20.7	21.4	22.0
9. Community, social and personal services	18.0	18.9	17.1	17.2	19.0	18.7	17.0	16.6	15.1	14.0	16.0
10. Activities not adequately defined	0.6	0.6	0.5	0.4	0.4	0.5	0.3	0.3	0.3	0.3	0.2

* less than 0.05 per cent.

Source: 1970–9, Census and Statistics Department (1982), *Estimates of Gross Domestic Product*; and 1980, rough estimates, Financial Secretary, *The 1981-82 Budget*, February 25, 1981.

Table 2.4 PERCENTAGE DISTRIBUTION OF WORKING POPULATION BY INDUSTRY, 1971, 1976 AND 1981

Industry	1971	1976	1981
	%	%	%
Manufacturing	47.0	44.8	41.2
Agriculture and fishing	3.9	2.6	2.0
Construction	5.4	5.6	7.7
Wholesale and retail trades, restaurants and hotels	16.2	19.5	19.2
Transport, storage and communication	7.4	7.4	7.5
Finance, insurance, real estate and business services	2.7	3.4	4.8
Services	15.0	15.4	15.6
Others and unclassifiable	2.4	13.0	2.0

Source: Census and Statistics Department, *Census Reports*, various years.

trade became a prosperous though not necessarily profitable business. China set up new trading corporations and expanded existing offices in Hong Kong. Foreign merchants also came to Hong Kong in a swarm to set up their offices. Table 2.5 shows the drastic increase in Hong Kong's domestic exports and re-exports to China in the period 1977–81. It is to be noted that the very big increases did not occur in 1977 and 1978 but in the year 1979 and after. In 1977 and 1978, China was concerned with the import of complete plants and other heavy industrial supplies directly from industrialized countries. In this case, Hong Kong was not important as an entrepôt. In the period 1979–81, compensation trade schemes, joint ventures and the Special Economic Zones were established. In all these, Hong Kong's participation has been by far the largest. Thus, the increased volume of trade between Hong Kong and China is largely accounted for by Hong Kong's active participation in industrial co-operation and real estate projects in China. A large part of the trade is in fact intra-industry trade in which raw materials and semi-manufactures are exported to China and final products imported from China. It is therefore important to note that the revival of entrepôt trade in Hong Kong in the past few years is not

Table 2.5 TRADE BETWEEN HONG KONG AND CHINA

Year	Hong Kong Exports to China	Re-exports to China	Total Exports to China	Imports from China	Trade Balance
			million HK dollars		
1960	13	107	120	1,186	−1,066
1970	30	34	64	2,830	−2,766
1976	24	122	146	7,761	−7,615
1977	31	175	206	8,082	−7,876
1978	81	214	295	10,550	−10,255
1979	603	1,315	1,918	15,130	−13,212
1980	1,605	4,642	6,247	21,948	−15,701
1981	2,924	8,044	10,968	29,510	−18,542

Source: Census and Statistics Department, *Hong Kong Trade Statistics*.

because Hong Kong has once again acted as a threshold for China trade, but as a consequence of Hong Kong's direct investment in China. With a decline in Hong Kong's industrial and real estate activities in China, it can be expected that Hong Kong's exports to and imports from China will fall. This has in fact proved to be the case in the first quarter of 1982, during which the growth of Hong Kong's direct investment in China slowed down and the volume of Hong Kong–China trade also experienced a much slower growth.

The revival of the China trade has undoubtedly led to the revival of Hong Kong as an international financial centre. To support and finance the increasing volume of Hong Kong–China trade, an expansion in financial services in Hong Kong was necessary. At the same time, China sees Hong Kong as a desirable focal point for the financing of China's overall foreign trade and investment. Thus, taking advantage of its proximity to China and closer cultural affinity, Hong Kong has been able to regain its comparative advantage over Singapore in the provision of financial services. Had there not been China's new economic policies, Hong Kong would not have undergone the structural change that it has experienced in the past few years. In fact, immediately after Hong Kong's recovery from the recession, the government, in 1977, was in favour of a new approach to industrial development and had no intention of specially promoting the financial sector. In October 1977, the Advisory Committee on Industrial Diversification (later, the word industrial was dropped) was asked to examine the factors which had been influential in attracting or deterring the establishment of new activities in the manufacturing and other sectors, and the role that the government could play in the diversification process. To some extent, this marked a change in the government's attitude towards industry. The reason was that the government recognized the increasing difficulties of Hong Kong in maintaining a high growth rate in its traditional manufacturing exports because of competition from other newly industrializing countries and the changing comparative advantage of Hong Kong itself. Even with a strong *laissez-faire* tradition in Hong Kong, the government had to admit that the private sector alone could not be expected to undertake a restructuring of the industrial sector. It was true that Hong Kong industrialists had been very successful in product diversification. But industrial diversification which involves the establishment of totally new activities is a different matter.

It took much longer than expected for the Diversification Committee to finish its report, which was eventually published in December 1979 after two years' work. It became clear why diversification instead of industrial diversification was the focal point of discussion. The reason was that the Committee or the government[20] saw that a switch to financial services could be more desirable than the establishment of new manufacturing activities in offsetting the decline in Hong Kong's traditional labour-intensive industries. This idea was surely a consequence of the new developments that could be observed in China at that time. The Diversification Report devotes a chapter to the discussion of Hong Kong's economic relationship with China. The report emphasizes the increasing importance of the visible and invisible trade with China and the possibility of Hong Kong becoming a logistic support base in connection with the exploitation of new oil fields in the South China Sea. The Committee is right in seeing that these new developments provide a golden opportunity for Hong Kong to regain its position as an international financial centre, but perhaps wrong in neglecting the other contributory factors of China's new developments to Hong Kong's industrial diversification. These factors will be discussed later in this chapter. Being preoccupied by the attractiveness of promoting the financial sector in Hong Kong, the Diversification Committee has given less than the necessary attention to the establishment of new manufacturing activities. Indeed, the Committee simply makes very general recommendations with regard to vocational training, and industrial support and technical back-up services, and shifts the responsibility of policy implementation to an Industrial Development Board which it recommends should be set up. The Diversification Report is surely one of the most important government documents dealing with the direction of economic changes in Hong Kong in the 1980's. Interestingly, the writing of this report was greatly influenced by what happened in China during 1977–9.

In the two years following the publication of the Diversification Report, important measures were taken to reform and streamline the financial sector of Hong Kong. In the 1981 Budget Speech, the Financial Secretary proposed a series of changes to regulate the financial markets. They deal with company law, disclosure of shareholdings, take-overs, insurance law, unification of stock exchanges, the formation of a Hong Kong Association of Banks, and the establishment of a three-tier banking sector which now includes three categories of financial institutions, that is, licensed banks, licensed deposit-taking companies, and registered deposit-taking companies. This is not the place to discuss these changes in detail. The essence is that these changes have the effect of strengthening the financial sector and making it more attractive to those who have an interest in it. In 1982, the last obstacle to the development of financial services in Hong Kong was removed; the interest tax on foreign currency deposits was finally abolished. That on local currency deposits was also reduced from 15 per cent to 10 per cent.

What, then, are the implications of Hong Kong's economic restructuring, which is geared towards the increasing importance of financial services? In the short run, there is no question that the Hong Kong economy benefits and will benefit from the income-generating capacity of the financial sector in the face of the shrinking overseas demand for Hong Kong's manufacturing exports at this phase of the business cycle. The growth rate of Hong Kong in these years would surely have been lower had there not been a rapid growth of the financial sector. But in the long term an overemphasis on financial services as a major source of income is not without problems.

First, as far as long-term economic growth is concerned, the overemphasis on financial activities may not be in line with Hong Kong's comparative advantages, which have been and most likely will still be the dynamism of entrepreneurs and the productivity and docility of the labour force. With a suitable investment environment and ample training opportunities, these advantages will enable Hong Kong to excel more in manufacturing industries than in financial services.

Second, an overdependence on financial activities will give rise to greater economic instability and uncertainty. To provide incentives to investors and to maintain an attractive environment for short-term capital inflows, Hong Kong will be more constrained in controlling its tax base, monetary base, interest rates and exchange rates, and therefore its macro-economic stability.

In addition, there are socio-economic implications of an overdependence on financial activities. Obviously, employment absorption is a problem if the importance of manufacturing gives way to financial services. Currently, the financial sector contributes to 22 per cent of GNP but employs only 4.8 per cent of the labour force. No matter how flexible the labour market is and how significant the indirect effects are, there is no way to avoid considerable unemployment in this situation.

Lastly, it is expected that income inequality will increase with the rising importance of the financial sector. In the 1960's, evidence shows that the rapid economic growth of Hong Kong was accompanied by decreases in income inequality.[21] But since the early 1970's, the situation has changed. While growth rates were still high during 1971–81 (except for the recession years of 1974 and 1975), income inequality tended to increase. In 1971, the poorest 20 per cent had a 5.7 per cent share of total income and the Gini Coefficient was 0.459; in 1976, the corresponding figures were 5.1 and 0.456; and in 1981 the poorest 20 per cent had only a 4.5 per cent share of total income and the Gini Coefficient had increased to 0.462.[22] One major reason for a decrease in income inequality in the 1960's was the rising importance of the manufacturing sector, which generated a large amount of employment and, as a rule, had a low within-sector degree of inequality. The financial sector, on the other hand, has not only a much lower employment generation capacity, but also a much wider within-sector income inequality. Greater income equality is no less an objective of development than rapid income growth. More importantly, a reasonable measure of income equality is an important source of social stability and therefore of economic prosperity.

The above analysis does not imply that development of the financial sector in Hong Kong should be deliberately checked. The rising importance of financial services in the Hong Kong economy in the face of the recent new developments in China is perhaps unavoidable and to some extent desirable. But the crucial fact is that Hong Kong should not see promotion of the financial sector as a short cut, and as an administratively convenient policy for promoting the prosperity of Hong Kong. The government should be able to recognize the potential of Hong Kong's industrial sector and give assistance in a more positive way to facilitate the transformation of Hong Kong's industrial structure. As we have seen, the Hong Kong Government has taken very positive measures to streamline the financial sector, and a similar effort should be devoted to the industrial sector.

China and Hong Kong's Industrial Development

By the time the Diversification Report was published, the situation in China had in many ways changed. The Great Leap Outward movement had already ended, and China had started to move towards economic readjustment and reform. At the same time, China opened its door to foreigners, and especially to Hong Kong investors, to participate in China's various industrial activities including manufacturing, construction and real estate, and tourism. Had the Diversification Committee been able to take these new developments into account, the report would not have overemphasized the role of financial services in the face of China's modernization, and would have taken a more positive and optimistic look at Hong Kong's industries in the 1980's. It is thus unfortunate that the Diversification Report was largely written on the basis of China's Great Leap Outward, and not on the basis of China's economic readjustment and reforms which will last at least until the mid-1980's. In this sense, the report was outdated when it was published. In 1980–2, in line with the spirit of the Diversification Report, positive measures were taken to foster the financial sector in Hong Kong. It was not until early 1981 that the Hong Kong Government began to recognize the changed situation in China and the likely impact on Hong Kong. Since early 1981, the government has been more positive than before in promoting the industrial sector. For instance, a special technology section was created in the Trade Industry and Customs Department; the Hong Kong Productivity Centre was given a much larger grant; an electronics testing centre was established; and a Department of Technical Education and Industrial Training was set up. These measures are still largely uncoordinated, and even if effective it will be a considerable time before the benefits are felt.

Potentially, the modernization programmes as they are being undertaken by the Chinese authorities have considerable favourable effects on Hong Kong's industrial sector in general and on the process of industrial diversification in particular.

First, China could be an important market for the products of Hong Kong's potential new industries, which are presumably technology- and capital-intensive. With the emphasis on economic adjustment, China will increasingly look for appropriate technology and products. Hong Kong surely has the capabilities, and perhaps a comparable advantage, in developing appropriate technology and products for developing countries. With the possibility that China can become a stable market for some of Hong Kong's heavier industrial products such as telecommunications equipment, ships and oil rigs, and machinery and tools, the development of these industries in Hong Kong will be stimulated. It is expected that as regards the production of heavier industrial products in Hong Kong, the products, at least in the initial period, will find more ready markets in developing countries than in developed countries.

Second, with the emphasis of China on readjustment and reform as regards agriculture and the production of industrial raw materials and semi-manufactures, Hong Kong should be able to secure a more certain and ample supply of food, fuels and industrial materials from China.

Third, the establishment of four Special Economic Zones and the opening up of China for joint-venture projects are beneficial not only to China, but also to Hong Kong's industrial development. This should be looked at from the viewpoint of Hong Kong's involvement in foreign direct investment.[23] For a long time, developing countries acted only as host countries for multinational activities or foreign direct investment. But now, multinational activities are no longer monopolized by developing countries. Since the late 1960's, many newly industrializing countries have been undertaking foreign investment, at first in other developing countries and later in developed countries as well. It is now thought that foreign direct investment from both developed and developing countries can be explained by the eclectic approach.[24] According to this approach, the propensity of a country's enterprises to engage in foreign direct investment is determined by three conditions. First, the enterprises must possess certain assets which their competitors do not possess or do not possess in the same degree or on the same terms. These assets or ownership-specific advantages include technology, marketing, management, access to inputs and markets. Second, the enterprises must find it worthwhile to exploit these advantages themselves (that is internalize them) rather than sell them or sell the right to use them to foreign firms. Third, the enterprises must find a location outside their own country which is attractive enough for the exploitation and internationalization of their ownership-specific advantages. Should all these conditions be fulfilled, the enterprises will engage in foreign direct investment.

In such industries as textiles, garments, electronics and plastics, many Hong Kong enterprises, with their long experience and high productivity, possess all the ownership-specific advantages of technology, management and marketing. Specifically, the advantages of management and marketing are particularly great and are more profitable and more easily exploited through internalization (that is setting up subsidiaries to form an internal market). Thus, whenever an attractive location is found, Hong Kong enterprises will expand their activities abroad by setting up overseas subsidiaries. Hong Kong began its foreign direct investment activities in the mid-1960's, and has by now become the most important foreign investor among the developing countries. Before the open-door policy of China, Hong Kong enterprises invested mainly in Indonesia, Taiwan, Malaysia and Singapore. At present, it is estimated that the amount of Hong Kong's direct investment in China falls behind that in Indonesia and Taiwan, but is above that in Malaysia and Singapore.[25] China, and in particular its Special Economic Zones, offers attractive location advantages. The tax rate is even lower than in Hong Kong, and the land and labour costs are also lower. More importantly, the supply of labour, and in particular that of manual labour, is much more plentiful than in Hong Kong. When compared with other host countries, China is both geographically and culturally closer to Hong Kong. Thus, the opening up of China has greatly facilitated the foreign direct investment activities of Hong Kong industries.

Table 2.6 shows the results of a survey conducted in early 1982. The sample consists of 32 industrial firms which are of Hong Kong origin and which have set up subsidiaries in other countries.[26] Exactly one-half of the 32 sample firms have set up subsidiaries in China. This table reports the results regarding the motivations for foreign direct investment. The managers of the sample firms were asked to rank the importance of a list of factors supplied to them on a scale of 0 (no importance) to 10 (extremely important). Table 2.6 gives two sets of scores: the overall scores and the scores of China investors. Each of the overall scores represents the average of the scores given by all the 32 sample firms; and each of the scores of the China investors represents the average of the scores given by the 16 firms in our sample which have set up subsidiaries in China. The table shows that firms investing in China are much more concerned with the shortage of labour, the high labour cost, and the high land cost and rent in Hong Kong. In addition, firms investing in China indicated that they were more concerned with the exploitation of their technical know-how and marketing and managerial skill than firms investing in other countries. It is generally believed that an important motive for Hong Kong firms' direct investment in China is the dumping of the participants' outdated machinery, but this does not seem to be the case; although firms investing in China did give an average score higher than the

Table 2.6 MOTIVATIONS FOR FOREIGN DIRECT INVESTMENT: HONG KONG MANUFACTURING MULTINATIONALS

Motivations	Score	
	Overall	China Investors
Shortage of labour supply in Hong Kong	5.6	6.3
High labour costs in Hong Kong	5.2	6.0
To facilitate the export of products to another country	5.0	4.0
High land costs and rents in Hong Kong	4.9	5.3
To open up new markets by directly investing there	4.3	2.6
Lack of technical and skilled labour force in Hong Kong	3.8	1.2
To circumvent tariffs and quotas imposed by developed countries	3.6	1.5
Defending and/or expanding the existing market by directly investing there	3.3	2.0
To avoid or reduce the pressure of competition from other firms in Hong Kong	2.8	3.5
To further exploit the advantage of the managerial and marketing skill of your Hong Kong parent firm	2.6	4.0
Diversification of products and/or risks	2.5	2.2
High capital costs in Hong Kong	2.0	1.5
To further exploit the advantage of the technical and production know-how of your Hong Kong parent firm	1.6	2.6
As a means of managing the financial assets of your Hong Kong firm (that is, establishing a subsidiary overseas is similar to investing in the financial markets overseas)	1.4	0.2
Lack of higher levels of technology in Hong Kong	1.1	0.2
To make use of the outdated machinery used in the Hong Kong firm	0.9	2.6
Lack of management manpower in Hong Kong	0.4	0.3

overall average. This may be related to China's recent policy of stopping such practices by Hong Kong firms.

The operation of Hong Kong-based firms in China has one characteristic which is not normally shared by Hong Kong investment elsewhere. This is the close relationship between the Hong Kong parent firm and the subsidiary in China. In particular, the parent firms attempt to build a vertically integrated structure with the Chinese subsidiaries. Elsewhere, the Hong Kong-owned subsidiaries might be producing different classes of products (usually less sophisticated products) from those produced by the parent firm, but the subsidiaries, in most cases, are responsible for producing the complete products, which are ready for export or for sale in the local market. On the other hand, it is typical that the Chinese subsidiaries are responsible for only one stage of the production process, usually the labour-intensive stage. This is very similar to the investment of many United States and European multinationals in the developing countries, and quite unlike Hong Kong investment in other countries.

In general, the opportunities for Hong Kong industrial firms to invest in China have given some advantages to Hong Kong's overall industrial development, in addition to the benefits that accrue to individual firms. First, Hong Kong firms are given access to cheaper land and an ample supply of manual and semi-skilled labour, implying that Hong Kong firms can now relocate some of the production in China and concentrate on more sophisticated products or production processes in Hong Kong. This is in line with the changing comparative advantages of Hong Kong industries. The possibility of relocating some or all of the existing production processes or products stimulates the adjustments towards such changing comparative advantages in Hong Kong. Second, the vertical integration established between the Hong Kong parent firms and the subsidiaries in China should have the effect of cost reduction, and should therefore increase the competitiveness of Hong Kong's traditional exports. These advantages are, however, potential rather than actual at present. Hong Kong firms investing in China have been encountering various difficulties which include government inefficiency, low labour productivity and poor infrastructure. For the time being, most of the industrial projects in China financed (wholly or in part) by Hong Kong firms are small. The actual impact on Hong Kong's industrial development has so far been limited. Table 2.7 reports the survey results regarding the criteria for

Table 2.7 CRITERIA FOR SELECTING HOST COUNTRIES

Criteria	Score
Political stability	8.2
Availability of labour	6.9
Cheap land	6.8
Cheap labour	6.6
Good infrastructure (for example, good transportation and communication networks)	6.4
Government efficiency	6.3
Tax concessions	6.2
Absence of foreign exchange controls and the possibility of repatriating profits	5.6
Possibility and facility for exporting to the developed countries	5.2
Availability of technical and skilled manpower	5.0
Geographical location	4.9
Language and cultural affinity	4.8
Availability of material components and semi-manufactures	4.5
Loan availability	4.3
Size and potential of the host country's market	3.8
Business and family connections	3.6
Availability of advanced technology	3.4

selecting host countries. The methodology and sample are the same as those used for the derivation of Table 2.6. It can be seen that while China satisfies many of the high-score criteria, it fails to comply with others, such as good infrastructure and government efficiency. In addition, it is still unclear how politically stable China will be in the near and more distant future.

Two other matters should perhaps also be mentioned in connection with the impact of China on Hong Kong's industrial development. First, there is China's investment in Hong Kong's industries. No systematic information and statistics are available as to the importance of China's participation in Hong Kong's industries. Scattered reports show that China has an equity participation in a cement plant, an electronics firm producing sophisticated products, a ship-building company, some machinery and tool plants, and the manufacturing of beverage containers. On the part of China, these activities enable China to secure a more certain supply of industrial materials and equipment, and to acquire managerial and marketing skills and technical know-how. Of course, these activities can also be a profitable business from which China can earn extra foreign exchange. On the part of Hong Kong, such industrial co-operation arrangements in Hong Kong help to build up the confidence of Hong Kong industrialists engaged in heavier and more sophisticated industrial products which require a longer pay-off period. Moreover, such co-operation may help to explore the China market for the products they produce.

Another development worth noting is the exploitation of the oil fields in the South China Sea. At first, there were high hopes that Hong Kong could become a back-up base. Land has in fact been set aside for the possibility of developing oil storage and oil refinery activities in Hong Kong. But in early 1982, the Chinese Government announced that the oil field back-up bases mut be located within China, and China has in fact assigned a bay (Chiwan) in Shekou as the oil field back-up base. What remains for Hong Kong is therefore a number of third- or fourth-line supporting services such as financing, insurance, information-collecting and technical consultancy. Of course, it is also possible that the ship-building industry in Hong Kong can contribute to the supply of oil rigs and other exploration and exploitation equipment.

Conclusion

The modernization of China since 1977 has come at a time when the Hong Kong economy is about to undergo another transformation after its change from an entrepôt to an industrial city in the 1950's. The Great Leap Outward of China in 1977–9 led Hong Kong to believe that it should put greater emphasis on the development of financial services to take advantage of the growing Hong Kong–China visible and invisible trade. Later developments in China, such as its economic readjustment and reforms, and the establishment of Special

Economic Zones, suggest that Hong Kong's manufacturing industries can also benefit from China's modernization programmes. Specifically, Hong Kong can take this opportunity to expand its foreign direct investment activities in China and build up a vertical integrated network. This development should help to foster the introduction of new industries in Hong Kong and increase the competitiveness of Hong Kong's existing products. Unfortunately, China is not yet an ideal host country for Hong Kong investors in industry. The favourable impact of China's modernization on Hong Kong's industries at present is limited, although the potential is great. The outlook in the short term is certainly favourable in the sense that conditions in China will continue to improve in some ways and for some time, and Hong Kong industrial investors will have a chance to adjust themselves to the China environment. In the end, the development of Hong Kong's industries very much depends on the failure or success of China's experiments with the Special Economic Zones. Indeed, the entire future of Hong Kong may hinge on the fate of the Special Economic Zones. It is still too early to tell whether the Special Economic Zones will be a success or not. Meanwhile, the Hong Kong economy has to accept the fact of living with China and try to make the best of this situation.

Notes

[1] Central Intelligence Agency (CIA), United States Government, *China: International Trade*, December 1978.

[2] These figures are based on CIA estimates.

[3] CIA source; see A. Doak Barnett, *China's Economy in Global Perspective* (Washington D.C., The Brookings Institution, 1981), Part II.

[4] A speech delivered by Ye Jianying at the meeting in celebration of the thirtieth anniversary of the founding of the People's Republic of China, September 29, 1979.

[5] Zhou Shulian and Wu Jinglian, 'Heavy Industry in the Period of Economic Readjustment', *Jingji Yanjiu*, November 1981.

[6] See Zhao Ziyang (1982), *China's Economy and Development Principles* (Beijing, Foreign Language Press).

[7] Economists in China have written extensively on the subject of economic management reform since late 1979. See the numerous articles in *Jingji Yanjiu* and *Jingji Guanli*, and also Xue Muqiao, 'On Reforming the Economic Management System', *Beijing Review*, February 4, March 24, and April 7, 1980.

[8] *Renmin Ribao*, August 11, 1980.

[9] *Renmin Ribao*, April 24, 1980; *Zhongguo Jingji Nianjian 1981*, p. III–39.

[10] *Renmin Ribao*, April 24, 1980; *Zhongguo Jingji Nianjian 1981*, p. III–39.

[11] *Zhongguo Jingji Nianjian 1981*, pp. III–39, IV–6.

[12] *Renmin Ribao*, October 8, 1980.

[13] *Zhongguo Jingji Nianjian 1981*, p. III–39.

[14] *Renmin Ribao*, December 14, 1981.

[15] *Zhongguo Jingji Nianjian 1981*, p. III–39.

[16] *Renmin Ribao*, December 14, 1981.

[17] *Renmin Ribao*, February 14, 1981.

[18] For further discussions, see E. Szczepanik (1958), *The Economic Growth of Hong Kong* (London, Oxford University Press); and E.K.Y. Chen, 'The Economic Setting', in David Lethbridge (ed.), *The Business Environment in Hong Kong* (Hong Kong, Oxford University Press, 1980).

[19] Y.C. Jao has in various places traced in detail the development of financial services in Hong Kong; see for example, Y.C. Jao, 'Hong Kong as a Regional Financial Centre: Evolution and Progress', in C.K. Leung *et al.* (eds.), *Hong Kong: Dilemmas of Growth* (Canberra, Australian National University, 1980).

[20] The Diversification Committee was chaired by the Financial Secretary of the Hong Kong Government.

[21] See R. Hsia and L.C. Chau (1978), *Industrialization, Employment and Income Distribution: A Case Study of Hong Kong* (London, Croom Helm).

[22] The Gini Coefficient is a popular index for measuring inequalities in distribution. It ranges from 0 to 1; the lower the index, the more equal the distribution.

[23] For a study on Hong Kong manufacturing multinationals, see E.K.Y. Chen, 'Hong Kong Multinationals in Asia: Characteristics and Objectives', in K. Kumar

and M. McLeod (eds.), *Multinationals from Developing Countries* (Lexington, D.C. Heath, 1981).

[24] See J.H. Dunning, 'Explaining Changing Patterns of International Production: In Defence of the Eclectic Theory', *Oxford Bulletin of Economics and Statistics*, November 1979; and J.H. Dunning, 'Explaining Outward Direct Investment of Developing Countries: In Support of the Eclectic Theory of International Production', in K. Kumar and M. McLeod (eds.), *Multinationals from Developing Countries* (Lexington, D.C. Heath, 1981).

[25] For further details, see E.K.Y. Chen, 'Hong Kong Manufacturing Multinationals', in S. Lall (ed.), *Third World Multinationals* (London, Wiley), forthcoming.

[26] This survey was undertaken for a project sponsored by the Institute for Research and Information on Multinationals in Paris. The results will be published in my article in *Third World Multinationals*.

3. Industrial Co-operation between China and Hong Kong*

JOSEPH CHAI

Introduction

The opening up of China since 1978 has resulted in two significant developments in the Asian-Pacific region: the reintegration of China's economy into the international economy, and increased industrial co-operation between Hong Kong and China.

Both these developments are likely to have far-reaching implications for the neighbouring developing countries in the region. The re-emergence of China on the international economic scene means that these countries are likely to face increased competition from China in the near future, both in the market for foreign capital and investment and in the overseas export market for labour-intensive manufactures. The increased industrial co-operation between Hong Kong and China further enhances the danger of competition from China for these countries. For China has tremendous labour resources which will, by 1990, consist of around 500 million literate, healthy and work-

* In writing this paper I am deeply indebted to Professor A.J. Youngson who read the original draft, improved the English of my manuscript and made helpful suggestions which enabled me to improve the final version of this paper. I am also indebted to Mr T.W. Wong of the Federation of Hong Kong Industries, Mrs Cecilia Fung of the Hong Kong General Chamber of Commerce, Mr J.P. Lee of the Chinese Manufacturers' Association and Mrs May Tam of the Hong Kong Trade Development Council for their generous assistance and valuable comments. Needless to say, I take full responsibility for mistakes and views expressed in this paper.

oriented people in the most productive age groups between 20 and 45.[1] This will be nearly twice as much as the combined literate labour force of the United States, Japan and Western Europe. Hong Kong is one of the world's leading exporters of labour-intensive manufactured goods. With the aid of Hong Kong's experience, financial resources, equipment, technology and know-how, China's tremendous labour force could be used as the basis for the development of one of the world's largest export-oriented manufacturing economies.

The purpose of this chapter is to analyse the main development of Hong Kong's involvement in China's industrial co-operation with the West since late 1978. Motives of and the problems encountered by both Hong Kong and Chinese firms are discussed. The impact of industrial co-operation on China's economy and the resulting increased interdependence between the economies of China and Hong Kong are examined. The chapter concludes with an assessment of the potential for increased industrial co-operation in the near future.

For the purpose of this chapter the definition of industrial co-operation provided by the United Nations Economic Commission for Europe is adopted.[2] Accordingly, industrial co-operation refers to the economic relations and activities arising from contracts extending over a number of years between enterprises belonging to different economic systems which go beyond straightforward export/import operations. It includes a set of complementary and matching arrangements in production, in the development and exchange of technology, and in marketing between the two economies.

The classification of the various types of industrial co-operation in this chapter is based on Chinese practice[3] which recognizes five general classes of industrial co-operation agreements (ICAs) listed below roughly in ascending order of complexity of co-operation relations:

(a) processing;
(b) assembly;
(c) compensation trade;
(d) co-production; and
(e) joint venture.

Processing is a 'lower' form of ICA in which foreign firms provide samples and the necessary raw materials for Chinese enterprises to produce goods according to the required quality and specifications.

The finished products will be sold by the foreign firms while the Chinese enterprises charge only processing fees.

Assembly is another 'lower' form of co-operation usually involving such products as machinery, electrical appliances and electronics. Foreign firms provide samples and necessary parts and components for Chinese enterprises to assemble the finished products according to the required quality and designs. Foreign firms are responsible for selling the products and paying the Chinese firms for their assembly services.

In both processing and assembly arrangements foreign firms usually provide Chinese firms with certain equipment and machinery as well. The cost of the equipment and machinery provided is defrayed by the Chinese firms by instalments out of their processing and assembly charges. Thus, to a certain extent, processing and assembly overlap with another form of ICA — compensation trade.

Compensation trade involves the supply of plant and/or equipment as well as technical services to Chinese firms, and the acceptance by foreign firms of payment in the form of resultant products. Compensation trade in China is further divided into (a) large-scale and (b) medium- and small-scale according to the size of the projects. Large-scale compensation trade involves key construction projects undertaken by the state, negotiations for which are handled by Chinese ministries and state commissions. Medium- and small-scale compensation trade involves projects other than those undertaken by the state, negotiations for which are handled by the Foreign Trade Corporations and the Foreign Trade Bureaux or Industrial Bureaux of the local authorities concerned.

Co-production represents a 'higher' form of co-operation which involves a certain division of labour in the manufacturing of parts and components for final products. Each partner specializes in the production of certain parts of the final product which is then assembled by one of the partners or both, each to meet the requirements of its assigned market area. Under this type of agreement the Chinese partner usually manufactures the simpler or more labour-intensive parts, and foreign firms the more intricate or more capital-intensive parts.

Joint venture is the most advanced form of co-operation which involves a pooling of assets, joint management and sharing of profits and risks according to a commonly-agreed formula. Joint venture is further subdivided into three categories: equity joint venture, contractual joint venture and joint oil exploration. In the manufacturing sector, China participates mainly in equity and contractual joint venture. In the equity joint venture, two partners take a certain ratio of shares in the equity capital to form a new and distinct business entity and agree to share the profits and the risks in proportion to their capital participation. In the contractual joint venture, no equity capital is involved. Association is based entirely on a contract in which foreign firms agree to supply funds, equipment and technology, while Chinese firms supply sites, labour, management personnel, raw materials and other services. Risks and profits arising from the joint venture are shared between partners, not in relation to their capital share, but according to a formula as agreed in the contract, which usually takes the form of an allotted ratio of products, sales volume and profits. This type of joint venture, which represents an alternative to equity joint venture, is more flexible for both partners as it provides no equity ownership for the foreign partner.

The topics covered in this chapter and their analysis have been restricted in several respects. First, to narrow the analysis to manageable proportions, this chapter focuses primarily on China's ICAs in the manufacturing sector, leaving aside agreements in agriculture, mining, transportation, hotels, tourism, real estate and other sectors of the economy. Second, it focuses exclusively on the industrial co-operation projects located in China. Discussion of projects located in Hong Kong and third countries must be left to others. Third, it does not examine the impact of Hong Kong–China ICAs on the Hong Kong economy — a subject covered elsewhere in this book. Finally, as China has just started its industrial co-operation with Hong Kong recently, most of the requisite information is still in the hands of Hong Kong and Chinese firms and has not been made public in the quantity and detail necessary for serious research. Consequently, this chapter should be treated as a hypotheses-generating study. Its conclusions are very tentative and are to be confirmed when more data becomes available.

The Role of Hong Kong in China's Industrial Co-operation with the West[4]

China moved with extraordinary speed in its development of industrial co-operation with Western firms. Industrial co-operation had been officially endorsed in July 1978. Within a few months, several hundred agreements had already been concluded. As indicated in Table 3.1 and Table 3.2, the agreements concluded experienced a sharp increase in number in 1979 and 1980. By 1981, however, the growth tempo appeared to have slowed down.

Despite this recent slowing down, China's record of industrial co-operation performance is very impressive indeed. In less than four years China is estimated to have concluded some 20,000 ICAs. In contrast, its Eastern European counterparts, which pioneered the development of ICAs with the West, had concluded only 1,000 agreements by the end of 1975 after almost one decade of development.[5]

Although the number of China's ICAs dwarfs figures for any Eastern European country, the dollar value of its agreements was relatively small. As indicated in Table 3.3, 95 per cent of China's ICAs involved simple forms of co-operation — processing and assembly with unit values which averaged only US$17,000. Higher forms of co-operation with relatively higher unit values played only an insignificant role.

No figures for a detailed breakdown of China's ICAs by industry are available. However, press reports indicate that most of the processing, assembly, small- and medium-scale compensation trade and co-production agreements, and 15 out of the 29 equity joint ventures approved as of the end of August 1981, involved manufacturing.[6] Large-scale compensation trade agreements were mainly connected with mining (coal)[7], and contractual joint ventures were mainly centered around non-manufacturing activities: real estate, hotels, tourism, transportation and other service industries.[8] Thus, in terms of the number of agreements, manufacturing must have accounted for at least 60 per cent of China's total ICAs as of the end of 1981. However, since most of the manufacturing ICAs are small- and

Table 3.1 CHINA'S ICAS BY YEAR[a] (accumulative number)

Type of Agreement	1978	1979	1980	1981
Processing and assembly	200[b]	3,200[c]	10,320[d]	19,220[d]
Compensation trade:				
medium- and small-scale	38[b]	195[e]	400[e]	500[g]
large-scale			3[e]	3
sub-total	38	195	403	503
Co-production			12[h]	12
Joint-venture:				
equity			20[e]	39[f]
contractual			300[e]	400[i]
joint oil exploration			4[j]	4
sub-total			324	443
Total	238	3,395	11,059	20,178

a. All figures are approximate numbers as reported in the press.
b. Light industry only. *Ta Kung Pao*, February 9, 1979.
c. Ji Chongwei, 'Questions Concerning China's Utilization of Foreign Investment and Relevant Economic Law', paper presented to a seminar on *New China's Economic Trend*, October 1980, p. 3.
d. *Ta Kung Pao*, April 4, 1982.
e. *The Annual Economic Report of China*, 1981, pp. IV–132–134.
f. Figure given by Rong Yiren, Chairman of China International Trust and Investment Corporation. See *Economic Reporter*, February 1982, p. 15.
g. *Renmin Ribao*, October 3, 1981.
h. *China Economic News*, August 3, 1981, p. 2; *China Trade Report*, February 1981, p. 7.
i. *World Economic Herald*, January 25, 1982.
j. Ji Chongwei, 'A Brief Introduction to the Forthcoming China Investment Promotion Meeting', mimeograph, p. 1.

medium-scale projects, they accounted for at most 40 per cent of China's total ICAs in terms of value.

Within the manufacturing sector, press reports indicate that China's ICAs were dominated by the textile, garments and other light

Table 3.2 CHINA'S ICAS BY YEAR (yearly concluded agreement)

Type of Agreement	1978	1979	1980	1981
Processing and assembly	200	3,000	7,120	8,900
Compensation trade:				
medium- and small-scale	38	157	205	100
large-scale			3	
sub-total	38	157	208	100
Co-production			12	
Joint venture:				
equity			20	19
contractual			300	100
joint oil exploration			4	
sub-total			324	119
Total	238	3,157	7,664	9,119

Source: Derived from Table 3.1.

industries and, to a lesser extent, by electronics. Chemicals, machinery and transport equipment played only an insignificant role.[9]

Hong Kong is by far the leading foreign partner in China's ICAs. Again, although no exact figure is available, press reports indicate that approximately 60 per cent of all China's processing and assembly agreements concluded during 1978 and 1979 were accounted for by Hong Kong and Macau firms.[10] Of China's 29 equity joint ventures in the manufacturing and non-manufacturing sectors approved as of the end of August 1981, 55 per cent involved Hong Kong firms,[11] and most of the contractual joint ventures involved Hong Kong and Macau capital.[12]

The pattern of Hong Kong ICAs with China can be seen from the foreign investment agreements concluded in Shenzhen. As of August 1981, 814 agreements had been concluded, involving a total of US$465 million pledged foreign investment in Shenzhen (excluding Shekou), of which 91 per cent originated from Hong Kong.[13] Tables

Table 3.3 UNIT VALUE OF CHINA'S ICAS AND THEIR DISTRIBUTION BY TYPE OF AGREEMENT, 1979–81
(thousand US dollars)

Type of Agreement	Unit Value	Percentage Distribution
Processing and assembly	17[a]	95
Compensation trade:		
medium- and small-scale	506[b]	2
large-scale	29,000[b]	negligible
sub-total	680	
Co-production	5,833[c]	negligible
Joint venture:		
equity	5,128[d]	negligible
contractual	1,250[d]	2
joint oil exploration	125,000	negligible
sub-total	2,709	
Total	96	100

a. Valued in terms of processing and assembly fees.
b. Valued in terms of machinery, equipment and know-how compensated.
c. Value of the contract.
d. Foreign share of investment.

Source: See Table 3.1.

3.4 and 3.5 show that, in terms of number of agreements, foreign investment in Shenzhen was mainly in the form of processing and assembly ICAs and in the manufacturing sector. However, when analysed in terms of value, most of them were found to be in the higher form of co-operation — contractual joint venture — but in the non-manufacturing sector. Real estate, tourist-related industries, commerce and transportation accounted for three-quarters, and manufacturing for only 16 per cent, of the total pledged foreign investment in Shenzhen.

Table 3.4 FOREIGN INVESTMENT IN SHENZHEN BY TYPE OF INVESTMENT[a]

	Percentage Share (in terms of number of projects)	Percentage Share (in terms of pledged investment)
ICAs:		
processing and assembly	62.2	2.3
compensation trade	0.6	1.8
co-operation in agriculture and fishing	25.4	3.3
contractual joint venture	9.0	56.8
equity joint venture	1.0	2.8
Total	98.2	67.0
100 per cent equity investment	1.9	33.0

[a] As of August 1981.

Source: *Economic Reporter*, November 11, 1981, p. 8.

Table 3.5 FOREIGN INVESTMENT IN SHENZHEN BY INDUSTRIAL BRANCH[b]

	Percentage Share (in terms of number of projects)	Percentage Share (in terms of pledged investment)
Manufacturing	66.1	16.3
Agriculture, fishing and animal husbandry	26.0	4.1
Trade	1.5	7.9
Tourism	2.5	28.3
Real estate	2.8	39.5
Transportation	0.9	0.2
Other	0.3	3.6

[a] As of August 1981.

Source: See Table 3.4.

The Experiences of Hong Kong and Chinese Firms

A. A Survey of the Experiences of Hong Kong Firms

In order to assess the experiences of Hong Kong firms, a survey was carried out among members of the Federation of Hong Kong Industries. A total of 1,500 questionnaires were sent out. As expected, the rate of response was low. Only 38 firms responded, of which 18 indicated that they had either no co-operation experience or only sales contracts with Chinese firms. Only 20 have been positively identified as having ICAs with Chinese firms. These 20 firms are involved in approximately 129 ICAs with China.

Despite the low response rate the results of the survey are not entirely meaningless. Firstly, although the overall response rate is low, the response rate among member firms which do have co-operation experience with China is much higher. This is because, according to the Deputy Chairman of the Federation of Hong Kong Industries, only about 100 of the Federation's member firms are known to be involved in such trade.[14] Secondly, the results of the survey agree broadly with that carried out by the Hong Kong General Chamber of Commerce among its member firms in 1980.

Nevertheless, in view of the small sample, the results should be treated as preliminary hypotheses to be confirmed by a more representative survey and detailed case studies in the near future.

1. *A Profile of Sample Firms and their ICAs with China*

Of the 20 firms which responded, 12 are manufacturing firms, 3 are trading firms and 5 are engaged in both activities. They vary in size: 5 firms employ less than 49 persons, another 5 employ between 50 and 99 persons, and the rest employ more than 100 persons.

The distribution of the sample ICAs concluded by the firms by type of agreement is almost identical with that of all China's ICAs shown in Table 3.3. As indicated in Table 3.6, of 129 sample agreements, 96 per cent involve processing and assembly; only 3 per cent involve compensation trade. Other forms of agreement play an insignificant role.

Table 3.6 DISTRIBUTION OF ICAS SURVEYED BY TYPE OF AGREEMENT, 1981

Type of Agreement	Unit Value (thousand US dollars)	Number of Agreements
Processing and assembly	43	124
Compensation trade	2,564	4
Joint venture	5,000	1
	Average Unit Value	
All agreements	160	129

Table 3.6 also shows the unit value of the sample ICAs. As expected, due to the predominance of medium and large firms in the sample, the average unit value of the sample processing and assembly agreements as well as that of compensation trade agreements is much higher than for all China's ICAs.

The sample ICAs cut across major areas of the manufacturing sector. As indicated in Table 3.7, most of the contracts are centred on light industry, pharmaceuticals and electrical appliances and electronics with relatively low unit values. Contracts in heavy industry (metal manufactures and transport equipment), although they amounted to only three, account for more than one-half of the total value of the sample ICAs.

2. Motives

Table 3.8 analyses the motives of both Hong Kong and Chinese firms according to the Hong Kong respondents. To reflect the value difference of their agreements, the firms' responses are weighted both according to the number of agreements signed as well as their relative money values.

Table 3.8 reveals two significant differences. First of all, it confirms the hypothesis that the motives of Chinese firms differ from those of Hong Kong firms. The interests of Hong Kong firms are mainly micro-oriented: cost and accessibility advantages, better utilization of existing capacity, and an increase of export market share in China.

Table 3.7 DISTRIBUTION OF ICAS SURVEYED BY INDUSTRIAL BRANCH, 1981

Industrial Branch	Number of Agreements	Relative[b] Unit Value
Food industry	1	24.2
Pharmaceuticals	50	0.04
Metal manufactures	2	29.7
Transport equipment	1	11.0
Electrical equipment and electronics	20	0.79
Light industry[a]	55	0.30
Total	129	

[a] Textiles, garments, footwear, furniture, plastic manufactures, toys, watches and clocks.

[b] Ratio of average unit value of ICAs in each industrial branch to their overall unit value.

Table 3.8 MOTIVES ACCORDING TO HONG KONG FIRMS SURVEYED (the same firm may report more than one motive)

	Hong Kong Firms		Chinese Firms	
	A	*B*	*A*	*B*
Financial			121	66.5
Employment			33	62.1
Cost and accessibility advantages	128	104.4		
Better utilization of existing capacity	64	20.7		
Technology transfer			71	111.3
Export promotion	22	115.4	11	103.7
Other motives	16	33.7		

A = number of ICAs.

B = number of ICAs weighted by their relative values.

The motives on the Chinese side are dominated by macro-considerations: foreign exchange earnings, technology transfer, and an increase in export and employment opportunities.

Secondly, the motives of Hong Kong firms with more valuable ICAs with China differ from those with less valuable ICAs. The main objectives of the latter group of firms are to take advantage of China's low factor cost and raw material accessibility, as well as to achieve better utilization of their existing production capacity in Hong Kong. The main objective of the former group of firms is, however, to use the ICA as a tool for export promotion to China. Evidently they are hoping that by initiating industrial co-operation with China their position in the marketing of complementary products to China will be improved, or that they will at least be able to gain a competitive edge against other competitors in China's market. Cost and other accessibility advantages are also considered as important motives; but their significance is less than that of export promotion.

3. *Problems*

Hong Kong respondents were asked about explicit problems regarding the negotiation for and the implementation of the ICAs. Their opinions, weighted by the number of agreements signed as well as their relative values, are presented in Table 3.9.

Table 3.9 reveals that there are both common as well as unique problems encountered by the two groups of Hong Kong firms. Transportation difficulties were the most frequent problem common to both groups of firms. These centered around the lack of transportation facilities, the exorbitant transportation charges, and the carelessness and red tape involved in cargo-handling and shipments, and so on.

The second most frequent and common problem concerned delivery times and related problems, such as failure to deliver, and the inflexibility of Chinese firms as regards changes in quantity, date of delivery, and so on. Co-ordination problems were also a frequent and common complaint. Co-ordination between the two partners was made difficult by information and communication problems and lack of decision-making power on the Chinese side. Last but not least, both groups of firms also frequently complained about the slowness of Chinese firms in absorbing Western technology.

Table 3.9 MAJOR PROBLEM AREAS ACCORDING TO HONG KONG FIRMS SURVEYED

	Number of ICAs			Number of ICAs Weighted by their Relative Values		
	Number	*Percentage*	*Rank*	*Number*	*Percentage*	*Rank*
1. Negotiation for agreement:						
information problems on the Chinese side	61	47	(8)	53.0	41	(9)
Chinese shortage of foreign exchange	8	6	(13)	77.0	60	(8)
Chinese lack of decision-making power	114	88	(3)	96.0	74	(6)
availability of fuel and raw materials	53	41	(9)	16.0	12	(13)
2. Technology transfer:						
slow assimilation of Western technology	97	75	(5)	80.8	63	(7)
3. Quality	36	28	(11)	122.1	95	(2)
4. Supply problems:						
delivery problems on the Chinese side	111	86	(4)	117.5	91	(4)
transportation problems	123	95	(1)	126.0	98	(1)
5. Prices	32	25	(12)	119.5	93	(3)
6. Marketing:						
'psychological barrier' against Chinese products	64	50	(7)	25.9	20	(11)
difficulty in obtaining certificate of origin in Hong Kong	117	91	(2)	27.5	21	(10)
7. Management and co-ordination:						
co-ordination between partners	73	57	(6)	114.6	89	(5)
management and co-ordination problems on the Chinese side	47	36	(10)	20.6	16	(12)

Quality and pricing were major problems unique to the firms with more valuable ICAs. These concerned the low quality of Chinese products/parts and components and the dispute over both the level and adjustment of prices between the two partners. Firms which are involved in only a small-scale ICA with China appear to be least concerned about quality and pricing. They are more concerned with marketing problems. The difficulty of getting the certificate of origin in Hong Kong and the difficulty of marketing the Chinese products in Hong Kong, as well as in overseas markets, because of a 'psychological barrier' against Chinese products were two of their major complaints. Difficulties for their co-operating Chinese partner in procuring the necessary fuel and raw materials in China were also a frequent complaint by this group of firms.

The above survey findings agree broadly with those of a similar survey carried out by the Hong Kong General Chamber of Commerce in 1980. The Chamber's survey findings were based on responses from 46 firms. It should be noted that the results of the Chamber's survey are not strictly comparable with those mentioned above. First of all, the Chamber's survey was conducted among its members, which include a high proportion of non-manufacturing firms. Secondly, the survey included all co-operation ventures both in the manufacturing and the non-manufacturing sectors. Thirdly, the survey did not explicitly ask about pricing problems and included no questions relating to technology transfer. Finally, the responses of the firms were neither weighted by the number of agreements concluded nor by the relative value of the agreements.

Table 3.10 indicates that the most frequent problems, according to the Chamber's survey, were those relating to management decisions, punctuality of delivery, productivity of workers, product quality and availability of raw materials. Cost of delivery and other related transportation problems, such as red tape for the remittance of materials and for outgoing shipments, as well as labour discipline, were also major problem areas. It should be noted that low productivity of workers was not reported as a major problem area by the firms in our survey. It is not known whether this is due to the different sample size or due to the difference in the time period during which the two samples were taken.

Table 3.10 SURVEY OF HONG KONG'S ICAS BY THE HONG KONG GENERAL CHAMBER OF COMMERCE, 1980: MAJOR PROBLEM AREAS

	Number of Firms Reported
1. Quality	13
2. Supply problems:	
punctuality of shipments	17
cost of delivery	8
red tape for remittance of materials and parts	7
red tape for outgoing shipments	3
3. Infrastructural facilities:	
supply of electricity	6
supply of water	1
4. Productivity of workers	14
5. Marketing:	
quota for textile products	6
6. Management and co-ordination problems:	
management decisions	19
control of workers	9
availability of raw materials	13

Source: Unpublished information, made available to the author by the Hong Kong General Chamber of Commerce.

When the major problems frequently encountered by Hong Kong firms are analysed according to their origin, it appears that many of them are symptoms of differences between the two economic systems: plan versus market. It is well known that the ways of conducting business are different under the two systems. The way of doing things in a planned economy is known to be highly bureaucratic and inflexible which explains many of the management and co-ordination problems, and the delay in delivery as well as the inflexibility of Chinese firms in changing their delivery schedules, as was frequently complained of by

Hong Kong firms. Furthermore, Chinese firms are accustomed to producing for the plan rather than for the market. Thus they tend to neglect quality and prompt delivery. The ideological barrier to firing workers and to adopting a less egalitarian system of wages also makes it difficult to maintain labour discipline and a high working morale among the work force. Last but not least, the lack of a market mechanism means that there are no meaningful prices for many inputs such as land, labour and other non-traded goods. Thus Chinese firms have difficulty in valuing equipment, technology and know-how brought in by Hong Kong firms; and Hong Kong firms have difficulty in valuing what the Chinese provide. Consequently this gives rise to a lot of price disputes between the two partners.

Overall Assessment

The overall results of their ICAs with China, as can be seen from Table 3.11, were rated as 'acceptable' by most of the Hong Kong firms. Similar results were also reported in the survey carried out by the General Chamber of Commerce: of the 46 firms which responded, 67 per cent regarded the results of their ICAs with China as 'satisfactory, but hoped to have improvements in certain areas', 17 per cent reported full satisfaction and no major problems, and the rest indicated that it was too early for them to comment.

The assessments of the firms differ with respect to the value of their ICAs. Firms with more valuable agreements appear to be more satisfied with the overall results than those with less valuable agreements, as the most frequent assessments by the former group of firms

Table 3.11 SURVEY OF HONG KONG'S ICAS WITH CHINA, 1981: OVERALL ASSESSMENT

	Number of Agreements	Number of Agreements Weighted by their Relative Values
1. Unsatisfactory	48	19
2. Acceptable	66	75.4
3. Good	13	31.2
4. Very good	2	3.1

were 'acceptable' and 'good', whereas those by the latter group were 'acceptable' and 'unsatisfactory'.

To uncover the factors which affect the overall outcome of the firms' agreements, correlations between the overall results and the characteristics of the firms and their ICAs are shown in Table 3.12.

It was found that two factors — the involvement of Hong Kong firms in trading activities and the number of Chinese partners involved

Table 3.12 SURVEY OF HONG KONG'S ICAS WITH CHINA, 1981: THE ZERO-ORDER CORRELATION BETWEEN THE OVERALL ASSESSMENT AND THE CHARACTERISTICS OF THE FIRMS AND THEIR ICAS

1. Characteristics of Hong Kong firms:	
firm involved in trading or not[a]	−0.54****
size, small[b] or not[a]	−0.40**
previous business experience with China or not[a]	0.025
2. Characteristics of Chinese firms:	
located in Special Economic Zones or not[a]	−0.03
commune- or brigade-run enterprise or not[a]	−0.23
3. Characteristics of co-operation agreements:	
number of Chinese partners involved in each agreement	−0.53***
initiative for co-operation taken or not by Hong Kong firm[a]	0.29*
processing and assembly agreement or not[a]	−0.23
equipment transferred to China or not[a]	−0.19
training for Chinese workers or not[a]	0.15
parts and components received from China or not	0.10

* Significance at 0.10 level
** Significance at 0.05 level
*** Significance at 0.025 level
**** Significance at 0.001 level

[a] These variables are defined as binary variables with values 1, 0 in this order.
[b] A small firm is defined here as one employing less than 50 persons.

in each ICA — were most strongly correlated with the overall results. Both factors appear to have had a negative effect on the results. Firms involved in trading were probably handicapped by their lack of adequate manufacturing and production management experience. The greater the number of Chinese partners involved in each of the agreements, the greater seem to have been the risks of conflict and co-ordination problems.

The size of Hong Kong firms appears to be significantly correlated with the results. Big firms appear to be more successful than small firms. Although the correlation between the initiative taken by Hong Kong firms and the results is only indicative, it is reasonable to assume that a firm taking the initiative might create favourable conditions for successful co-operation.

Neither the location nor the type of Chinese firms were related to the results. Both commune- and brigade-run enterprises, as well as state enterprises and firms located within and outside Special Economic Zones, appear to have been equally successful (or unsuccessful). Similarly, the results appear to be independent of the previous business experiences of Hong Kong firms with China, the form of co-operation, the kind of products Hong Kong firms received from China, and the kind of technology transferred to China.

One could have expected that some of the most frequent problems as reported by the firms would be related to the results. However, no significant correlation was found. It seems that Hong Kong firms either expected such problems and learned to live with them, or the cost arising from such problems was regarded as tolerable in relation to the substantial saving the firms derived from the lower factor cost in China. Furthermore, several firms regarded co-operation as a means to the promotion of other exports to China, and consequently were willing to accept substantial costs in order to achieve this objective.

B. Evaluation of the Experiences of Chinese Firms

In order to assess the experiences of Chinese firms an attempt has been made to conduct a similar survey to that carried out among the

Hong Kong firms. However, as confirmed by the Hong Kong firms' experiences, China's bureaucracy proved to be formidable; and to date the questionnaires designed for the survey are probably still held up somewhere in China's bureaucratic machinery. Consequently the following assessment of Chinese firms' experiences has to depend entirely on case studies and on a survey done by Chinese economists and reported in the Chinese press and economic journals. Due to the fragmentary nature of the available evidence, the conclusions again must be seen as largely tentative.

1. *Motives*

It is useful to make a distinction between the different levels of bureaucracy in China as their motives are not always the same. The driving force behind industrial co-operation is generally on the macro-level, that is the State Planning Commission, the Foreign Economic Relations and Trade Ministry, and so on. Their main motives behind industrial co-operation are, as confirmed by Hong Kong firms in the survey, macro-considerations such as technology transfer, increase of exports, hard currency earnings and employment opportunities. The motives at the micro-level — the local authorities and the firms — are mainly micro-oriented. However, unlike the Western firms, they are not aiming at profit maximization or an increase of market share. Their motivation is mainly oriented towards fulfillment of plans and directives handed down from above so as to maximize the rewards or concessions granted by the state.

In order to encourage a high volume of ICAs, the Chinese Government has introduced several measures since 1978. One of these is the decentralization of the management of industrial co-operation by giving local authorities and firms increased autonomy to deal with foreign firms directly. Thus, according to the decree issued by the State Council in September 1979,[15] Chinese firms are allowed to invite foreign firms to China to hold business talks, to take a direct part in negotiations and to join Foreign Trade Corporations in signing agreements concerning processing, assembly and compensation trade. Agreements worth less than US$1 million which do not involve the utilization of China's export quota and which do not affect the national balance for fuel and raw materials supply need only be approved by the local authorities.

Another measure is the introduction of a comprehensive incentive programme to stimulate the interest of local authorities and of Chinese firms in co-operation.[16] The main incentive is the foreign exchange bonus. Enterprises and their local authorities are entitled to 15 per cent of net foreign exchange earnings through processing, assembly and compensation trade agreements, which share they can use to import any equipment and material they need or to finance study tours abroad. Another type of incentive is the exemption from taxation on their net income and from the need to turn in any part of their profits for the first three years. Other incentives include priority given in the supply of raw materials and capital funds, exemption from customs duties in importing raw materials and equipment, and a preferential exchange rate (higher than the average rate) offered by the Chinese bank when converting their foreign exchange earnings into Rmb, and, finally, subsidies by the state in the case of losses for the first two years.

2. Problems

China's experience of ICAs, like Hong Kong's experience, has not been without numerous problems. The crude incentive system mentioned above, coupled with decentralization measures, has led to peculiar and often dysfunctional behaviour by Chinese local authorities and firms in their conduct of industrial co-operation with foreign firms. First, in an attempt to conclude as many ICAs as possible in order to reap the benefits of privileges and concessions granted by the state in connection with ICAs, local authorities and Chinese firms tended to neglect the cost and profitability considerations of ICAs.[17] This was revealed in the low profitability and even losses involved in industrial co-operation business as frequently reported by the Chinese firms.[18] Second, local authorities and firms tended to undercut each other in terms of processing and assembly fees in competing for ICAs, leading to a general reduction of foreign exchange revenues for the state.[19] Third, many ICAs involved traditional trade which was disguised as 'co-operation' in order to reap the benefits from the incentive scheme, leading to trade diversion rather than trade creation.[20]

The decentralization measure itself has led to the participation of many small- and medium-size enterprises, particularly at commune and brigade level, in direct negotiation and the concluding of agreements with foreign firms. Due to their low expertise and level of information, these firms were said to be constantly cheated by foreign firms with regard to processing and assembly fees, the age of technology introduced, and other terms of agreement. Thus, one of the frequent complaints was that foreign firms taking advantage of the ignorance of Chinese firms had imposed a processing or assembly fee which was way below the Hong Kong standard and, in some cases, even below the actual processing or assembly cost incurred.[21]

Furthermore, Chinese firms are also said to have been constantly cheated with regard to the age and price of the machinery and equipment introduced under the compensation trade agreement. Thus, it was discovered that most of the machinery and equipment imported into Guangdong under compensation trade agreements was obsolete and was being phased out in Hong Kong, and some items were even archaic pieces dating back to 1924 and 1926. [22] The prices charged for such machinery and the interest rate for the loan were found to be unreasonably high. Many enterprises reportedly had difficulties in meeting the payment schedule because of their low and unstable revenues from processing and assembly fees.[23]

Finally, numerous cases of default by Hong Kong businessmen have also been reported, which have caused Chinese firms to suffer substantial financial losses as they have failed to check the credit-worthiness of Hong Kong businessmen before signing the contract.[24]

The inherent instability of the market economy also posed problems for the Chinese firms as they had had very little previous experience with the market economy. Thus, they were unaware of the market risks caused by demand fluctuation and failed to take precautions to introduce into the agreements a compensation clause which they could rely on whenever there were not enough orders forthcoming from the foreign firms. Consequently, during the recession in Western economies, they found their revenues dwindling and had to subsidize the wages and salaries of their workers and staff as, contrary to

Western practice, they could not lay them off during a recession.[25]

The inflexibility of China's supply system also created problems. Despite the preferential treatment promised by the government, Chinese firms often complained about the difficulties in obtaining the necessary raw materials, spare parts, packaging materials, and so on, necessary for the implementation of the agreements.[26]

Problems due to lack of experience were easily solved by Chinese firms through learning by doing. Thus, Chinese firms have now learned to protect themselves against the risk caused by market uncertainties by including a clause in the agreement specifying the amount of compensation due from foreign firms in times of reduced orders due to business recession in the West.[27] They have also learned to protect themselves from being cheated in processing and assembly fees by introducing a trial production period during which Chinese firms have ample opportunity to test the profitability of the proposed arrangements.[28]

Problems related to the inflexibility of China's supply system have proved more difficult to solve. They are sometimes circumvented. Thus, the difficulty of obtaining domestic raw materials, spare parts, packaging materials, and so on, is simply solved by Chinese firms by requesting that foreign firms provide whatever cannot be obtained within China. Such a solution is evidently contrary to the macro-objectives of increased exports and foreign exchange earnings.

Problems related to incentive schemes and decentralization measures have proved particularly difficult to solve as they involve an optimal degree of centralization or decentralization as well as an optimal incentive system, both of which have been found to be extremely difficult to achieve in a planned economy.

To avoid cut-throat competition, disguised co-operation and other related problems, China has lately recentralized the management of ICAs through 'unified planning' and 'unified pricing'.[29] Furthermore, to induce firms to strive for optimum instead of maximum ICAs, China plans to introduce 'profitability' as an additional success indicator in evaluating the firms' performance in ICAs.[30] It will be fascinating to see what will be achieved in the years ahead.

The Effect of Industrial Co-operation on China's Economy

A. Static Gains

Foreign exchange earnings have been considered as the most important static gain for China from ICAs. Few would dispute the extremely high marginal value of foreign exchange to the Chinese planners. The Chinese reliance on ICAs as a source of foreign exchange earnings is, however, frequently exaggerated. Taking the sum of processing and assembling fees earned, the value of machinery and equipment imported under the compensation agreements, and the foreign share of total investment in joint ventures as a proxy, foreign exchange revenues arising from all ICAs amounted to US$1,172 million in 1980, contributing only 5 per cent of China's total gross foreign exchange earnings as indicated in Table 3.13. This 5 per cent is most probably a maximum figure as foreign pledged investment in equity and contractual joint ventures, instead of actual investment expenditure, has been counted as part of foreign exchange revenues from industrial co-operation. Compared with China's other major sources of foreign exchange earnings such as exports, invisible trade and foreign borrowings, the significance of ICAs is still rather limited. The contribution of ICAs in the manufacturing sector is probably even smaller, as most of them are centered around small- and medium-scale co-operation projects as mentioned earlier.

The significance of ICAs as a source of domestic capital formation appears to be even smaller. Total gross investment in China was estimated at US$74 billion by the IMF in 1980.[31] Assuming that all foreign exchange revenues arising from ICAs were spent in real capital formation, this amounted to only 1.5 per cent of total gross investment in China. Hong Kong's share is probably much less than this and its significance also much more limited, because a substantial proportion of the real investment arising from Hong Kong ICAs is concentrated in the real estate and services-related sector which has only a limited productive capacity-creating impact.

Table 3.13 CHINA'S ESTIMATED GROSS FOREIGN EXCHANGE EARNINGS, 1980 (million US dollars)

Category	Value	Percentage Share[i]
Exports (fob):	18,130[a]	77.0
processing and assembly fees	112[b]	
Invisible earnings:	2,227	9.4
tourist revenues and other invisible trade earnings	1,200[c]	
remittances	700[c]	
export of labour	327[d]	
Capital imports:		
loan receipts	2,260[e]	9.6
investment capital arising from:	1,060	4.5
compensation trade	100[f]	
equity and contractual joint ventures	670[g]	
joint oil exploration	290[h]	

a. JETRO, *China Newsletter,* November–December 1981, p. 12.

b. *Ta Kung Pao*, April 4, 1982.

c. World Bank's estimate cited in *The Seventies*, 1981, No. 10, p. 30.

d. Planned revenues for all contracts signed in 1980, *Ta Kung Pao*, March 26, 1982

e. *Renmin Ribao*, September 13, 1980.

f. Machinery and equipment actually imported, *Economic Reporter*, April 1, 1981 p. 8.

g. Pledged investment, *Economic Reporter*, April 1, 1981, p. 8.

h. Exploration cost, *China Trade Report*, July 1980, p. 8.

i. Figures do not add up to 100 due to rounding.

Job creation is very often regarded as yet another important static gain for China from ICAs. Again its real significance often appears to be overstated. A crude estimate based on the sample average employment effects of various categories of ICAs in Table 3.14 indicates that the direct employment impact of ICAs concluded during the last three years or so (from late 1978 to 1981) probably amounted to only 598,000 jobs.[32] Total new employment in the urban sector created by

Table 3.14 THE DIRECT EMPLOYMENT EFFECT OF ICAS IN CHINA, 1978–81

Form	Number of Agreements	Number of Workers Engaged	Average Employment per Agreement
Processing and assembling[a]	9,000 +	200,000	22
Compensation trade (small and medium)[b]	113	20,000	177
Equity joint ventures[c]	3	4,600	1,533

a. *Ta Kung Pao*, September 29, 1981. Data refer to Guangdong during the period from late 1978 to the first half of 1981.

b. *Ta Kung Pao*, November 29, 1981. Data refer to Shanghai during the period from late 1978 to October 1981.

c. *Ta Kung Pao,* July 8 and October 4, 1981, *China Newsletter*, January–February 1982, p. 20. Data refer to Tianshan Woollen Textile Company, China-Schindler Elevator Company and Fujian Hitachi TV Ltd.

the government during the same period was reported to be 26 million.[33] Hence ICAs contributed only 2 per cent of the total urban employment created during the period under discussion.

As indicated in Table 3.14, the direct employment impact of lower forms of ICAs, such as processing and assembling, is very small when compared with more advanced forms of ICAs such as equity joint ventures. It also appears that the direct employment effects of ICAs in the manufacturing sector are likely to be substantially larger than those in services and other non-manufacturing branches. Since Hong Kong's ICAs with China are mainly dominated by the lower form of ICAs and a large proportion of Hong Kong's higher forms of ICAs are confined to the non-manufacturing sector, particularly in real estate and tourist-related industries, Hong Kong's contribution towards solving China's unemployment problem is perhaps even more limited. The limited direct employment effect of Hong Kong's ICAs can be observed in Shenzhen where, as mentioned earlier, more than 90 per cent of foreign investment connected with ICAs comes from Hong Kong. Up to the first half of 1981, a total of 802 ICAs had been concluded and the employment created amounted to 15,000 plus.[34] Thus the overall average direct employment effect per agreement was about 18.7 persons only.

B. Dynamic Gains

Though the static gains of ICAs may be small because of the enormous size of China's economy in relation to the scale of foreign investment resulting from ICAs, their dynamic gains could nonetheless be considerable.

Of all the presumed dynamic benefits to China from increased industrial co-operation, the import of Western technology is considered to be the most important. Carl H. McMillan's study of Eastern European experiences in East–West industrial co-operation shows that ICAs are potent media for technology transfer.[35] Of the 129 Hong Kong agreements surveyed, all involved technology transfer from Hong Kong to China in some form or another, as indicated in Table 3.15.

The issue of technology transfer is not only of academic interest, but is also of vital importance to China as well as Hong Kong and other developing countries in the Asian–Pacific region. Realization of this potential dynamic gain will narrow the technological gap between China and the advanced countries, and will bring China a step closer to its modernization goal. For Hong Kong and other developing countries in this region, large-scale technology transfer to China from

Table 3.15 PATTERN OF TECHNOLOGY AND COMMODITY FLOWS IN HONG KONG ICAS SURVEYED, 1981 (number of agreements)

	Frequency	Hong Kong to China only	China to Hong Kong only	Reciprocal
Embodied technology (hardware)	58	58	0	0
Disembodied technology (software)	129	129	0	0
Deliveries of parts and components	129	115	0	14
Deliveries of finished products	115		113	2

Hong Kong and the West raises the issue of whether China will use this technology to enhance its future export competitiveness vis-à-vis Hong Kong and other developing nations, and take away their overseas manufactured export markets.

To gauge the potential of this dynamic gain for China let us consider (a) the scale of technology transfer through ICAs, and (b) the potential of its utilization and diffusion in China's economy.

1. The Scale of Embodied Technology Transfer

Technology transfer in the form of product or embodied technology transfer can be evaluated in terms of machinery and equipment imports through ICAs.

Table 3.16 uses officially released data to measure the magnitude of embodied technology flow through various forms of ICAs. It shows that the dominant forms of China's ICAs, processing and assembly as well as compensation trade, are not an important medium for embodied technology transfer as the average value of machinery and equipment imports connected with these kinds of ICAs averaged only US$8,000 and US$645,000 respectively. Statistics regarding the value of machinery and equipment imports through higher forms of ICAs such as joint venture are not available. As indicated in Table 3.3, the average foreign investment for the 39 equity joint ventures concluded by the end of 1981 was about US$5 million, and for the some 400 contractual joint ventures, only US$1.3 million. However, there are indications that the average value of machinery and equipment imports per joint-venture agreement is probably much less than the average investment figures. First, a survey of the contract details of some of the equity joint ventures reveals that the equity capital contribution of the foreign partner is not solely in the form of machinery and equipment imported, but also includes building construction, working capital and know-how. Second, most of the contractual joint ventures are located in the non-manufacturing sector, particularly in real estate and hotels which involved very little transfer of machinery and equipment. The contribution of Hong Kong ICAs to embodied technology transfer to China is probably even more limited because most of its ICAs are of the 'lower' form, and its 'higher' forms of ICAs are centered in the real estate and services-related industry. This can be seen from the relatively low value of machinery and equipment imports per agreement (including 100 per cent equity ventures) in Shenzhen, which averaged only US$37,000 (see Table 3.16). It can also be seen from the survey findings given in Table 3.15 that only 45 per cent of the Hong Kong ICAs surveyed included machinery and equipment transfer.

Table 3.16 CHINA'S MACHINERY AND EQUIPMENT IMPORTS THROUGH ICAS, 1979–81[a]

Form of ICAs	Number of Agreements	Value of Machinery and Equipment Imported (million US dollars)	Average Value of Machinery and Equipment Imported (thousand US dollars)
Processing and assembling[b]	19,020	157	8
Compensation trade[c]	465	300	645
All ICAs (Shenzhen only)[d]	914	34	37

[a] All figures are approximate.

[b] *Ta Kung Pao*, April 4, 1982.

[c] *1979-1981, World Economic Herald*, January 25, 1982.

[d] As of October 1981. *China Economic News*, December 28, 1981, p. 7.

Hong Kong's contribution to embodied technology transfer to China through ICAs is also limited by the age of its technology. Hong Kong is not an original innovator, and its technological level lags behind that of Western industrialized nations. Much machinery and equipment transferred from Hong Kong to China in connection with ICAs was either imported from Western industrialized countries or taken from industries which were being phased out in Hong Kong, as has been mentioned earlier in our discussion of Chinese firms' experiences. This is also confirmed by our survey findings that in most of the Hong Kong ICAs surveyed the technology embodied in the machinery and equipment transferred to China was rated as 'intermediate', and in some cases was even regarded as out-of-date (see

Table 3.17). In one, perhaps rare, instance a piece of leather-processing machinery brought into Shenzhen was later found to have actually been made in China in the 1950's.[36]

Table 3.17 THE AGE OF EMBODIED TECHNOLOGY TRANSFER IN HONG KONG ICAS SURVEYED, 1981

	Number of ICAs	Number of ICAs Weighted by their Relative Value
Advanced	7	29
Intermediate	46	94
Obsolete	76	6

2. The Scale of Disembodied Technology Transfer

The study by Carl H. McMillan shows that ICAs are less important as a way of obtaining machinery and equipment than as a means of acquiring disembodied technology or know-how.[37] As shown in Table 3.15, all Hong Kong ICAs surveyed carried some form of know-how transfer. However, very little useful information is available about the effectiveness and intensity of such transfer. The OECD's survey of East–West technology transfer suggests that the actual performance of ICAs in this regard can be partly gauged in terms of the following two indices.[38] First, transfer is likely to be more effective and intense if the inter-firm relationship is a long-term one. Second, transfer is likely to be more effective and intense if the Western partner is anxious to see that know-how is properly mastered and applied by the less-developed partner.

In terms of the above two criteria, Hong Kong's ICAs are unlikely to become a powerful medium for disembodied technology transfer. As has already been mentioned, Hong Kong's ICAs in the manufacturing sector are dominated by small- and medium-scale 'lower' forms of co-operation. In such forms of co-operation the inter-firm relationship is relatively loose and short in duration. There is neither capital participation nor sharing of profits and losses in Chinese firms by Hong Kong firms. Thus the interest of the Hong Kong partner in the effective application of his technology and know-how by the Chinese partner is unlikely to be great.

Finally, the range of know-how transferred appears to be rather restricted, as the activity of Chinese firms in most of the 'lower' forms of co-operation is almost totally devoted to production, to the exclusion of marketing or research and development.

3. The Absorption of Transferred Technology

Although the scale of technology transfer through ICAs may be rather limited, such technology transfer may nevertheless become a catalyst in China's modernization process if it can be put to work effectively and diffused successfully within the domestic economy.

China's historical record of assimilation of imported advanced technology is largely negative.[39] Her performance during the 1950's was somewhat better, probably because of massive Soviet assistance in planning and execution. The lead-times needed to acquire, install and begin operating the imported machinery and complete plants during that time were, according to planned schedule, from two to eight years depending on the size of the project.[40] Also, most of the plant and equipment was utilized at its normal rate of output. Performance during the 'self-reliance' period in the 1960's and from 1970 to 1979 deteriorated rapidly. Two-thirds of the machinery and equipment imported during the 1960's and between 1970–7 was subject to excessive lead-times and very low utilization rates. 50 per cent of the machinery and equipment imported in 1970–7 operated at less than half the normal output level, and the giant Wuhan iron and steel complex reached only 30 per cent of the rate guaranteed by the supplier.[41] Most of the agreements on plant and technology imports during 1978–9 were cancelled, postponed or frozen. Around US$2 billion worth of equipment already imported was reportedly lying idle in the warehouses due to recent retrenchment.[42]

Numerous factors have been cited as being responsible for the low assimilation capacity in the past. One group of factors was related to political campaigning, especially during the 1960's: the beating up of foreign technicians and engineers, the disruption of plant construction and installation by political turmoil, and so on.[43] Others were related to inexperience on the Chinese side, such as the inability of workers and management to cope with the new technology. But some of the factors appear to be systemic ones: long lead-times and a low utilization rate were caused by the lack of supporting infrastructural facilities and the shortage of matching funds, raw materials, fuel, power, and even demand for the resultant products. All these were symptoms of a faulty decision-making structure and co-ordination mechanism in China's economic system.

Very little is known about the actual performance of the Chinese absorption of transferred technology under ICAs. Theoretically, there ought to be substantial improvement with the help of foreign partners. Available evidence, however, indicates that the Chinese absorption capability has not improved very much. This is confirmed by our survey findings given in Table 3.9, which indicate that the slowness of Chinese firms in absorbing Western technology was one of the frequent complaints of Hong Kong firms. Independent case studies of ICAs in Guangdong, and particularly in Shenzhen, by Chinese economists have also revealed that the rate of utilization of equipment introduced under compensation agreements was low. For example, the equipment utilization rate of the Shenzhen Vehicle Assembly Plant introduced under a compensation agreement reached only 40 per cent of its targeted rate in 1981.[44] The utilization rate of the Xiang Zhou Wool Spinning Mill in Chuhai after massive consolidation and reorganization was still below its targeted rate in 1981.[45] Chinese partners have tended to attribute the low output level to the failure of Hong Kong partners to provide raw materials in sufficient quantity and quality. However, it seems that at least part of the failure of Hong Kong partners to provide sufficient raw materials can be attributed, in turn, to the failure of Chinese partners to meet the quality standards which caused marketing problems for the Hong Kong partners.

4. *The Diffusion of Transferred Technology*

Diffusion of embodied technology usually takes the form of replicating imported machinery and equipment and series-manufacturing the items, and their subsequent adoption by other domestic enterprises.

Only during the 1950's was China able to copy successfully the machinery and plants imported. Average lead-times in reverse engineering usually took less than 10 years.[46] During the self-reliance period China had difficulty in digesting the imported technology, let alone imitating it. In the case of a few successful reproductions, the lead-times had been extended to something between 10 and 20 years.[47]

China's ability to diffuse the imported embodied technology under the pragmatic economic policies of the new leadership should improve, but there is room for scepticism about the Chinese performance in this respect in the near future. First of all, China has yet to formulate a long-term strategy for the absorption and diffusion of the imported technology, and she has also yet to establish an institutional mechanism to implement such a strategy.[48] Secondly, there are the well-known institutional hindrances to the spread of successful reproduction of Western technology in a centrally planned economy.[49] Despite the much publicized economic reform, the role of market forces is still limited and centralized planning still dominates China's economic system.[50] The direction of the reform in the next decade or so is toward 'an improved system of centralized planning' rather than 'market socialism' as revealed in a seminar on economic reform held by economists in Beijing recently.[51]

Under the existing economic system, Chinese enterprises are neither adequately equipped nor motivated to introduce new technology. Producing enterprises are dissociated from research and development institutes and hence have difficulty in obtaining the necessary capital funds and research and development services for innovation.[52] The essential materials are still subject to centralized rationing which creates problems for the enterprises trying to obtain the required inputs in sufficient quantity and quality to carry out innovation.[53] Furthermore, sufficient price and income incentives have not been offered to enterprises who innovate successfully. Firms have been allowed limited autonomy in pricing decisions in certain non-essential commodities in recent economic reform experiments, but rising inflationary pressure during the last two years soon led the government to withdraw much of the price autonomy granted. So far there has been very little discussion of the inadequacy and the reform of pricing principles for new products. The major sources of managerial and worker bonuses continue to be the basic bonuses earned primarily by fulfilling the eight basic enterprise plan targets. The special financial rewards for the act of innovation are of only minimal importance.

Owing to the weak incentives for Chinese enterprises to innovate, the diffusion of new technology in the near future, as in the past, will have to rely heavily on 'pressure from above'. One of the problems that the Chinese authorities are likely to encounter in this kind of diffusion mechanism is the limited amount of resources available to replicate and mass-produce the imported machinery and equipment. At present, only 0.5 per cent of China's GNP is spent on research and development in civilian technology.[54] The Cultural Revolution retarded the development of a technical labour force with skills and educational standards comparable to those of the West.[55] The recent educational reforms have just started to correct some of the past deficiencies. However, Western experience shows that it would take China decades to develop such a technical labour force.[56] The machinery industry is another weak line in China's diffusion process. It has been much neglected in China's programme of imported Western technology since 1960. Its share in imported Western machinery and plant did not exceed 15 per cent during the 1960's and 1970's.[57] Consequently its technological level was largely frozen at its 1940's and 1950's level. The machinery sector suffered another heavy blow in the recent economic retrenchment programme. Investment in this sector has been severely cut back. Many enterprises have been forced to stop production and some were reorganized so as to turn out durable consumer goods instead of capital goods.

Another problem with the policy of forced diffusion from above is that it is unlikely to result in the adoption of optimal technology, as the planner is unlikely to be familiar with the situation at the local and enterprise level.

There is still very little information available about the practice of diffusion of disembodied technology transferred through ICAs in China. According to Chinese past experience as well as Eastern European experience, presumably this will assume the following form: job rotation of managerial and technical personnel, as well as of workers, in the co-operating enterprises so as to provide 'in-plant training' and 'advanced experience sharing'. However, such frequent changes of personnel are likely to interfere with the smooth operation of the co-operation enterprises and reduce their operational efficiency, thus creating further conflict between the Chinese and foreign partners.

5. Other Dynamic Effects

Other dynamic effects of ICAs include the spillover effects of ICAs in the Chinese economy. Available evidence indicates that the contribution of ICAs in this respect, especially those associated with Hong Kong, is likely to be limited for the following reasons.

First of all, there appears to be a narrow geographical concentration of Hong Kong's ICAs in China. Though no legal restriction has been imposed on other localities accepting ICAs with foreign firms, most of the ICAs, particularly those associated with Hong Kong, are concentrated in certain localities — the three municipalities of Beijing, Shanghai and Tianjin; and the two southern coastal provinces of Guangdong and Fujian. Table 3.18 shows that in terms of number of agreements, around 81 per cent of China's ICAs were concentrated in these localities. Within these localities Guangdong accounted for 64 per cent of China's ICAs. Within Guangdong, Guangzhou, Shantou, Foshan and the Special Economic Zones accounted for more than half of the province's total ICAs.

Although, in terms of number of agreements, the Special Economic Zones' share of China's total ICAs was only 6 per cent, their significance in terms of the value of agreements was much higher: according to *Renmin Ribao*, by the end of 1981, the total pledged foreign investment in ICAs (including 100 per cent equity investment) concluded in Shenzhen reached US$1,366 million.[58] The total pledged foreign investment for all China's ICAs concluded by the end of 1981, as estimated from Table 3.1 and Table 3.3, was US$1,939 million. Thus Shenzhen, with its ICAs and 100 per cent equity investment, accounted for 71 per cent of the value of all China's ICAs by the end of 1981.

The regional distribution of Hong Kong ICAs follows a similar pattern. The survey by the Hong Kong General Chamber of Commerce in 1980 found that 65 per cent of all Hong Kong ICAs surveyed, both in the manufacturing as well as in the non-

Table 3.18 REGIONAL DISTRIBUTION OF CHINA'S ICAS AS AT THE END OF 1981 (number of agreements)

Localities	Number of Agreements	Percentage Share
Guangdong		
Guangzhou[a]	2,598	
Foshan[b]	2,267	
Shantou[c]	1,248	
Special Economic Zones:		
Shenzhen[d]	989	
Chuhai[e]	129	
Shekou[f]	24	
Guangdong[g] total	12,827	64
Fujian[h]	1,126	6
Shanghai[i]	2,093	11
Beijing[j]	125	
Tianjin[k]	117	
Guangdong, Fujian, Shanghai, Beijing and Tianjin total	16,288	81
Grand total	20,178	100

a. As of June 1981. *Ta Kung Pao*, February 12, 1981; March 12, 1981; and September 26, 1981.

b. As of March 1981. Data refers to processing and assembly only. See *Ta Kung Pao*, March 21, 1981.

c. *Ta Kung Pao*, November 8, 1981.

d. Includes 100 per cent equity ventures. *Renmin Ribao*, March 17, 1981.

e. As of end of 1980. *Gangao Jingji*, 1981, No. 2, p. 31.

f. *The Asian Wall Street Journal*, February 8, 1982.

g. *South China Morning Post*, December 6, 1981; and *Ta Kung Pao*, December 17, 1981.

h. *Ta Kung Pao*, January 29, 1982.

i. *Ta Kung Pao*, January 31, 1982.

j. *Ta Kung Pao*, November 29, 1981.

k. As of June 1980. Processing and assembly only. See *Caimao Jingji Congkan*, 1981, No. 1, p. 26; and *China Economic News*, March 24, 1980, p. 6.

manufacturing sector, were located in the above-mentioned localities. Within these localities Guangdong took the lion's share (see Table 3.19). Our survey of Hong Kong manufacturing ICAs in 1981 indicates an even heavier concentration in these localities: 96–98 per cent were found to be within these localities. Within these areas, Guangdong accounted for 95 per cent of the total number and 74 per cent of the total value of ICAs surveyed. Within Guangdong, Special Economic Zones accounted for over half of the value of ICAs surveyed.

There are several factors behind the heavy concentration of Hong Kong ICAs in certain localities, and in Special Economic Zones in particular. Apart from geographical proximity in the case of Guangdong, and better infrastructural facilities and the availability of skilled labour in the case of the three municipalities, the most important reason is undoubtedly the government's deliberate policy of allowing these localities to offer special financial incentives and greater business freedom to foreign firms.

Table 3.19 REGIONAL DISTRIBUTION OF HONG KONG ICAS SURVEYED

Localities	Survey 1980[a]	Survey 1981[b]	
	(number of agreements)	(number of agreements)	(number of agreements weighted by their relative value)
Guangdong total	44	122	95.4
Special Economic Zones	17	6	67.4
Fujian	0	0	0
Shanghai, Beijing and Tianjin	18	2	31.4
Guangdong, Fujian, Shanghai, Beijing and Tianjin total	62	124	126.8
Other localities	18	5	2.4
Unidentified	15	0	0
Total	95	129	129

[a] Survey of the Hong Kong General Chamber of Commerce. ICAs in non-manufacturing sector are included.

[b] Manufacturing sector only.

As has already been mentioned, one of the major obstacles to China increasing its industrial co-operation with foreign firms has been its rigid economic system. One way to solve the problem is to allow the traditional centres for the country's economic exchange with foreigners, such as Guangdong, Fujian, Shanghai, Tianjin and Beijing, to move a step ahead of other localities in economic reform. Specifically, they are given more freedom in conducting their foreign trade and industrial co-operation with foreign firms. For example, according to Ji Chongwei, a leading member of China's Foreign Economic Relations and Trade Ministry, local authorities in Beijing, Tianjin, Shanghai and Liaoning have been given powers to approve co-operation projects involving an investment not exceeding US$5 million.[59]

Guangdong and Fujian were granted an even greater degree of local autonomy than the three municipalities. First, the two provinces were given more power in planning, price and wage determination, labour management and external economic relations. For instance, as disclosed by Ji Chongwei, the two provinces can approve projects of any value provided that such projects do not affect the national balance for fuel and raw material supply, and do not utilize China's export quota.[60] Second, the two provinces were given more financial and particularly foreign exchange autonomy. For example, under the new fiscal and foreign exchange consignment system, Guangdong undertakes to guarantee the delivery of a fixed amount of its fiscal and foreign exchange revenues to the central government. This amount is based on past years' experience and remains unchanged for a period of time in the future. Hence, the province is motivated to maximize its fiscal and foreign exchange revenues because it is allowed to retain the surplus for its own disposal.[61] Last, but not least, the two provinces were given the green light to set up Special Economic Zones in their territories to provide a quasi-free enterprise environment for foreign firms. In such special zones, foreign firms are not only given a greater degree of business freedom, but also special financial incentives.[62] Thus, they are allowed to own and run their factories in the form of 100 per cent equity investment without Chinese participation. They are allowed to import the raw materials and equipment, and export the finished products, without paying any customs duties. They are also given considerable freedom in hiring and firing their workers and in the determination of the wage system. The various financial incentives include: (a) a lower profit tax rate of 15 per cent for foreign investment in the Special Economic Zones as compared with 33 per cent in the rest of the country; (b) exemption from profit tax on profits reinvested in the special zones for five years or longer; (c) special prices for China-made products and raw materials; and (d) relative ease in the repatriation of after-tax profits.

The geographical concentration of foreign investment also allows the government to control the activities of foreigners more effectively and to insulate the rest of the domestic economy from the 'corruption effects' of capitalist ideology and practice. But, at the same time, it also limits the points of contact of the large domestic economy with modern industrial technology and management methods, and thus reduces the spill-over effects of foreign investment.

The spill-over effects are also limited by the structure and form of Hong Kong ICAs with China which generate only limited backward and forward linkages between the foreign sector and the domestic economy. As mentioned earlier, the bulk of Hong Kong ICAs are in the service sector, particularly in real estate and tourist-related services. The input demands of these industries are minimal, and their forward linkage is almost nil as their output mainly goes directly to foreign consumers. The limited number of Hong Kong ICAs in the manufacturing sector are concentrated in 'lower' forms of co-operation in the consumer goods industries. The limited forward and backward linkages of these kinds of ICAs are also obvious: their inputs are acquired mainly from Hong Kong and their output goes directly to Hong Kong as exports.

The Effect of Industrial Co-operation on Hong Kong–China Trade and Intra-industry Specialization

Hong Kong–China trade has registered a sharp increase in recent years. From 1978 to 1981, the average annual growth of Hong

Kong's domestic exports and re-exports to China was 231 and 235 per cent respectively; imports from China increased by 41 per cent annually, as shown in Table 3.20. As a result, mutual trade now makes up an increased proportion of the total trade of the two economies. The share of mutual trade in the total exports of the two economies has increased from 10 per cent in 1978 to 15 per cent in 1981, and the share of mutual trade in total imports has increased from 9 per cent in 1978 to 19 per cent in 1981. Thus the interdependence between the two economies has perceptibly increased. Trade in manufactures grew even faster, as indicated in Table 3.21, resulting in an increased share of manufactures in the mutual trade between the two economies from 49 per cent in 1978 to 69 per cent in 1981.

Table 3.20 HONG KONG'S TRADE WITH CHINA, 1978–81 (million HK dollars)

	Year				Annual Average Growth Rate (per cent)
	1978	1979	1980	1981	
Domestic exports	81	603	1,605	2,924	231
Re-exports	214	1,315	4,642	8,044	235
Imports	10,550	15,130	21,948	29,510	41

Source: *Hong Kong Trade Statistics*.

Table 3.21 HONG KONG–CHINA TRADE IN MANUFACTURES,[a] 1978–81 (million HK dollars)

	Year				Annual Average Growth Rate (per cent)
	1978	1979	1980	1981	
Domestic exports	72.3	515.3	1,393.9	2,628.9	231
Re-exports	117.2	1,093.5	3,746.1	7,086.2	292
Imports	5,108.5	8,182.1	12,804.4	18,140.0	53

[a] SITC 5 to 8.

Source: *Hong Kong Trade Statistics*.

There are several factors behind the recent rapid expansion of Hong Kong–China trade in general and trade in manufactures in particular. The lifting of import restrictions on consumer durables by China in order to soak up the surplus purchasing power in the domestic economy has resulted in a sharp increase in Hong Kong's domestic exports and re-exports of consumer goods to China.

The increased indirect trade with South Korea and Taiwan has also boosted Hong Kong's re-export trade with China, as China has no diplomatic relations with these two countries and hence prefers to conduct its trade with them through Hong Kong. Last but not least, the increased industrial co-operation between the two economies has contributed substantially to the rapid expansion of Hong Kong–China trade in general and trade in manufactures in particular.

There are no official statistics on the precise share of Hong Kong–China trade accounted for by ICAs between the two economies. The Hong Kong Trade Industry and Customs Department introduced, in February 1981, an 'Outward Processing Arrangement' under which 'a certificate of Hong Kong origin may be issued in respect of a product if it can be established that despite certain intermediate processes of manufacture having been subcontracted out of Hong Kong, the terminal- or origin-conferring process has been carried out by a factory in Hong Kong registered with the Department for certification purposes.' Since the outward-processing arrangements of Hong Kong firms operate mainly between Hong Kong and China, the amount of exports accounted for by these arrangements can be taken as an indicator of the trade increase due to industrial co-operation. In 1981, about 52 factories had registered themselves and HK$27 million worth of goods had been exported under this scheme.[63] This amounted to less than 1 per cent of Hong Kong manufactured exports to and imports from China. However, this figure grossly underestimates the actual share of industrial co-operation in Hong Kong–China trade as a large proportion of Hong Kong's exports do not require a certificate of origin, and hence a substantial proportion of outward-processing arrangements between Hong Kong and China remains unregistered.

The Hong Kong Government acknowledged recently that a substantial proportion of Hong Kong's semi-manufactured exports to China was attributable to ICAs between Hong Kong and China.[64]

Semi-manufactures made up 73 per cent of Hong Kong's major domestic manufactured exports to China in 1981, as indicated in Table 3.22. If only one-third of this was due to ICAs between Hong Kong and China, the share of industrial co-operation in Hong Kong major domestic manufactured exports to China would amount to 24 per cent. Again, this percentage is very likely to be an underestimate of the importance of industrial co-operation in Hong Kong–China trade. For analysis of the semi-manufactured content of Hong Kong's major

Table 3.22 SEMI-MANUFACTURED CONTENT OF HONG KONG MAJOR DOMESTIC EXPORT COMMODITIES TO CHINA, 1981 (million HK dollars)

SITC	Total Exports	Semi-manufactures[a]	Percentage Share
65 Textile yarn, fabrics and made-up articles	628.9	623.81	99
885 Watches and clocks	372.4	227.0	61
764 Telecommunications equipment, n.e.s. and parts n.e.s.	301.0	296.2	98
762 Radio-broadcast receivers	148.9		
699 Manufactures of base metal, n.e.s.	73.5	67.4	92
84 Articles of apparel and clothing accessories	162.8	54.7	34
893 Articles, n.e.s., of plastic materials	102.8	32.1	31
899 Other miscellaneous manufactured articles	85.9	81.8	95
583 Polymerization and copolymerization products	107.0	107.0	100
894 Baby carriages, toys, games and sporting goods	66.9	0.6	negligible
Total	2,050.1	1,490.6	73

[a] Semi-manufactures include (a) industrial supplies, parts and accessories of capital goods and transport equipment as defined by the United Nations (UN, *Classification by Broad Economic Categories*, Statistical Papers Series M, No. 53, Rev.1, New York, 1976), and (b) parts and components of consumer goods.

Source: *Hong Kong Statistical Tables.*

domestic manufactured exports to China reveals that a large number of the following products can be identified as being closely linked to Hong Kong–China industrial co-operation arrangements: parts and accessories of watches and clocks, parts and accessories of telecommunications equipment, uncompleted garments, parts of lighters, umbrellas and sunshades, and electric motors for toys and models. As indicated in Table 3.23, trade in these commodities was virtually non-existent in 1977 but has greatly increased since 1978. The total export value of these commodities, however, already amounted to about 40 per cent of Hong Kong's major domestic semi-manufactured exports to China in 1981. Accordingly, the share of industrial co-operation in Hong Kong major domestic manufactured exports to China should amount to at least 28 per cent. If one further includes part of the industrial raw materials attributable to ICAs listed in Table 3.22, the share is likely to exceed one-third.

A significant proportion of Hong Kong's re-exports of semi-manufactures, machinery and equipment to China was also attributable to the processing, assembly and compensation trade agree-

Table 3.23 SELECTED LIST OF COMMODITIES IN HONG KONG MAJOR DOMESTIC SEMI-MANUFACTURED EXPORTS TO CHINA, 1977, 1978 AND 1981 (million HK dollars)

Commodities	1977	1978	1981
Parts and accessories of watches and clocks[a]	–	0.7	227
Parts and accessories of telecommunications equipment[b]	–	0.4	296
Incomplete garments[c]	–	0.09	55
Parts of lighters, umbrellas and sunshades[d]	–	0.1	0.7
Electric motors for toys and models[e]	–	–	0.6

a. SITC: 885131–139, 885140, 885251–259, 885260, 885298–299.

b. SITC: 764911–999.

c. SITC: 845938, 845958, 845978, 845998, and 847194–198.

d. SITC: 899349, 899729.

e. SITC: 894639.

Source: *Hong Kong Statistical Tables.*

ments between Hong Kong and China. However, as China is known to import a large quantity of industrial raw materials and machinery from third countries through Hong Kong for its own needs, it is difficult to differentiate between genuine re-exports and those connected with ICAs, and hence impossible to determine the exact share of Hong Kong's re-exports to China attributable to ICAs between the two countries.

Increased industrial co-operation between Hong Kong and China has also resulted in increased industrial specialization between the two economies. The trend towards specialization can be deduced from changes in the commodity export composition in each case. To discover what kinds of specialization have actually occurred one could seek to ascertain the increase of inter- or intra-industry trade and the degree of similarity of export structure between China and Hong Kong.

The commodity flow pattern of the Hong Kong ICAs surveyed and given in Table 3.15 shows that there was always a flow of parts and components from Hong Kong to China, and a corresponding flow of finished products from China to Hong Kong in most of the agreements. Only in 11 per cent of the agreements was there a reciprocal flow of parts and components between the two countries. Thus, one could have expected that ICAs would lead to inter-industry trade and specialization. However, according to Grubel and Lloyd,[65] international assembly and processing is bound to give rise to intra-industry trade because in many countries, and at most aggregation levels, the parts and assembled products are classed in the same statistical category. To test this hypothesis, the average intra-industry trade ratio has been computed. Since specialization based on processing and assembly also enters entrepôt trade according to the definition of Hong Kong trade statistics,[66] re-exports to China are also included in the measurement of the intra-industry trade ratio.

Table 3.24 confirms the hypothesis by Grubel and Lloyd. It was intra-industry trade which increased during the period, indicating a trend towards increased intra-industry specialization between the two countries. Inter-industry trade increases, if any took place, clearly exerted a less important influence. The share of intra-industry trade in total trade jumped from 5.8 per cent in 1978 to 38.9 per cent in 1981.

Table 3.24 INTRA-INDUSTRY TRADE AND THE SIMILARITY BETWEEN HONG KONG EXPORTS TO AND IMPORTS FROM CHINA (annual averages)

	1978	1981
Share of intra-industry trade in total trade, unadjusted for the overall balance:[a]		
at three-digit level of aggregation	5.8	38.9
at six-digit level of aggregation[b]	3.0	18.5
Cosine coefficient:		
at three-digit level of aggregation	0.38	0.51
at six-digit level of aggregation[b]	0.058	0.069

a. The difference between the adjusted and unadjusted average share is so large that it is meaningless to use the adjusted average measure.

b. Only major import and export commodities with a value exceeding HK$1 million are included.

Source: *Hong Kong Statistical Tables*.

As expected, intra-industry trade is reduced by almost half when the indices are calculated at the greater degree of disaggregation at the six-digit level. However, the trend toward an increased intra-industry trade is unmistakable even at this lowest level of aggregation.

The trend towards increased intra-industry trade and specialization is also confirmed by the increased cosine coefficient which measures the similarity of product composition of the two sets of exports on a scale from 0 (complete dissimilarity) to 1.0 (complete identity of structure). As shown in Table 3.24, at the three-digit level of aggregation, the cosine of similarity of the total exports of each country to the other had increased from 0.38 in 1978 to 0.51 in 1981 indicating a clear trend towards greater similarity of export structure, and hence a greater degree of intra-industry specialization between the two countries. The trend is less clear when computed at the six-digit level of aggregation. Nevertheless, a slight increase in the degree of similarity can still be observed even at this lowest level of aggregation.

Conclusion and Future Prospects

From the above discussion, it is clear that over the past few years Hong Kong and China have increased their degree of economic interdependence. Industrial co-operation between the two countries in the manufacturing sector has increased significantly. The main forms of co-operation have been processing, assembly, and medium- and small-scale compensation trade. The main trade of co-operation has been light industry, especially textiles, garments and electronics.

The increased industrial co-operation between the two countries has resulted in a dramatic increase in Hong Kong–China trade in general and in manufactured trade in particular. Mutual trade now makes up an increased proportion of the total trade of the two economies. The share of manufactured trade in the mutual trade between the two economies has risen rapidly. A substantial proportion of Hong Kong–China trade is now accounted for by industrial co-operation. This increased industrial co-operation has also resulted in increased intra-industry trade and specialization between the two economies, as indicated by the increased intra-industry trade ratio and increased similarity of export structures recorded during this period.

However, despite the rapid increase noted, industrial co-operation in the manufacturing sector has not reached the potential level, as suggested by the complementarities existing between the two economies. This study shows that Hong Kong's involvement in the manufacturing sector is still small when compared with its involvement in real estate, tourism and other services-related industry. So far only lower forms of co-operation have been involved in the manufacturing sector, the unit value of which was low and the duration of which was limited.

The slow progress towards more meaningful, substantial and long-term co-operation in the manufacturing sector is apparently linked to the mediocre results achieved so far by both partners. Our survey of the experience of both partners reveals that the overall outcome has not been very satisfactory for either side. On the Hong Kong side, firms surveyed indicated that their ICAs with China had not been as profitable as expected. On the Chinese side, the study shows that the actual performance of ICAs in terms of cost and effectiveness in achieving the given goals as proclaimed by the Chinese planners has been disappointing.

The cost of ICAs to China appears to be on the high side, as suggested by the low profitability and even losses experienced by the Chinese enterprises in their co-operative ventures. The effectiveness of ICAs in achieving certain macro-objectives as proclaimed by the Chinese authorities remains doubtful. ICAs have made a useful but not a very significant contribution to Chinese foreign exchange earnings, capital formation and employment programmes, due to the fact that investment arising from ICAs was a comparatively small input in an economy as large as that of China. The potential dynamic gains also appear to be rather limited. The role of ICAs as a potent media for technology transfer was found to be restricted by the form and structure of Hong Kong ICAs. It was also found to be restricted by China's relatively long lead-times in utilizing and diffusing the imported technology. Other dynamic gains such as the spill-over effects of ICAs in China's economy were found to be limited by both the narrow geographical concentration of Hong Kong ICAs in certain localities, particularly in Guangdong, and in Special Economic Zones, and by the form and structure of Hong Kong ICAs. This implies that China cannot rely mainly on Hong Kong and overseas Chinese capital to achieve its modernization goals. It also implies that, at least in the near future, the fear of competition from China in overseas export markets affecting either Hong Kong or the developing countries in the Asian-Pacific region is largely unfounded.

For the future, there is every reason to believe that Hong Kong–China industrial co-operation will continue to grow as both sides have a very strong incentive for co-operation. The relatively high cost of land and labour will continue to force Hong Kong firms to relocate the land- and labour-intensive parts of their operations to China. China's ambitious programme of renovating the existing 300,000 or so industrial enterprises during the current Sixth Five-Year-Plan period and beyond, in order to improve industrial efficiency and achieve 'intensive' growth, as well as its reluctance to borrow substantially from international capital markets for fear of being burdened with an increased debt service ratio, will force China to continue to look to industrial co-operation with Hong Kong for a large part of the necessary capital and technology.

However, the future development of more meaningful and substantial co-operation in the manufacturing sector based on long-term inter-firm relationships is likely to depend very much on the solution of certain problems experienced by both sides in their co-operative ventures so far. The first type of problem relates to the lack of experience of each partner in operating in the other's completely different economic system. This should be comparatively easy to solve. As industrial co-operation is a learning process for both sides, the growth of mutual confidence between partners and increased familiarity with each other's economic system over time must make this problem less of an obstacle in the future.

The second type of problem is related to the lack of supporting infrastructure, particularly transportation and public utilities. The solution of this problem is, again, a matter of time. The infrastructure of the Special Economic Zones is scheduled to be completed within the next three to four years. Several giant Hong Kong projects are under way to solve the problem, including the development of a new town in Fuk Tin, and the construction of a 240-kilometre expressway linking Shenzhen, Guangzhou and Macau. There is also the development of an electronic-processing industrial city in Man Kam To and a 'science city' in Deep Bay.[67]

Problems related to the institutional environments affecting the co-operating partners are likely to be more difficult to solve. These involve the inflexible and bureaucratic decision-making structure, the irrational pricing system, inadequate incentive scheme and overall planning difficulties in China's economic system which create co-ordination problems for both partners, as well as quality, pricing and delivery problems. The creation of special zones where a market economy can be operated is one way to solve the problem. However, China cannot rely mainly on industrial co-operation in special zones to realize its modernization goals. This is substantiated by the fact that of the 130 industrial co-operation projects in the manufacturing sector which China plans to introduce in the Sixth Five-Year-Plan period, only three appear to be located in Special Economic Zones.[68] Hence, to facilitate the future development of industrial co-operation China appears to have few options other than comprehensive economic reform throughout the whole country.

Notes

[1] International Labour Office (1977), *Labour Force, 1950-2000*, vol. 1, p. 62.

[2] F. Levcik and J. Stankovsky (1979), *Industrial Co-operation Between East and West* (White Plains, New York, M.E. Sharpe), p. 6–7.

[3] *China Economic News*, February 11, 1980, pp. 4–6.

[4] The terms 'East' and 'West' used here signify two fundamentally different economic systems. The 'West' comprises the systems of market-economy countries and the 'East' the systems of centrally-planned economies.

[5] E. Zaleski and H. Wienert (1980), *Technology Transfer between East and West* (Paris, OECD), p. 99.

[6] *Ta Kung Pao*, October 18, 1981.

[7] *The China Business Review*, March–April, 1979, p. 73; and *China Newsletter*, June 1980, p. 28.

[8] *Annual Economic Report of China*, 1981, p. IV–134.

[9] *Economic Reporter*, January 23, 1980, p. 28.

[10] *China Economic News*, February 11, 1980, p. 4.

[11] *Ta Kung Pao*, October 18, 1981.

[12] *China Newsletter*, November and December, 1981, p. 5.

[13] *Economic Reporter*, November 11, 1981, p. 8.

[14] *Ta Kung Pao*, February 9, 1982.

[15] *Zhongguo Gongye Jingji Faqui Huibian 1949-81* (A Collection of China's Industrial Law and Regulations, 1949–81) (Beijing), 1981, pp. 633–4.

[16] *Zhongguo Gongye Jingji Faqui Huibian 1949-81*.

[17] *Xueshu Yanjiu* (Academic Research), 1981, No. 6, p. 44.

[18] *Caimao Jingji Congkan* (Finance and Trade Journal), 1980, No. 4, pp. 54–6.

[19] *Guoji Maoyi Wenti* (Issues in International Trade), 1980, No. 2, pp. 41–2.

[20] *Xueshu Yanjiu*, 1981, No. 6, p. 43.

[21] *Guoji Maoyi Wenti*, 1980, No. 2, pp. 41–2

[22] *Gongye Jingji Guanli Congkan* (Journal of Industrial Management), 1981, No. 4, p. 50.

[23] *Gongye Jingji Guanli Congkan*, 1981, No. 4, pp. 48–9.

[24] *Gongye Jingji Guanli Congkan*, 1981, No. 4, 1981, p. 48.

[25] *Gongye Jingji Guanli Congkan*, 1981, No. 4, 1981, p. 48.

[26] *Guoji Maoyi Wenti*, 1980, No 1, pp. 58–9.

[27] *Guogye Jingji Guanli Congkan*, 1981, No. 4, pp. 53–4.

[28] *Gongye Jingji Guanli Congkan*, 1981, No. 4, pp. 53–4.

[29] *China Economic News*, September 14, 1981, p. 13.

[30] *Ta Kung Pao*, January 29, 1982.

[31] Estimate by IMF cited in *The Seventies*, November 1981, p. 65.

[32] The direct employment effect is estimated by multiplying the total number of ICAs concluded during 1978–81 in Table 3.1 by the average employment effect given in Table 3.14. The average employment effect of contractual joint-venture agreements is estimated by using the average number of workers engaged in each building construction site in Hong Kong (see *Shui On Quarterly*, December 1981, p. 27) as a proxy, since most of the contractual joint ventures are in fact in housing and hotel construction. Not included in the estimate are the direct employment effects of the 3 large-scale compensation projects, 12 co-production agreements and the 4 oil exploration joint ventures, as their average employment effect is not known.

[33] *Renmin Ribao*, March 22, 1982.

[34] *Xueshu Yanjiu*, 1981, No. 6, p. 42.

[35] Carl H. McMillan, 'East–West Industrial Co-operation', in *Eastern European Economies Post-Helsinki — A Compendium of Papers* (Washington D.C., Joint Economic Committee, U.S. Congress), 1977, pp. 1192–3.

[36] *Xueshe Yanjiu*, 1981, No. 6, p. 44.

[37] Carl H. McMillan, pp. 1192–3.

[38] E. Zaleski and H. Wienert, pp. 97–9.

[39] *Gongye Jingji Guanli Congkan*, 1981, No. 5, pp. 44–54; also No. 6, pp. 39–48.

[40] *Gonye Jingji Guanli Congkan*, 1981, No. 5, p. 46.

[41] *Gonye Jingji Guanli Congkan*, 1981, No. 5, pp. 51–2.

[42] *Gonye Jingji Guanli Congkan*, 1981, No. 5, p. 54.

[43] *Gonye Jingji Guanli Congkan*, 1981, No. 5, p. 48.

[44] *Xueshu Yanjiu*, 1981, No. 6, p. 45.

[45] *Gangao Jingji* (Hong Kong–Macau Economy), 1981, No. 2, p. 38.

[46] *Gongye Jingji Guanli Congkan*, 1981, No. 15, p. 46.

[47] *Gonye Jingji Guanli Congkan*, 1981, No. 6, p. 41.

[48] *Ta Kung Pao*, March 22, 1982.

[49] The details of such institutional barriers are analysed in Joseph S. Berliner, 'Prospects for Technological Progress', in U.S. Congress, Joint Economic Committee, *Soviet Economy in a New Perspective* (Washington D.C., U.S. Government Printing Office, 1976), pp. 431–46.

[50] See C.H. Chai, 'Reports vs. Reality in Chinese Reform', *China Newsletter*, December 1980, pp. 6–13.

[51] *Ta Kung Pao*, March 22, 1982.

[52] *Gongye Jingji Guanli Congkan*, 1981, No. 6, p. 43.

[53] *Gongye Jingji Guanli Congkan*, 1981, No. 6, p. 45.

[54] *Gongye Jingji Guanli Congkan*, 1981, p. 6, p. 43.

[55] Hans Heymann, Jr., 'Acquisition and Diffusion of Technology in China', U.S. Congress, Joint Economic Committee, *China: A Reassessment of The Economy* (Washington D.C., U.S. Government Printing Office, 1975), p. 705.

[56] Hans Heymann, Jr., p. 705.

[57] *Gongye Jingji Guanli Congkan*, 1981, No. 6, Table 1, p. 48.

[58] *Renmin Ribao*, March 17, 1982.

[59] Ji Chongwei (1982), 'A Brief Introduction to the Forthcoming China Investment Promotion Meeting', mimeograph, p. 5.

[60] Ji Chongwei, p. 5.

[61] *Zhongguo Baike Nianjian* (China Yearbook), 1981, p. 202.

[62] *Zhongguo Gongye Jingji Faqui Huibian 1949-81*, pp. 642–3; and *Ta Kung Pao*, December 24, 1981.

[63] *Ta Kung Pao*, February 27, 1982.

[64] *1981 Economic Background* (Hong Kong), January 1982, p. 12.

[65] H.G. Grubel and P.J. Lloyd (1975), *Intra-industry Trade: the Theory and Measurement of International Trade in Differentiated Products* (London, Macmillan), p. 115.

[66] This point is well illustrated by a diagram in an article in *Hang Seng Economic Quarterly*, January 1982, pp. 15–16.

[67] *South China Morning Post*, December 23, 1981.

[68] *Ta Kung Pao*, March 25, 1982.

4. Hong Kong in China's Foreign Trade: A Changing Role

JOHN C. HSU

I. Introduction

Since the early 1970's, the foreign trade of China has expanded rapidly. This expansion, along with the possibility of further large-scale expansion and development, has attracted considerable attention in some Western countries.[1] This is because these countries consider China either as a potentially large market for their exports, or as a strong competing exporter in the international market for light industrial products. It has been mainly the industrialized countries which have benefited from China's enlarged import capacity; the export-oriented and newly-industrializing countries, such as Hong Kong, Taiwan, South Korea and Singapore, have, on the other hand, suffered strong destabilizing effects from the rise of China as a large exporter of textiles, clothing and other relatively unsophisticated industrial products. If China continues to promote its foreign trade under its existing outward-oriented trade policy, the impact of its trade expansion on these newly-industrializing countries will certainly increase unless they can dramatically change their existing export structures.

China's trade development has been, and will continue to be, a matter of major concern for Hong Kong. This is so not only because of the destabilizing effects that China's exports may have on the foreign trade of Hong Kong, but also because the political future of Hong Kong is widely believed to be closely related to the role that Hong Kong plays in China's foreign trade. In the past three decades, Hong Kong was China's most important source of foreign exchange earnings, a role considered to be the major reason why China has been willing to tolerate an economy with an entirely different ideology existing on soil historically regarded as part of China. Hsueh and Woo, in their study of the trade between Hong Kong and China, maintain that 'there has been some decrease in the degree of interdependence between China and Hong Kong', and they observe that 'since the 1970's the proportion of China's exports to Hong Kong in her total exports to non-Communist countries has declined.'[2] In other words, they consider that the importance of Hong Kong as an earner of foreign exchange for China has gradually diminished with the expansion of China's foreign trade, so that China has become less dependent on Hong Kong than before. Whether this is the case and how Hong Kong's position has changed with changes in China's foreign trade policy are the subjects of our investigation in this study. In Section II of this chapter, we discuss the functions of Hong Kong in China's economic development. Section III examines the changes in the structure of China's exports to Hong Kong in the course of the expansion of China's foreign trade in the 1970's, while Section IV shows how the changes in the structure as well as the growth rate of China's exports to Hong Kong were related to changes in China's foreign trade policy. Finally, Section V concludes this chapter and looks at the future trade relationship between China and Hong Kong.

II. The Position of Hong Kong in China's Foreign Trade

As a major point of contact between China and the world market, Hong Kong, with her rapidly growing and diversified market economy, is conveniently placed to provide China with some indispensable facilities to meet with the West. These facilities include not only an economically different environment in which China can undertake some economic activities which it would find awkward or inefficient to carry on within its own political and economic framework, but also the contacts and arrangements which enable China to obtain large amounts of foreign exchange earnings through trade with other Western countries.

For the present, Hong Kong is still an important contact point between foreign traders and Chinese trade representatives, in spite of the fact that foreign traders can freely enter China and negotiate with China's trade authorities. China's international trade is controlled by the Ministry of Foreign Trade and by provincial governments, and is conducted through a number of specialized foreign trade corporations.[3] These trade corporations act as intermediaries between end-users and foreign traders in imports, and as sales agents for Chinese producers of exports. Therefore, foreign traders in most cases must go through these corporations if they are to buy Chinese products or sell their products to China. Their contacts with these trade corporations may take place through Hong Kong, where the agents of these trade corporations operate. These agents include:

(a) China Resources Corporation: the buying and selling agent of most of the national trade corporations and the government of China;
(b) Ng Fung Hong: the agent of the China National Cereals, Oils and Foodstuffs Import and Export Corporation;
(c) Teck Soong Hong Ltd.: the agent of the China National Native Produce and Animal By-products Import and Export Corporation;
(d) Hua Yuan Company: the agent of the China National Light Industrial Products Import and Export Corporation;
(e) Chinese Arts and Crafts (H.K.) Ltd.: the agent of the China National Arts and Crafts Import and Export Corporation;
(f) Fujian Enterprises Company Ltd.: the agent of the Fujian Foreign Trade Corporation; and
(g) Guangdong Enterprises Ltd.: the agent of the Guangdong Foreign Trade Corporation.

Apart from setting up agents in Hong Kong as a direct use of Hong Kong's trade facilities, China also makes use of these facilities indirectly. For instance, China holds its trade fairs regularly in Guangzhou to attract foreign buyers who usually prefer to stay in Hong Kong, where modern hotels and a Western style of life can be provided. Also, some of China's trade is facilitated by the fact that some foreign traders have stationed their representatives in Hong Kong so that they can make regular trips to China as may be required in their trade with that country.

A more important function of Hong Kong in China's foreign trade is to help to provide the large proportions of hard currencies that China has earned through its trade with Hong Kong. Given the underdevelopment of China's foreign trade, Hong Kong is not only a relatively large market, but also an entrepôt for China's exports. Being more developed than China, Hong Kong has, despite its size, been able to digest large volumes of imports from China, and its import capacity has been growing rapidly with the growth of its national output. China's traditional exports, such as rice, vegetables, fish and unsophisticated manufactures, have found their outlets in the predominantly Chinese community of Hong Kong. Because of its geographical proximity to China, as well as the loyalty of its Chinese population to Chinese products, Hong Kong is a unique market for those Chinese products which are not marketable in other parts of the world.

Another important function of Hong Kong in China's trade is the former's entrepôt facilities, which allow China to export to Hong Kong without being seriously limited by the size of the Hong Kong market. Traditionally, China prefers to trade directly with its partners so that it can use trade as a means to achieve its political goal as well. Nevertheless, when foreign exchange is badly needed, its political goal may be temporarily sacrificed in order that its economic goal may be achieved. Indirect trade is then promoted and Hong Kong's trade relationship with other countries is made use of. Thus Hong Kong's entrepôt function has in fact added considerable flexibility to the foreign trade of China.

The importance of the above functions to China is unlikely to remain unchanged in the wake of the rapid expansion of China's foreign trade in the past decade. Nor can it remain unchanged in the future if China further expands its foreign trade. Our analysis of the changes in the role of Hong Kong in China's foreign trade in the past decade should shed some light on the direction in which the importance of these functions to China may change in the future.

III. Structural Changes in China's Exports to Hong Kong

This section examines the extent to which the changes in the composition of China's exports to Hong Kong, in the period from 1971 to 1980, were related to changes in Hong Kong's domestic demand as well as to changes in China's overall export structure in that period. In the discussion below, China's exports to Hong Kong are classified, according to *Hong Kong Trade Statistics*, into four main categories: foodstuffs, raw materials, manufactures and chemicals.[4] For the time being, we will not make any effort to exclude re-exports from each category, so that a structural change in China's exports to Hong Kong referred to here could arise from a change in either the composition of the part retained by Hong Kong, or in the composition of the part re-exported, or both.

The changes in the composition of China's exports to Hong Kong during the period from 1971 to 1980 were quite significant. Foodstuffs, as shown in Table 4.1, were the most important item of China's exports to Hong Kong in the early and mid-1970's, and they contributed as much as around 50 per cent of the total in the years from 1971 to 1974. However, the share of this item began to decline uninterruptedly from 1975 onwards. The decline was most precipitous in 1978, 1979 and 1980, when foodstuffs represented respectively only 37, 30 and 26 per cent of China's total exports to Hong Kong. As from 1978, the dominance of foodstuffs in China's exports to Hong Kong was taken over by manufactures, the share of which rose from below 40 per cent in most of the years before 1978 to 45 per cent in 1978, 49 per cent in 1979, and 53 per cent in 1980. Significant changes in the share of raw materials also occurred during the 1970's as it rose from an annual average of around 6 per cent in the period from 1971 to 1974 to an average of greater than 13 per cent in the years from 1975 onwards. Chemicals were the only item which did not change significantly in share and remained at around 3 to 5 per cent of China's exports to Hong Kong throughout the period concerned.

The significant drop in the share of foodstuffs and the correspondingly rapid increase in the share of manufactures had little to do with changes in China's overall export structure. As Table 4.1

Table 4.1 THE COMPOSITION OF CHINA'S EXPORTS TO HONG KONG AND TO THE WORLD, 1970–80

Year	Foodstuffs		Raw Materials		Manufactures		Chemicals	
	Hong Kong	World	Hong Kong	World	Hong Kong	World	Hong Kong	World
1970	51.63	31.46	39.12	41.70	6.33	20.98	2.69	5.12
1971	51.89	30.64	38.20	43.69	6.46	19.67	3.12	5.38
1972	48.82	31.10	41.04	43.04	6.50	19.97	3.38	5.07
1973	43.38	30.85	47.36	45.56	5.84	17.74	3.14	5.14
1974	52.13	31.20	34.90	40.41	8.98	21.60	3.67	6.09
1975	48.04	29.60	34.56	38.16	13.03	27.09	4.01	4.18
1976	43.65	26.83	39.03	42.21	13.14	24.90	3.87	4.55
1977	42.28	24.35	39.74	45.09	13.80	25.65	3.91	5.09
1978	36.81	22.49	44.68	46.69	14.47	25.72	3.73	4.70
1979	29.82	19.23	49.07	44.97	14.80	29.51	4.99	5.85
1980	25.82	–	53.38	–	15.66	–	4.95	–

Note: Percentage shares for each year do not add up to 100 because the share of the 'other' item is not shown.

Sources: 1. Census and Statistics Department, Hong Kong Government (1972–80), *Hong Kong Trade Statistics, Annual Supplement* (Hong Kong, Government Printer);

2. Census and Statistics Department, Hong Kong Government, *Hong Kong Review of Overseas Trade*, various issues (Hong Kong, Government Printer);

3. National Foreign Assessment Centre, Central Intelligence Agency, *People's Republic of China: International Trade Handbook*, October 1976 (Washington, D.C.); and

4. National Foreign Assessment Centre, Central Intelligence Agency, *China: International Trade Quarterly Review*, various issues (Washington, D.C.).

indicates, the share of foodstuffs did not suffer as substantial a decline in China's overall exports as in China's exports to Hong Kong. Furthermore, as a contrast to the rapid increase in the share of manufactures in China's exports to Hong Kong, the share of manufactures in China's overall exports increased only marginally by 1 per cent over the period from 1971 to 1979. Such differences in structural changes occurred mainly after 1977, following a rapid expansion of China's foreign trade in that period. As shown in Table 4.2, in the years from 1971 to 1977, China's foodstuff exports to Hong Kong and to the world increased by about the same percentage.

Table 4.2 THE GROWTH OF CHINA'S FOODSTUFF AND MANUFACTURING EXPORTS TO HONG KONG AND TO THE WORLD (percentage)

	Foodstuffs		Manufactures	
	Hong Kong	World	Hong Kong	World
1971–7	156	165	228	244
1978–9	23	34	115	69

Source: See Table 4.1.

This was also true in the case of China's manufactured exports. However, considerable differences occurred in the years from 1978 to 1979: on the one hand, China's manufactured exports to Hong Kong increased by 115 per cent, which is much higher than the 69 per cent increase of China's overall manufacturing exports; on the other hand, the increase of 23 per cent in China's foodstuff exports to Hong Kong was considerably slower than the 34 per cent growth of China's overall food exports. This drastic divergence of the structural changes in China's exports to Hong Kong from the structural changes in China's overall exports must have concerned the nature of Hong Kong as a market as well as an entrepôt of China's exports.

The change in the composition of Hong Kong's imports from China could be closely related to the development both of Hong

Kong's domestic demand for China's products, and of Hong Kong's re-export of China's products. These two developments may be used to explain why the pattern of change in the composition of Hong Kong's imports from China differed significantly from the pattern of change in the composition of China's exports to the world. Thus, we will now look at the change in the composition of Hong Kong's retained imports from China (RIC) and compare it with the change in the composition of Hong Kong's total imports, retained imports plus re-exports, from China (TIC).

Since the data on Hong Kong's retained imports from China for individual categories are not available, we will carry out the following estimation. First, we assume that Hong Kong's foodstuff re-exports, for which published data are available, came entirely from China, the major foodstuff supplier to Hong Kong. Their values are shown in Table 4.3 as Hong Kong's re-export of foodstuffs from China. Second, Hong Kong's re-export of raw materials and chemicals is assumed to be minimal and thus negligible, based on the consideration that these two categories did not constitute significant proportions of China's exports to Hong Kong before 1974, and that the increase in their relative importance from 1974 was due primarily to the dramatic increase in China's petroleum exports to Hong Kong, a component which was mainly for Hong Kong's domestic consumption. Based on these two assumptions, Hong Kong's re-export of China's manufactures is approximated by the difference between Hong Kong's re-export of China's products and Hong Kong's re-export of foodstuffs from China. The estimation is shown in Table 4.3. Making use of these re-export estimates, we can obtain the estimates of Hong Kong's retained imports from China as presented in Table 4.4. The last two rows in the table show how close our estimated total retained imports are to their actual values.

The pattern of change in the composition of our estimated RIC differs rather significantly from the pattern of change in the composition of TIC (Table 4.1). Most noticeable is the item of manufactures, whose share in TIC was far greater and rising more rapidly than in RIC. The former increased from 38 per cent in 1971 to 53 per cent in 1980, while the latter increased from 34 per cent in 1971 to only 37 per cent in 1980. Such a difference indicates that the rapid rise in Hong

Table 4.3 HONG KONG'S RE-EXPORT OF CHINA'S PRODUCTS AND THEIR ESTIMATES IN SELECTED GROUPS
(million US dollars)

	1971	1972	1973	1974	1975	1976	1977	1978	1979	1980
Total	126	173	308	312	353	490	535	781	1,132	1,676
Foodstuffs*	61	72	105	112	124	211	196	208	281	343
Manufactures**	65	101	203	200	229	279	339	573	851	1,333

Notes: * Hong Kong's re-export of foodstuffs from China is approximated by Hong Kong's re-export of foodstuffs.
** Hong Kong's re-export of manufactures from China is estimated by deducting foodstuffs from the total in the table.

Source: Census and Statistics Department, Hong Kong Government.

Kong's re-export of manufactures from China accounted for the rapid growth of the share of manufactures in TIC, particularly in the years from 1978 to 1980, when re-exports accounted for more than 50 per cent of Hong Kong's manufactured imports from China. It also indicates that the relatively small domestic market of Hong Kong was a restrictive factor in the growth of Hong Kong's retained manufactures from China. Turning to another notable item, raw materials, we observe that its share in RIC increased from around 8 per cent in the years before 1974 to above 20 per cent in the years from 1977 to 1980. This increase is much greater than the corresponding increase from 6 to 15 per cent of the share of this item in TIC. Since this item is mainly for Hong Kong's domestic consumption, the relatively fast increase in its share in RIC reflects the ample import capacity that Hong Kong had for China's petroleum products. China's promotion of the sale of this item to Hong Kong was the predominant factor contributing to the rise in the share of this item in both RIC and TIC. With regard to chemicals, their shares in TIC and RIC are fairly low and stable as China was still relatively underdeveloped in its heavy industrial sector. Finally, the shares of foodstuffs in RIC appear to change systematically with those in TIC, indicating that the restrictive domestic market of Hong Kong was the major cause for the decline of this item in China's exports to Hong Kong.

Table 4.4 ESTIMATES OF CHINA'S EXPORTS RETAINED BY HONG KONG AND THEIR COMPOSITION

Year	Foodstuffs	Raw materials	Chemicals	Manufactures	Estimated Total	Actual Total
1971	225	36	17	145	423	425
	(53.19)	(8.51)	(4.02)	(34.28)		
1972	285	45	23	180	533	512
	(53.47)	(8.44)	(4.32)	(33.77)		
1973	370	64	34	315	783	785
	(47.25)	(8.17)	(4.34)	(40.23)		
1974	503	106	43	212	864	868
	(58.22)	(12.27)	(4.98)	(24.54)		
1975	538	180	55	247	1,020	1,024
	(52.74)	(17.65)	(5.39)	(24.22)		
1976	480	208	61	339	1,088	1,092
	(44.11)	(19.12)	(5.61)	(31.16)		
1977	537	239	68	350	1,194	1,199
	(44.97)	(20.02)	(5.70)	(29.31)		
1978	621	326	84	433	1,464	1,470
	(42.42)	(22.27)	(5.74)	(29.58)		
1979	621	448	151	633	1,853	1,892
	(33.51)	(24.18)	(8.15)	(34.16)		
1980	796	690	218	1,022	2,726	2,738
	(29.20)	(25.31)	(8.00)	(37.49)		

Note: Figures in parentheses represent the percentage shares of individual items in the estimated annual total.

In sum, there were three major factors which resulted in significant changes in the composition of China's exports to Hong Kong: the small size of the domestic market that severely restricted the growth of China's foodstuff exports to Hong Kong, the abrupt increase in China's petroleum exports to Hong Kong from 1974, and, most importantly, the rapid expansion of Hong Kong's re-export of manufactures from China. The first and the third factors explain why the pattern of change in the composition of China's exports to Hong Kong differed significantly from that of the composition of China exports to the world during the period from 1977 to 1979. They also explain why Hong Kong continued to import around 22 per cenr of China's total exports, while the retained component gradually decreased from 18 per cent in 1971 to 14 per cent in 1979 (Table 4.5). The particularly restrictive domestic market of Hong Kong slowed down the growth of its retained as well as foodstuff imports from China, but the rapid expansion of Hong Kong's re-export of China's manufactures prevented the share of China's total exports to Hong Kong in China's total exports to the world from declining.

Table 4.5 CHINA'S EXPORTS RETAINED BY HONG KONG AS A PERCENTAGE OF CHINA'S TOTAL EXPORTS TO HONG KONG

Year	China's Total Exports to Hong Kong	China's Exports Retained by Hong Kong
1971	22.8	17.6
1972	22.4	16.7
1973	22.1	15.8
1974	18.0	13.2
1975	19.2	14.3
1976	21.8	15.1
1977	21.4	14.9
1978	22.3	14.8
1979	22.9	13.8
1980	22.3	13.8

Source: See Table 4.1.

IV. The Evolution of China's Exports to Hong Kong and Changes in China's Foreign Trade Policy

A change in China's foreign trade policy can have a significant impact on the growth of its overall as well as its sectoral exports. The reason is that foreign trade in China is under the direct or indirect control of the central authority, which may change its view on the importance of foreign trade to the country once there is a change in its own political leadership. When foreign trade is regarded as unimportant or even harmful to the country, China will keep its imports of capital equipment and technology at a relatively low level and, in the meantime, maintain a level of exports only high enough to finance its imports. Conversely, when foreign technology is considered important to China's economic development, China will promote its exports and imports at a rate considerably faster than when an inward-looking policy is adopted.

In this section, we examine the causes of the variations in the growth rate of China's exports to Hong Kong by studying the interaction between changes in the growth of the demand of Hong Kong for China's exports[5] and changes in China's foreign trade policy. In order to account for the changes in China's foreign trade policy, we will follow the widely adopted notion that China's foreign trade varies closely with the ups and downs of its two political factions: the radicals (ideologists) and the moderates (pragmatists).[6] According to this notion, China's foreign trade will expand when the moderates are in power and contract when they are replaced by the radicals.

China's exports to Hong Kong at any one time are determined, on the one hand, by China's foreign trade policy and, on the other hand, by Hong Kong's demand for imports from China. Therefore, a change in China's foreign trade policy may not necessarily result in a change in the growth rate of China's exports to Hong Kong unless Hong Kong's demand plays a minimal role in determining the level of its imports from China. If a change in Hong Kong's demand for imports from China has an important effect on the growth of China's exports to Hong Kong, it would be difficult to determine the extent to which a change in China's foreign trade policy might affect China's exports to Hong Kong. In the discussion below, we will show that changes in China's foreign trade policy, in comparison with changes in the demand of Hong Kong for China's exports, were a dominant factor in determining the growth of China's exports to Hong Kong in the period from 1971 to 1980. This was so because there was a relatively large and ready market in Hong Kong for China's exports in the early 1970's, and gradually expanding indirect markets to which China could export through the use of the transshipment facilities of Hong Kong in the late 1970's.

Our discussion divides the period from 1971 to 1980 into three: 1971–3, 1974–7, and 1978–80. During the first and third periods, the annual growth rate of China's exports to Hong Kong was relatively high and on an upward path, whereas during the second period the annual growth rate of China's exports to Hong Kong declined.

1. Rapid Growth in 1971–3

As shown in Table 4.6, the annual growth rate of China's exports to Hong Kong increased rapidly from 18 per cent in 1971 to 24 per cent in 1972, and further to 60 per cent in 1973, pushing China's foreign exchange earnings up from US$467 million in 1970 to US$1,094 million in 1973. To some extent, of course, this growth was inflated by the depreciation of the US dollar in 1972 and by Hong Kong's rising prices in 1973, but the real gain of about 50 per cent[7] from 1970 to 1973 was still quite substantial.

Some political changes in China in the early 1970's were favourable to China's expansion of its trade with and through Hong Kong. In 1971, the fall of Lin Biao, China's Defence Minister, marked the end of the military regime which had emphasized military build-up to counter the Soviet threat, but had ignored the need to develop the economy. Following Lin Biao's fall, China started to establish its trade and diplomatic relations with a large number of Western countries from whom China wished to receive help in modernizing the economy. The most notable steps in China's diplomatic offensive were its entry into the United Nations in 1971 and Nixon's visit to China

Table 4.6 THE GROWTH RATES OF CHINA'S EXPORTS TO HONG KONG IN SELECTED GROUPS (percentage)

Year	Total	Retained in Hong Kong	Re-exported by Hong Kong	China's Foodstuff Exports to Hong Kong	China's Manufactured Exports to Hong Kong
1971	17.92	20.27	10.61	18.53	15.15
1972	24.41	19.97	38.07	17.06	33.69
1973	59.68	54.03	78.16	41.87	84.22
1974	7.87	10.54	13.23	29.62	−20.50
1975	16.74	17.99	13.23	7.58	15.60
1976	14.89	6.60	38.82	4.40	29.73
1977	9.54	9.70	9.13	6.09	11.55
1978	29.90	22.67	46.11	13.08	46.04
1979	34.30	28.64	44.96	8.81	47.50
1980	45.85	44.35	48.06	26.30	58.65
1970–3	134.26	122.23	171.72	96.84	183.60
1973–7	58.47	52.62	73.35	54.45	32.99
1977–80	154.36	128.00	213.60	55.41	241.74

Note: The growth rates are calculated on the basis of the US dollar value of China's exports.

Source: See Table 4.1.

in 1972, both of which had a profound impact on China's foreign trade development in later years. Internally, the moderate faction led by Zhou Enlai came to power, and it launched the ambitious Fourth Five Year Development Plan which emphasized, among other things, the import of foreign technology as a means to achieve the goal of modernization. In financing the acceleration of technological imports, China resorted mainly to the expansion of its exports to Western countries, and to Hong Kong, China's long-time major trade partner.

The rapid expansion of China's exports to Hong Kong, as shown in Table 4.6, was due partly to the rapid increase in the re-exported component, and partly to the rapid growth of the portion which was retained in Hong Kong. Hong Kong's re-export of Chinese goods shot up to US$308 million in 1973 from US$114 million in 1970, an increase of more than 170 per cent in three years. Hong Kong's retained imports from China rose from US$354 million in 1970 to US$786 million in 1973, an increase of more than 120 per cent in three years.

While the rapid growth of Hong Kong's re-exports of Chinese goods was an immediate result of China's adoption of an outward-oriented trade policy, the rapid growth of Hong Kong's retained imports from China in this period was made possible not only by the change in China's trade policy, but also by the existence of an ample and readily available market in Hong Kong for China's products. Such a market existed because, first, China was plagued by political turmoil at home in the 1960's and did not at that time make full use of the market opportunities available in Hong Kong, and second, Hong Kong's national income grew rapidly in the early 1970's, further expanding the market for China's exports.[8] Because of the demand of the Hong Kong market, China's traditional foodstuff exports to Hong Kong, for instance, increased by nearly 100 per cent in three years (Table 4.6). The retained imports of Hong Kong also showed a marked increase of 122 per cent in these three years. Had Hong Kong already been saturated with China's exports, the rate of growth would have been much lower, and the growth of China's foreign earnings from Hong Kong would have depended much more heavily on its indirect export trade through Hong Kong.

2. Sluggish Growth in 1974–7

The annual growth rates of China's exports to Hong Kong in the period from 1974–7, ranging from 7 to 17 per cent, were much lower than the average of about 34 per cent in the previous period (Table 4.6). Eckstein indicates that the decline was not due to any change in China's foreign trade policy, but mainly to changes in the world economic situation, which was severely depressed by the dramatic increase in the price of oil in 1973–4.[9] This reasoning, if correct, may also be applied to explaining the drop in the growth rate of China's exports to Hong Kong in 1974 and 1975. Indeed, these were the years in which Hong Kong suffered severe depression as a result of the oil crisis, and the growth rate of its real GDP was only around 2 per cent per year, compared with 16 per cent in 1973. This low rate of output growth, together with the foreign exchange shortage created by high oil bills, greatly limited Hong Kong's capacity to import from China. This explains why Hong Kong's retained imports from China went up by only 10 per cent in 1974 and 18 per cent in 1975, compared with 54 per cent in 1973. Furthermore, the depression in the world market dampened the growth of Hong Kong's re-export of Chinese goods, which recorded an increase of 9 per cent and 13 per cent in 1974 and 1975 respectively, both being much lower than the 78 per cent of 1973. Therefore factors on the demand side were largely unfavourable to the growth of China's exports to Hong Kong in 1974 and 1975.

As for China's foreign trade policy, which affected the supply side of China's exports, the evidence seems to support Eckstein's view that little change occurred during these two years. One piece of evidence is China's promotion of its petroleum exports, a prohibited item in China's foreign trade in the past, to Hong Kong and to the rest of the world. China's export of crude oil and petroleum products rose sharply from a negligible level in 1973 to US$525 million in 1974, and further to US$890 million in 1975. This increase was to compensate for the decline in China's export earnings from other items of export and to sustain China's heavy demand for imports of complete plants and technology from Western countries. Had China altered its trade policy during 1974 and 1975, it would not have started to export this long-prohibited and highly treasured item and, to narrow its trade gap, would have dramatically lowered its imports without having to promote the export of petroleum. Apart from this evidence, the political stability in China during 1974 and 1975 also indicates that there was no significant change in China's trade policy during these two years. In 1975, Zhou Enlai delivered a speech to the Fourth National People's Congress, in which the need for China to continue to pursue the goal of the four modernizations (industry, agriculture, defence, and science and technology) was still stressed. His speech could have been a response to the strong undercurrent of opposition to his economic policy from the radical faction, but it is clear that the moderate faction led by Zhou was still firmly in power and that there was no fundamental change in China's view on the importance of foreign trade to China.

In 1976 and 1977, China's exports to Hong Kong continued to be sluggish, growing at the rate of 15 per cent and 10 per cent respectively (Table 4.5), despite the recovery of the Hong Kong economy from the previous recession. China's failure to take advantage of the rapid growth of the Hong Kong economy by boosting its exports can be seen clearly from the unusually low rates of growth of Hong Kong's retained imports from China, recorded at 7 per cent in 1976 and 10 per cent in 1977. As shown in Table 4.5, these were the lowest rates recorded among those in the period from 1971 to 1980, in spite of the fact that China was maintaining relatively stable export prices during these two years. Had China responded fully to the increase in Hong Kong's domestic demand, which expanded rapidly as real GDP increased by 19 per cent in 1976 and by 10 per cent in 1977, its exports retained by Hong Kong would have increased by 20 per cent in 1976 and 17 per cent in 1977,[10] assuming that the income elasticity of the import demand of Hong Kong was 1.0367 as obtained from the following estimate of Hong Kong's import demand function:[11]

$$\ln \frac{M}{P_m} = -0.3203 + 1.0367 \ln \frac{GDP}{WPI} - 1.2939 \ln \frac{P_m}{WPI}$$

$$(-1.0821) \quad (20.4605) \qquad\qquad (-5.9482)$$

$$R^2 = 0.9810$$

$$DW = 1.1604$$

where M = Hong Kong's total imports;
P_m = the import price index; and
WPI = the wholesale price index.[12]

Our estimates of the potential growth rates of China's exports retained by Hong Kong in response to the growth of the Hong Kong economy could be on the high side, considering the fact that China's exports to Hong Kong comprised mainly foodstuffs and raw materials, for which the demand usually has low income elasticities. However, even if we assume that the income elasticity was as low as 0.5, the estimated potential growth rates for 1976 and 1977 are still greater than the actual growth rates in these two years. Therefore, it is obvious that there was some change in China's foreign trade policy which resulted in a slowing down in the growth of China's exports to Hong Kong during these two years.

Indeed, political uncertainty developed in China upon the deaths of Zhou and Mao, the two most powerful political leaders in China's recent history, in 1976. Taking advantage of the political vacuum created by Zhou's and Mao's deaths, the radicals, rallying behind the Gang of Four, began openly to attack the prevailing trade policy for its subjection of China's economy to the violent fluctuations of the world economy.[13] They disputed Deng Xiaoping's pro-foreign trade stand, criticized him for selling China's precious raw materials to foreign countries, and accused him of being a running dog of the capitalists. The clash between the two factions culminated in October 1976 when the Gang of Four was purged and the moderates, led by Deng Xiaoping, regained their political dominance. China, however, did not fully recover from the political turbulence until late 1977 when Deng Xiaoping, instead of the then Premier and Party Chairman Hua Guofeng, gained power. This was why China's foreign trade suffered from political indecision on the part of its trade authorities in both 1976 and 1977.

3. Strong Revival in 1978–80

The rate of growth of China's exports to Hong Kong, as shown in Table 4.6, went up to nearly 30 per cent in 1978 from a low of below 10 per cent in 1977, and further to 34 per cent in 1979 and 46 per cent in 1980. Such high rates of growth can be attributed largely to the rapid growth in the items of raw materials and manufactures, which gained 189 per cent and 242 per cent respectively during these three years. Foodstuffs, a traditionally important item, went up by only 55 per cent and, unlike the period from 1971 to 1973, contributed very little to the growth of China's overall exports to Hong Kong.

The increase in the relative importance of manufactures in China's exports to Hong Kong, from 40 per cent in 1977 to 53 per cent in 1980, would not have been that significant, however, had it not been for an improvement in their competitiveness. Historically, low quality and lack of marketing skills were major obstacles to the expansion of China's exports. Most Chinese industries had by then shut themselves off from the rest of the world for too long to keep up with the growth of technology in the West. They used outdated machinery, designs, and packaging in the production of manufactures, turning out goods which were consumed only by the low-income groups of the more developed countries. Worse still, producers and people in charge of foreign trade in China had long been in the position to determine what would be produced and what the majority of the Chinese population should consume; they found it difficult to accept that in international trade they had to be told how much they should produce by foreign buyers. Because of their disregard of the demand in foreign markets, China's low-quality manufactured exports soon reached a bottleneck and could rarely command good prices. From 1978 onward, the Chinese began to become aware of the problem and to tackle it. As China's trade minister Li Qiang indicated, China was now willing to accept foreign buyers' trade marks, specifications, materials, packaging, and tools and machinery in the production of export goods. Furthermore, China began to promote exports by sending trade delegations and holding Chinese trade exhibitions abroad, having consignment sales with foreign importers, and monitoring closely the variations in international prices. In 1979, Li Qiang further indicated that China was interested in expanding compensation trade and joint ventures with Western countries with a view to improving the quality and expanding the volume of its exports.

The success of this export-promoting practice may be seen from the fact that China's exports to Hong Kong have more than fully taken advantage of the expansion of the Hong Kong market. Based on the assumption that the income elasticity of Hong Kong's demand for China's exports is, as estimated earlier, 1.0367, China's exports retained by Hong Kong would, as a result of the increase in Hong Kong's national income, have increased by 16 per cent, 24 per cent and 22 per cent in 1978, 1979 and 1980 respectively,[14] compared with the acutal growth rates of 23 per cent, 29 per cent and 44 per cent for these three years. These relatively high rates of growth for Hong

Kong's retained imports from China reflect China's success in breaking through some areas of the Hong Kong market which were previously inaccessible to China because of the low quality of its products or because of its lack of skill in international marketing. In addition to this success, China was also particularly successful in expanding its indirect export trade through Hong Kong, which re-exported US$1,676 million of Chinese products in 1980. This marked a 214 per cent increase over that of 1977. The rapid increase in Hong Kong's re-exports of Chinese goods was undoubtedly related to China's efforts to improve its international marketing skills and the quality of its exports. However, another increasingly important factor was also contributing to the expansion of re-exports. Since China set up Special Economic Zones and negotiated joint ventures with foreign firms in 1978, compensation trade as well as subcontracting between Hong Kong and China have expanded rapidly. As a result, there has been an increasing amount of raw materials and semi-finished products exported from Hong Kong to China for processing, and, in return, of finished products shipped back to Hong Kong to be re-exported to other countries.

Hong Kong's increased shipment of raw materials and semi-finished goods to China in the years from 1978 to 1980 was mainly in the form of re-exports, since Hong Kong itself relied heavily on such imports as well. The increase of the shipments, as shown in Table 4.7, was particularly dramatic in 1979 and in 1980. In 1978, its volume amounted to only US$46 million, but it shot up to US$263 million in 1979, and further to US$933 million in 1980. Taiwan, Japan and South Korea

Table 4.7 HONG KONG'S EXPORTS TO CHINA, 1978–80
(US dollars million)

	1978	1979	1980
Hong Kong's domestic exports to China	17	121	323
Hong Kong's re-exports to China	46	263	933
Total	63	384	1,256

Source: Economic Research Department, Hang Seng Bank, 'Hong Kong–China Trade', *Hang Seng Economic Quarterly*, January 1982.

were among the major sources of such shipments in 1980. Hong Kong's domestic exports to China represented a relatively small portion of Hong Kong's total exports to China in each of these years. Nevertheless, the increases in such transactions were by no means small, as they went up quickly from US$17 million in 1978 to US$121 million in 1979, and further to US$323 million in 1980.

The finished goods shipped back from China to Hong Kong were mainly for re-export. However, they were recorded in Hong Kong trade statistics either as Hong Kong's retained imports from China or as Hong Kong's re-exports of China's products, depending on the extent to which the products were processed in Hong Kong before they were re-exported. A considerable proportion of them could have been classified as Hong Kong's retained imports from China due to the final manufacturing processes in Hong Kong that were regarded by the Hong Kong Government as having changed permanently the shape, nature, form, or utility of the products. As a matter of fact, there were incentives for such processes to take place in Hong Kong as products labelled as 'Made in Hong Kong' would carry better prices in the international market than if they were labelled as 'China-made'. The rest of the shipments which did not go through such manufacturing processes were classified into Hong Kong's re-exports of China's products. It is thus clear that the rapid increases in Hong Kong's re-exports of China's products, as well as in Hong Kong's retained imports from China in 1979 and 1980 as presented in Table 4.6, can largely be attributed to the expansion of compensation trade, joint ventures and subcontracting between the two economies.

In sum, because of China's encouragement of compensation trade, export processing, and joint ventures in 1978, there has been a rapid expansion of the following items as recorded in Hong Kong's trade statistics in recent years: (a) Hong Kong's re-exports to China, (b) Hong Kong's domestic exports to China, (c) Hong Kong's retained imports from China, and (d) Hong Kong's re-exports of China's products.

As in 1971–3, China's drive to export in this period was due to its enthusiasm to import Western technology in the hope of achieving its goal of the four modernizations. In 1978, the first year of its ambitious modernization plan, China set an investment target of US$600 billion for the coming eight years, and initially negotiated US$40 billion and later actually signed US$7.8 billion of cash contracts with foreign firms for the import of complete plants, mainly in the fields of iron and steel, oil exploration and petrochemicals. This ambitious import plan was modified and partly cancelled in 1979, as it was found that a large proportion of the machinery imported either duplicated other machinery or could not be efficiently used. The Chinese planners began to realize that the installation of foreign machinery required not only foreign exchange to pay the initial purchasing costs, but also the co-ordination of other sectors, such as energy, transportation, educated technical personnel, upstream products and downstream users. By now, China had shifted its emphasis from complete plant imports to the import of individual technical items which could be used in existing factories. Imports of heavy machinery and equipment also gave way to imports of machinery for agricultural and light industries, in which China had a comparative advantage in foreign trade. As a result of these changes, the import of complete plants was kept at a level as low as US$1.8 billion in 1979 and US$2.6 billion in 1980.

Despite the retrenchment of China's foreign trade in 1979 and 1980, China remained adamant in its pursuit of the goal of modernization, and continued to promote its exports in order to finance its growing demand for imports. Most notable was its programme to decentralize its foreign trade system. In the programme, local trade corporations were set up and authorized 'to bypass the centralized foreign trade corporations and deal directly with foreign firms to conduct trade negotiations.'[15] Individual exporting firms and local trade authorities were allowed to keep a certain proportion of their foreign exchange earnings so that they could import whatever machinery they deemed necessary. In worker management, export industries gradually adopted the piece-rate payment system and were empowered to dismiss their employees. In addition to this decentralization programme, China set up several Special Economic Zones in Guangdong and Fujian to attract foreign investments and to promote export processing. All these changes either widened the range, or improved the quality, of the goods China exported, and helped the expansion of China's exports to Hong Kong as well as to the rest of the world.

The above discussions show that the growth of China's exports to Hong Kong in the period from 1971 to 1980 was determined mainly by China's foreign trade policy except during 1974–5, when Hong Kong and the rest of the world were in severe depression. From 1971 to 1973, China's outward-oriented trade policy, coupled with the ample domestic market of Hong Kong for China's exports, enabled China's exports to Hong Kong to grow rapidly. In the following years, however, firstly Hong Kong's depressed demand, and secondly political uncertainty in China resulted in a setback to their expansion. Vigorous growth resumed in 1978 as China again adopted an outward-oriented trade policy which allowed significant increases in China's exports through Hong Kong to take place.

V. Conclusion

The function of Hong Kong as China's major foreign exchange earner was, contrary to Hsueh and Woo's findings, almost unaffected by the expansion of China's foreign trade in the 1970's. Throughout the period, Hong Kong imported around 22 per cent of China's overall exports, and this share did not show any sign of declining. However, this does not mean that Hong Kong remained as unique a market for China's exports as in the 1960's, when China's foreign trade was low and when foodstuffs constituted the major proportion of China's exports. Upon the expansion of China's foreign trade, its foodstuff exports, which were in large part not widely marketable and depended considerably on the Hong Kong market, became less and less important, while its raw material and manufactured exports, which had much wider acceptance in the international market, gained increasingly important places in China's overall exports. Such a change has in a sense reduced China's dependence on the Hong Kong market for the earning of foreign exchange even though China's foreign exchange earnings from Hong Kong remain as an unchanged proportion of China's total exports.

Nevertheless, China's keeness to export has increased its reliance on the international transshipment facilities of Hong Kong, which is equipped with advanced international marketing skills, strong trade relations with other countries, and a good natural harbour with modern port facilities. In statistical terms, the proportion of China's exports going through Hong Kong went up from 5 per cent in 1971 to 8 per cent in 1979, and is likely to have exceeded 10 per cent in 1981. Such a significant increase in indirect trade would not have occurred if China had been keen on using trade as a political tool. However, when foreign trade was used mainly as a means to develop the economy, the dependence of China on Hong Kong to re-export its products increased, because China was more concerned with how much foreign exchange it could earn than with how foreign exchange could be earned. To some extent, Hong Kong was unique in providing China with its entrepôt facilities, which earned considerable foreign exchange that China needed and which could not be easily replaced by those of other countries which are situated much farther away from China.

Hong Kong's involvement in China's foreign trade in the late 1970's went deeper than functioning as a market and an entrepôt for China's exports. The increase of joint ventures and subcontracting arrangements with China made some of China's exporting firms depend entirely on Hong Kong for the import of raw materials and the export of finished products. Furthermore, Hong Kong became the front line of international trade for some of the newly established provincial and municipal trade corporations, which stationed their agents in Hong Kong to widen their contacts with foreign traders. Both forms of contact between the two economies, apart from boosting China's exports, provided China with opportunities to learn from Hong Kong in production management as well as international marketing.

In sum, the role that Hong Kong has played in China's foreign trade has been related less and less to what and how much the domestic market of Hong Kong can import from China and more and more to what Hong Kong can do to promote China's exports. The latter may not be measurable, but its importance to the long-isolated Chinese economy can not be overstated.

Future Prospects

China is likely to continue to depend on Hong Kong as an important foreign exchange earner and a gateway to the West in the near future, so long as China maintains its existing outward-oriented trade policy. For one thing, a large portion of the Hong Kong market for manufactures is still untapped by China, which has up to the present concentrated on the export of unsophisticated, light industrial products. By improving its production technology and by widening the range of its supplies, China can take advantage of its geographical proximity to Hong Kong and of the loyalty of the ethnic Chinese population in Hong Kong to China's products to become an important source of imports for Hong Kong. For another thing, some time must elapse before China can significantly improve its own international marketing skills and handle most of its trade relations with the West within its own social and economic framework — given that China is going to preserve its communism. China's export industries cannot acquire sophisticated marketing skills without direct contact with the world market, but even so the trade authorities are unlikely to furnish themselves with the flexibility and responsiveness that are needed for the full promotion of China's export trade. Therefore, Hong Kong can continue to function as a point of contact between China and the West and as a marketing agent, providing China with international market information through the re-export of China's products.

Notes

[1] Western countries are broadly defined here as non-Communist countries.

[2] See Hsueh and Woo (1981), pp. 13 and 22.

[3] China's major national foreign trade corporations include: China National Cereals, Oils and Foodstuffs Import and Export Corporation; China National Native Produce and Animal By-products Import and Export Corporation; China

National Textiles Import and Export Corporation; China National Light Industrial Products Import and Export Corporation; China National Arts and Crafts Import and Export Corporation; China National Chemicals Import and Export Corporation; China National Machinery and Equipment Import and Export Corporation; China National Metals and Minerals Import and Export Corporation; China Machinery Import and Export Corporation; China National Technical Import Corporation; China National Instruments Import and Export Corporation; China National Foreign Trade Transportation Corporation; China National Chartering Corporation; and China National Packaging Import and Export Corporation. Most of these national corporations have their branches in various provinces and agents in Hong Kong and Macau. Major local trade corporations include those of Shanghai, Tianjin, Beijing, Guangdong, Guangzhou, Fujian and Liaoning.

4 Trade goods in *Hong Kong Trade Statistics* are classified into 10 groups: (a) food and live animals chiefly for food; (b) beverages and tobacco; (c) crude materials, inedibles, except fuels; (d) mineral fuels, lubricants and related materials; (e) animal and vegetable oils, fats and waxes; (f) chemicals and related products, not elsewhere specified; (g) manufactured goods classified chiefly by material; (h) machinery and transport equipment; (i) miscellaneous manufactured articles; and (j) commodities and transactions not classified according to kind and transactions in gold and coins. In this study, (a) and (b) are grouped as foodstuffs, (c), (d) and (e) as raw materials, (f) as chemicals, (g), (h) and (i) as manufactures, and (j) is ignored as it is relatively insignificant in Hong Kong's trade with China.

5 Changes in Hong Kong's demand for China's exports may arise from changes in the market conditions in Hong Kong and in some of Hong Kong's major re-export markets.

6 See Morrison (1978).

7 The real growth is calculated on the basis of the fixed prices of China's exports to Hong Kong in 1971.

8 Hong Kong's real GDP expanded by over 25 per cent between 1970 and 1973.

9 See Eckstein (1977), p. 243.

10 These are the growth rates of the output-growth-induced real imports, adjusted for changes in import prices, that is:

$$G_m = G_y \eta_y (P_2/P_1) - (1 - P_2/P_1)$$

where

G_m = the growth rate of the value of the imports from China to Hong Kong that are induced by the growth of Hong Kong's national income;

G_y = the growth rate of Hong Kong's real GDP;

η_y = the income elasticity of Hong Kong's demand for imports;

P_1 = the price index of Hong Kong's imports from China in the previous period; and

P_2 = the price index of Hong Kong's imports from China in the current period.

Such estimates for the years from 1971 to 1980 are given as follows:

1971	1972	1973	1974	1975	1976	1977	1978	1979	1980
4.77%	11.76	49.21	34.46	10.42	19.49	16.99	15.76	23.54	22.28

[11] The period concerned is from 1966 to 1980.

[12] Since the wholesale price index is not available, we use the consumer price index as an approximation.

[13] China's foreign trade was in great difficulties in 1974 and 1975 as the severe world economic recession depressed its exports and soaring international prices swelled its expenditure on imports.

[14] Again, these estimates could be on the high side since Hong Kong's demand for imports from China could have an income elasticity much lower than 1.0367.

[15] See National Foreign Assessment Centre, Central Intelligence Agency, *China: International Trade Quarterly Review*, First Quarter, 1980, p. 7.

References

Batsavage, R.E., and Davie, L. (1978), 'China's International Trade and Finance', in Joint Economic Committee, Congress of the United States, *Chinese Economy Post Mao* (Washington D.C., U.S. Government Printing Office).

Beazer, W.F. (1978), *The Commercial Future of Hong Kong* (New York, Praeger Publishers).

Chen, N.R., 'China's Foreign Trade, 1950–74', in *China: A Reassessment of the Economy: A Compendium of Papers submitted to the Joint Economic Committee, Congress of the United States* (Washington D.C., U.S. Government Printing Office, 1975).

Eckstein, A. (1977), *China's Economic Revolution* (London, Cambridge University Press).

Gelber, H.G. (1978), 'Economics and Technology in China after Mao', *Asian Survey*, July.

Gatt, K.D. (1974), 'China's Foreign Trade Policies and Practices', in Patrick M. Boarman (ed.), *Trade with China: Assessment by Leading Businessmen and Scholars* (New York, Praeger Publishers).

Hsueh, T.T., and Woo, T.O. (1981), 'Trade between Hong Kong and China: Issues and Prospects', Centre of Asian Studies, University of Hong Kong, Contemporary Chinese Studies Seminar Programme, Working Paper No. cc 12.

Ishikawa, S., 'The Impact of the Emergence of China on Asian-Pacific Trade', in Kiyoshi Kojima (ed.), *Structural Adjustment in Asian-Pacific Trade, Paper and Proceedings of the Fifth Pacific Trade and Development Conference* (The Japan Research Centre, Tokyo, 1973).

Kravalis, H.H. (1978), 'An Analysis of China's Hard Currency Exports: Recent Trends, Present Problems, and Future Potential', in Joint Economic Committee, Congress of the United States, *Chinese Economy Post Mao* (Washington D.C., U.S. Government Printing Office).

Lupton, C.M. (1972), 'Hong Kong's Role in Sino-Western Trade', in Arther A. Stahuke (ed.), *China's Trade with the West: A Political and Economic Analysis* (New York, Praeger Publishers).

Mah, F.H. (1971), *The Foreign Trade of Mainland China* (Chicago and New York, Aldine-Atherton).

Morrison, K. (1978), 'Domestic Politics and Industrialization in China', *Asian Survey*, July.

Price, R.L. (1968), 'International Trade of Communist China, 1950-65', in Joint Economic Committee of the U.S. Congress, *An Economic Profile of Mainland China* (New York, Praeger Publishers).

Richman, B.M. (1974), 'Chinese Priorities and the Prospects for U.S.-China Trade', in Patrick M. Boarman (ed.), *Trade with China: Assessment by Leading Businessmen and Scholars* (New York, Praeger Publishers).

Usack, A.H., and Batsavage, R.E. (1972), 'The International Trade of People's Republic of China', in Joint Economic Committee, Congress of the United States, *People's Republic of China: An Economic Assessment* (Washington D.C., U.S. Government Printing Office).

5. Imports of Consumer Goods from China and the Economic Growth of Hong Kong

L.C. CHAU

Since it embarked on its export-led industrialization in the mid-1950's, Hong Kong has managed to sustain a high growth rate for nearly three decades. Through full employment and rising real wages, the fruits of growth have reached most of the population, which more than doubled during the period. This enviable record of growth has been achieved with minimum government intervention and restriction, and no outside aid or transfers. A commercial heritage, an institutional framework inducive to inflows of private capital, an adequate provision of infrastructure, along with the effective mobilization of an enterprising and hard-working population have provided the competitive edge, which took full advantage of the favourable world trade environment of the 1950's and 1960's. Economists are naturally interested in the applicability of the success of this 'Hong Kong model' to other developing economies. Many circumstances, historical and political, as well as cultural, that are peculiar to Hong Kong have been identified by observers, all of which purport to demonstrate that the experience of Hong Kong is 'unique'.

One particularly pertinent issue is the reliance of Hong Kong's trade success on the supply of foodstuffs, consumer goods and raw materials from China at prices much lower than world levels. While most observers readily include this as an important factor contributing to Hong Kong's success, few analyses on the magnitude of this advantage, and the precise way in which it has affected the course of Hong Kong's economic development, have been published.[1] If, indeed, the supply of imports from China at concessionary prices, as a result either of China's isolation coupled with the pricing behaviour of a socialist economy, or for political and other reasons, was crucial for its success, then the growth experience of Hong Kong is certainly unique.

It is the purpose of the present study to ascertain the degree of price advantage received by Hong Kong through its imports from China, and to analyse how different pricing policies pursued by China would alter the course of Hong Kong's economic development. In Section I we will portray the degree of dependency on imports of foodstuffs and wage goods from China, and how such dependency varies with household income. In Section II we will estimate how costs of food and goods imports from China would be affected by different hypothetical pricing policies and their impact on the cost of living. In the following section, the response of wage rates to rising costs of living over different phases of Hong Kong's development will be deduced in the context of Hong Kong's labour market and wage behaviour. The implication of this on the growth performance will be discussed in Section IV, followed by a brief summary.

I. Dependence on Food and Wage Goods Imports from China

Through necessity, Hong Kong, as a land-scarce city economy, has to depend on imports for its food supply. Because of geographical proximity, as well as ethnic and cultural ties, it is only natural that Hong Kong should turn first to China for supply. From Table 5.1 we note first that the degree of self-sufficiency for food has been quite stable since the early 1950's. Domestic production averaged 21 per cent of total consumption during 1976–80, precisely as in the 1950's. This indicates a remarkable development, considering that the population increased by about 70 per cent over the two decades, while both the extent of agricultural land and the agricultural labour force fell sharply.[2] Over the same period, there was an appreciable increase in dependency on food imports from China. As a percentage of total food imports, food imports from China went up from 43 per cent during

Table 5.1 SOURCES OF FOOD SUPPLY

Year	Total Food Imports	Exports and Re-exports	Domestic Production	Total Domestic Consumption
1952	1,010	437	–	–
1953	1,131	443	–	–
1954	833	313	157	677
1955	971	303	175	843
1956	1,029	335	202	896
1957	1,161	342	176	995
1958	1,255	374	213	1,094
1959	1,238	311	258	1,185
1960	1,353	311	291	1,333
1961	1,406	312	319	1,413
1962	1,610	379	321	1,552
1963	1,733	416	321	1,638
1964	2,013	480	292	1,825
1965	2,042	413	315	1,944
1966	2,217	453	342	2,106
1967	2,329	365	405	2,369
1968	2,468	426	493	2,535
1969	2,804	517	611	2,898
1970	3,051	500	732	3,283
1971	3,474	574	801	3,701
1972	3,679	604	874	3,949
1973	4,914	794	1,047	5,167
1974	6,111	812	1,124	6,423
1975	6,113	910	1,125	6,328
1976	6,687	1,478	1,357	6,566
1977	7,234	1,446	1,494	7,282
1978	8,207	1,584	1,694	8,317
1979	9,646	2,064	2,199	9,781
1980	11,558	2,231	2,311	11,638

Sources: Census and Statistics Department, *Trade Statistics*; and Agriculture and Fisheries Department, *Annual Reports*.

the first post-Korean War decade of 1954–63, to over 50 per cent between 1964–73. Since 1977, the share has been quite stable, at 47 per cent.

FOR HONG KONG, 1952–80

Food Imports from China	Degree of Self-Sufficiency (percentage)	Share of Imports from China (percentage)
380	–	38
382	–	34
384	23	46
458	21	47
457	23	44
525	18	45
711	19	57
507	22	41
538	22	40
430	23	31
585	21	36
720	20	42
1,002	16	50
1,130	16	55
1,242	16	56
1,105	17	47
1,218	17	49
1,349	21	48
1,413	22	46
1,709	22	49
1,863	22	51
2,404	20	49
3,100	17	51
3,240	18	53
3,352	21	50
3,366	21	47
3,883	20	47
4,520	22	47
5,624	20	49

Overall, from 1964 onward, about 80 per cent of foodstuffs consumed in Hong Kong were imported, half of them from China. For certain staples, the degree of dependency was considerably higher.

This is shown in Table 5.2. Among the six staple foods listed, 90 per cent of live animals and more than 60 per cent of meat and fish were brought in from China. Only in the case of cereals did importation from China fail to dominate until recent years. And this has resulted only from government policy. Through a licensing system, the import of rice was closely regulated by the Hong Kong Government. It has always been the policy to diversify the sources of supply for this major component of the local diet. Overall and in value terms, about 50 per cent of these staples were imported from China. Interestingly, there has been a steady decline in the import shares for the last four food groups, after a peak was reached during 1965–9. The import shares of

Table 5.2 IMPORTS FROM CHINA AS A PERCENTAGE OF TOTAL IMPORTS, SELECTED FOODSTUFFS

Year	Cereals and Cereal Preparations	Live Animals	Meat and Meat Preparations	Fruit and Vegetables	Fish and Fish Preparations	Dairy Products and Eggs
1959	17	63	53	49	62	41
1961	25	33	41	24	44	27
1963	22	71	40	40	50	53
1965	27	88	67	51	66	53
1967	21	85	59	50	64	51
1968	28	84	65	51	60	51
1969	25	84	63	48	60	49
1970	25	80	56	45	51	51
1971	26	84	58	42	53	50
1972	33	85	56	41	47	49
1973	42	83	52	37	44	49
1974	39	57	56	41	45	52
1975	41	91	59	42	50	50
1976	40	90	53	40	43	47
1977	35	89	47	39	35	44
1978	36	90	50	39	34	46
1979	35	91	51	39	37	47
1980	38	96	57	38	36	44

Source: Census and Statistics Department, *Trade Statistics*.

fish, fruit and vegetables, in particular, have shrunk most markedly. The reverse is true, however, for the first two groups. In sum, the items included account for about 80 per cent of total food imports.

Because of the Engel effect, dependency on imports from China varies a great deal among income classes. According to the 1963–4 Household Expenditure Survey, 65 per cent of households in the sample spent less than HK$600 per month. They spent between 50 to 60 per cent of their budget on food. Consider the expenditure class of HK$300–399, which was the modal class of the Survey and should also represent well the blue-collar workers in manufacturing.[3] They spent 57 per cent of their budget on food. Direct expenditure on the staples listed in Table 5.2 amounted to 44 per cent of total expenditure. If we allocate half of the cost of 'meals bought away from home' to these six food items, then the latter would account for 49 per cent of total expenditure.

The price effects also work to increase the dependency of wage earners on food imported from China. The Chinese have a strong preference for fresh meat and vegetables as against the chilled, frozen or canned varieties. Vegetables, meat and fish produced locally command considerable price premiums. For illustration, price differences for vegetables and meat are shown in Table 5.3. We note that vegetables produced in Hong Kong are about 40 per cent more expensive than imported vegetables, predominantly from China. Furthermore, there has been a clear long-term upward trend in this quality premium. For meat products, local products cost about 30 per cent more. The premium fluctuates, but there is no clear trend. It is only to be expected that lower-income households headed by wage earners would consume more of the lower priced imported food. Therefore, not only do they spend a higher proportion of their budget on food, but a higher proportion of their food bills are spent on food imported from China.

Imports from China are also an important source of supply for other wage goods. Most notable is clothing, of which about half of the imports came from China in the early years. Other wage goods dominated by Chinese imports are textile piece-goods, kitchen- and table-wares, furniture, and certain electrical appliances, such as electric fans.

Table 5.3 UNIT VALUE OF IMPORTED AND DOMESTIC FOODSTUFFS

	Fresh Vegetables: Price per ton (HK dollars)			Meat and Meat Preparations: Price per million lbs., Carcass Weight Equivalent (million HK dollars)		
	Domestic Production	Net Import	Price Premium (domestic/ imported)	Domestic Production	Imported	Price Premium (domestic/ imported)
1953	224	178	1.26	2.47	1.78	1.39
1954	229	173	1.32	2.19	2.01	1.09
1955	224	199	1.13	2.16	1.94	1.11
1956	218	185	1.18	2.27	1.75	1.30
1957	234	243	0.96	1.74	1.75	0.99
1958	244	196	1.25	2.43	1.56	1.56
1959	285	217	1.31	2.84	1.58	1.80
1960	308	224	1.37	2.79	1.53	1.82
1961	323	276	1.17	2.55	1.72	1.48
1962	281	230	1.22	2.31	1.63	1.42
1963	289	233	1.24	2.05	1.61	1.27
1964	350	284	1.23	2.17	1.57	1.38
1965	362	217	1.67	2.13	1.61	1.32
1966	472	274	1.72	–	–	–
1967	451	371	1.22	–	–	–
1968	552	380	1.45	2.08	1.21	1.72
1969	620	390	1.59	1.96	1.52	1.29
1970	816	456	1.79	2.14	1.59	1.35
1971	851	455	1.87	2.18	1.69	1.29
1972	1,005	550	1.83	2.23	1.67	1.34
1973	1,247	659	1.89	2.90	2.01	1.44
1974	1,144	873	1.31	3.13	2.66	1.18
1975	1,348	1,013	1.33	3.46	2.51	1.38
1976	1,437	1,039	1.38	3.80	2.70	1.41
1977	1,523	1,261	1.21	3.52	2.72	1.29
1978	1,834	1,559	1.18	3.38	2.76	1.22
1979	2,264	1,580	1.43	3.83	2.98	1.29
1980	2,212	1,668	1.33	4.39	3.37	1.30

Sources: Agriculture and Fisheries Department, *Annual Reports*; and Census and Statistics Department, *Trade Statistics*.

II. The Price Advantage of Food Imports from China

A steady supply of foodstuffs and wage goods from China, at stable and relatively low prices, has long been recognized as an important contributing factor to the success of Hong Kong's export-led industrialization.[4] It has been suggested that prices of such goods were always lower than world market prices.[5] In the 1950's and 1960's, in particular, stable prices of imported foodstuffs contributed to remarkably stable food price levels. A change in pricing policies is alleged to have occurred in the late 1960's. Import prices of foodstuffs started to rise rapidly, in line with a rapid increase in commodity prices the world over. Still, prices of food imported from China remained lower than those charged by other major suppliers.[6]

It is difficult to quantify price differentials between imports from China and those from other sources. A standard procedure is to compare unit values of a traded item, or group of items, as reported in Hong Kong's trade statistics.[7] But in a free market like Hong Kong, such a price differential for traded items must be largely the result of quality differences (including what is only subjective in the mind of some consumers). An orange from California commands a higher price than an orange from China because it is better. It could not be otherwise in a free market. Similarly, vegetables produced locally are sold at higher prices because they are fresher and have lower wastage. In products for which there is little difference in quality among different sources of supply, the dominant supplier will set the price and lesser producers will take the price and supply what they can produce with profit at that price.[8] In pork, for example, China sets the price, and only those local producers who can compete at that price stay in the business. In other cases, such as frozen poultry in the early 1960's, China was the price taker. In sum, price differentials cannot be established from traded items. To infer them among previously traded items, one has to run the gauntlet of allowing for exchange rate parity and domestic developments of potential suppliers. It is even less meaningful to project the impact of a cessation of imports from China on the basis of such price differentials. Aside from the dubious interpretation of such 'price differentials', the assumption that the observed prices of alternative sources of supply will stay put in the absence of imports from China[9] is simply inadmissible. For some food items, alternative sources of supply are not presently available. For many other items, information for inferring supply elasticity from other sources simply does not exist. Relative prices would change substantially, and with it the local consumption pattern. In short, the full impact of the cessation of food imports from China can hardly be gauged from a simple comparative static framework.

A more realistic and meaningful way in which to assess Hong Kong's special benefits from its trade relationship with China is to imagine that the socialist government of China had followed a different pricing policy for its exports to Hong Kong right from the beginning. Three alternatives come to mind. The most reasonable alternative is that China started matching her export prices to world market prices right from the early 1950's. A second alternative is that China acted as a revenue-maximizing monopolist, charging what the market could bear. A third alternative is that Hong Kong experienced the average rate of creeping inflation in living costs that occurred in cities of rapidly industrializing developing countries with market economies, as a result of changing terms of trade between the rural and the urban sector. We shall assess, in turn, the likely impact of each of these scenarios.

Prices of imported foodstuffs from China could be lower than world prices either because the price level was initially lower in the early 1950's, or because it moved upward more slowly than world prices, or both. We start by comparing the price trend of food imports from China with indexes of food prices in international markets. Data are presented in Table 5.4. An overall value index of food imports from China is available only since 1968. Unit value indexes for major food items are available as early as 1961. From such indexes, which account for a stable 83 per cent of total food imports from China over the period 1968–70, a value index was compiled by the author for 1961–7.[10] Before 1961, the retail price index for food items is considered as a proxy. As wage rates were quite stable during most of the 1950's, retail prices may be expected to move closely with import prices. For comparison, we consider prices for food exports in general, and those for food exports from developing countries in particular. To be sure,

Table 5.4 FOOD PRICE INDEXES OF LOCAL AND WORLD MARKETS

	Retail Price Index for Food Items (1953 = 100) (1)	Unit Value Index of Food Imports from China (1968 = 100) (2)	Unit Value Index, World Exports of Food (1953 = 100) (3)	Unit Value Index of Food Exports from Developing Countries (1953 = 100) (4)
1953	100		100	100
1954	95		108	121
1955	90		96	101
1956	95		95	98
1957	96		97	98
1958	93		94	90
1959	106		88	81
1960	98		86	79
1961	100	85	85	74
1962	96	88	85	72
1963	100	90	97	83
1964	103	88	100	88
1965	103	94	93	81
1966	108	93	96	80
1967	124	97	95	80
1968		100	92	80
1969		113	98	85
1970		118	101	96
1971		119	105	90
1972		124	116	101
1973		160	153	143
1974		224	192	208
1975		205	199	174
1976		208	199	205
1977		216	221	287
1978		227	239	240
1979		237	269	257
1980		258		

Sources: 1. Census and Statistics Department (1969), *Hong Kong Statistics 1947-1967*, p. 144.

Table 5.4 (continued)

Sources: 2. Census and Statistics Department, *Review of Overseas Trade*, various issues; statistics for 1961–7 were compiled by the author (see note 10).

3. United Nations, *Yearbook of International Trade & Development Statistics*, various issues.

4. UNCTAD, *Handbook of International Trade & Development Statistics*, various issues; data for 1976–9 were obtained by extrapolating the inflation rate of 'World export price indexes of food from developing market economies,' found in *1979 Yearbook of International Trade Statistics*, II, p. 1193.

the correspondence is rough, so a year-to-year comparison may not be very meaningful. Our interest is in seeing whether, over the long term, the price levels of food imports from China followed the broad trend of world prices.

For purposes of comparison we note first that the general price trend was quite similar, over most of this period, as between world food exports and food exports from developing countries (in both cases only market economies are covered). For both series, prices fell steadily after 1954, reached a trough around 1962, remained relatively stable until 1969, and rose quite sharply up to the mid-1970's. Over the entire 1961–74 period there was a close agreement in their year-to-year changes. This similarity in price behaviour is convenient to us, since Hong Kong draws substantial food imports from both developed and developing countries. For comparison with the local trend, consider first the period 1953–66. Local retail prices were essentially flat up to 1963, and thereafter rose moderately. The deflation in world food prices from 1958 to 1962 was not reflected in retail prices in Hong Kong. But wages for unskilled workers rose sharply in 1960 and 1963, which may well explain the higher retail prices locally. Thus, the observed local prices are broadly consistent with import prices similar to world prices. Most important, the stability of food prices over this period was a world-wide phenomenon.

For the period 1961–79 prices of food imports from China moved in close parallel to world prices until 1973. Between 1961 and 1973, prices of food imports from China went up by 88 per cent, compared with an 80 per cent increase in world export prices, and a 92 per cent increase in prices for food exports from developing countries. In 1974, prices of foodstuffs from China jumped by 40 per cent. Prices of food exports from developing countries also went up by 45 per cent. But prices of world exports of food went up by only 25 per cent. There was a retrenchment in Chinese prices during the next two years, while world prices continued their upward trend. During 1977–9, the rise of food prices from China was more moderate than that of world prices. For the entire period 1973–9, prices of food imported from China went up by 48 per cent, compared with a 76 per cent increase in world prices, and an 80 per cent increase in prices of food exports from developing countries.

It is widely believed that in the 1950's and 1960's foodstuffs were exported from China at prices below world levels, which constituted a form of subsidy for Hong Kong's economic development; and that in the 1970's, following the détente between China and the West, China began to adjust her export prices upwards so as gradually to eliminate these price gaps. The results from our comparison of price trends are at odds with this version of events. Up to 1972, there was no discernible deviation between the price trend of foods imported from China and the trend in world prices. Food prices were relatively stable in Hong Kong. So were food prices in world markets. After 1972, when China was supposed to be adjusting its relative prices upwards, we find that the increase in Chinese food prices was actually smaller than that for food exports from other countries. More precisely, for 1972–9 import prices from China went up by 91 per cent, compared with a 131 per cent price increase in world food exports, and a 166 per cent price increase in food exports from developing countries. Prices of food rose rapidly in Hong Kong after 1972, but prices in the international market rose even faster. If prices of foodstuffs from China were lower than world prices before 1972, this gap would have widened by the end of the decade.

Specifically, if prices of food imported from China had increased at the same rate as world prices in the 1970's, then in 1979 foodstuffs from China would have been 29 per cent more expensive than they actually were. Perhaps this may be considered as the lower limit of the cost advantage derived by Hong Kong from its imports of foodstuffs produced in China. Aside from such imported inflation, urban dwellers in rapidly industrializing economies face other well-known sources of rising costs of living.

We can compare the situation of Hong Kong with that of rapidly expanding major cities in developing countries. As the city grows rapidly in income and population, its terms of trade vis-à-vis its rural hinterland tend to deteriorate. With the increase in income and population, the demand for food goes up. At the same time, supply from the surrounding area falls due to loss of land and labour to urban encroachment and rural-urban migration. Foodstuffs now have to be brought in over longer distances at higher costs. And this is additional to forces released by rapid industrialization that tend to steer the terms of trade between industry and agriculture in favour of agriculture. The supply response of agriculture tends to be quite inelastic in under-developed economies, due to limitations in production capability. Furthermore, as rural incomes rise because of higher prices of primary products, rural food consumption may increase, putting additional constraints on the marketed surplus. Such supply constraints have been recognized as a crucial factor limiting industrial growth in developing countries[11], as well as being the major structural constraint contributing to inflation in less developed countries.[12]

Understandably, these market adjustments were not allowed to work in the trade relationship between Hong Kong and China. Prices in China were administered. Particularly, price stability was a major policy goal of the Chinese Government, which remembered all too clearly the ruinous impact of hyperinflation in the late 1940's. Food prices, in particular, were held down in order to stabilize the cost of living and industrial wage rates.[13] Consumption was controlled through rationing. With the return to normalcy and improvements in agricultural production in the post-Korean War era, there was an increasing marketed agricultural surplus. As the major source of badly needed hard currencies, the Hong Kong market was apparently allotted a high priority. The net result was that Hong Kong was blessed with a highly elastic supply of food and raw materials during the period of rapid industrialization after the mid-1950's. Thus, instead of having to contend with an inelastic domestic supply of foodstuffs and increasingly expensive imported food, as the rapidly growing urban centres in developing countries typically face, Hong Kong was blessed with a perfectly elastic supply of foodstuffs from the vast rural hinterland of China, anxious to meet Hong Kong's requirements at administered stable prices. We shall refer to this privileged position as Hong Kong's 'special China connection'.

Considerable advantages have also been enjoyed by Hong Kong in its imports of wage goods from China, and for largely similar reasons. These items include clothing and footwear, household durable goods such as furniture, kitchen wares and hardware, and miscellaneous goods, ranging from medicine to toilet requisites. Together, they accounted for about 10 per cent of the budget of low-income households. Imports from China accounted for a major share of the market, particularly for the lower end of the price range. In clothing, for example, more than 40 per cent of total imports were from China. In a typical Third World city many of these wage goods will be supplied by the so-called 'informal sector', produced by labour-intensive methods and using indigenous materials. If the process of development succeeds in absorbing the excess supply of labour, prices of such informal sector products rise rapidly, at least keeping pace with the increase in wages for unskilled workers. For most of the period under consideration it was possible for Hong Kong to obtain wage goods from China at stable prices.

Among the newly industrialized countries in the Pacific Region, the inflationary impact of an inelastic supply of foodstuffs was observed in South Korea. Between 1963 and 1973, for example, the growth of food grain production fell far short of the growth in consumption, resulting in a drastic increase in imports. Rising food prices were considered to be the leading factor in inflation in the second half of 1960's.[14] In Singapore and Taiwan, government policies succeeded in controlling inflation. Developing countries in Latin America, in general, sustained high rates of inflation.

It is clear that many developing countries had to cope with relatively high rates of inflation during their period of rapid growth. Hong Kong has been fortunate in that it was immune to various structural inflationary pressures: an agricultural bottleneck, foreign exchange constraints, export instability and fiscal constraints. In spite of rapid growth, the cost of living was relatively stable in the 1950's and 1960's. This would not have been the case had China chosen to assert a more aggressive pricing policy. Given the highly inelastic demand for many of the foodstuffs — empirically established[15] — for which alternative sources of supply are not available, China could have substantially increased its foreign exchange earnings by charging what the market could bear.

In sum, Hong Kong would have had to pay far more for its foodstuffs in any of the following three situations: (a) world export food prices prevailing in Hong Kong, (b) Hong Kong dependent on its domestic supply for food, or (c) China existing its monopolistic power as the sole supplier or price leader in many of the food items. It should be noted that the effect of (b) or (c), but not both, can be additional to (a). It is a highly conjectural matter to determine what the magnitude of the food price inflation would have been, if one or more of the alternative situations had prevailed. The actual experience of 1972–9 provides a guide. We have noted that prices of food imported from China would have been 29 per cent more expensive in 1979, had China adjusted its export prices upward at the same rate as world export prices over the period. The difference works out to be just under a compound rate of 3 per cent per annum. In view of the general stability of food prices before 1972, China would easily have added this rate of surcharge as a measure for revenue maximization. In other words, our tentative conclusion is that without the benefit of its 'special China connection' Hong Kong's inflation rate of foodstuffs and some wage goods could easily have been 3 per cent more. Given the expenditure pattern of low-income households, this would have resulted in a 1–2 per cent increase in their cost of living.

III. Wage Responses to Higher Food Prices

The effect on Hong Kong of a creeping increase in the cost of living, resulting from higher prices for its food imports, must depend, to a large extent, on the response of wage rates. A straightforward projection is that wages would rise as a direct consequence, thus eroding the competitive edge of Hong Kong's manufacturing exports and slowing down the pace of economic growth. This appears to be the general opinion, explicit or implicit, of most observers. But this consequence is by no means inevitable. How a change in the cost of living affects wages in general, and industrial wages in particular, depends on the tightness of the labour market and the level of real wages, as well as on institutional factors in the local labour market. It is appropriate, therefore, to consider the issue over different phases of post-war development.

1952-9

Export-led industrialization proceeded at a brisk pace after 1952, judging from the very limited information available on domestic exports and employment in key industries.[16] Between 1953 and 1959, industrial employment in registered and recorded establishments increased at an annual rate of 12 per cent. The estimated annual growth of population over this period was 4.9 per cent, and the growth in the working-age population was much lower.[17] But wage rates for unskilled and semi-skilled workers in manufacturing industries remained practically unchanged over this period.[18] As retail prices were stable, there was also no change in real wages. Hence an increase in employment much faster than that of the labour force was accomplished without an increase in the level of wages. This suggests that the supply of industrial workers at the time was perfectly elastic. There was also a large excess supply of workers in the early 1950's. Thus the Lewis model of unlimited supplies of labour applies to the situation. Under this circumstance, how much a creeping increase in the cost of subsistence would affect nominal and real wages hinges on how the minimum wage was determined. In the Lewis model, the minimum is set by the average product of farmers.[19] Other considerations are cost of subsistence and what may be termed 'efficiency wage'. According to the latter, a certain level of real wages, above the subsistence cost, is necessary to maintain the efficiency of industrial workers.[20] The farm income parity explanation was clearly not applicable in Hong Kong. Because of political barriers, most of the recent migrants could not, or would not, return to mainland China. Also in the mid-1950's, the standard of living of industrial workers in Hong Kong was already much higher than that of their counterparts in China.[21] In other words, the then ruling wages were considerably above the cost of subsistence. The efficiency wage argument was employed by Riedel to explain the observed wage level.[22] According to this argument, wage rates should move in line with the cost of living. And it appears that this view is supported by data. Food prices went up noticeably in 1956 and 1959 (Table 5.5). Wages went up a year later, in 1957 and 1960. In fact, this was largely a statistical result, and had rather little to do with market forces. The wage figures we have for the period before 1958 refer mostly to wages paid by European-owned firms — mostly in public utilities, transport, and the dockyard (large, Westernized industrial undertakings) — as well as by the government.[23] In addition to a basic wage, these employers also paid a variable cost-of-living allowance, which is reflected in the reported wage statistics. But such an escalator clause arrangement was not common. Indeed, a distinctly dualistic economy existed in Hong Kong at the time, befitting a colonial economy. Employers in the formal sector might choose to maintain stable wages higher than the going rate for one reason or another: monopolistic power, industrial peace, or efficiency. But only a decreasing minority of workers found employment in this sheltered sector. It was recognized that wages paid by smaller firms were much lower, and their range much wider.[24] In addition, there were large numbers of casual workers employed at daily or piece-rates in industrial establishments of all sizes. Many more women and children worked at home for industrial undertakings through the putting-out system. Wages for this majority group of workers were more flexible and responsive to market forces. Indeed, forces of demand and supply could assert themselves without disturbing the wage structure *per se*. With a short-run increase in demand, an employer might offer a *de facto* increase in wages, without changing the pay scales, by changing the composition of his work force through relaxing job specifications, by increasing fringe benefits, by offering more generous incentive pay, or by raising the pay rate for overtime.

Therefore, the effect of a rising cost of living on wage rates has to be analysed in terms of separate layers of the labour force. Its impact on wages in the open sector must be effected through demand and supply. As China was not a market for Hong Kong's products, an increase in prices for food and wage goods imported from China will obviously have no effect on the demand for labour. With substantive under-employment, its effect on the labour supply is likely to be small. The opportunity cost of labour is leisure. For impoverished workers, leisure is not valued highly. We deduce that a gradual increase in living costs would not have affected wage movements in any significant way in the 1950's, when the economy was absorbing its excess supply of labour and wages were already above subsistence level. Given that manufactures in Hong Kong were price-takers in the world market, the pace of employment expansion and the resulting wage increases would have to be dictated by demand factors: demand for Hong Kong's products in the world market and supply of capital and entrepreurship for industrial expansion within Hong Kong.

According to this analysis, a gradual increase in the price of foodstuffs and wage goods from China in the 1950's need not have materially affected the growth of employment and output in the export-oriented industrial sector. The functional distribution of income would have changed little. Workers would have been relatively worse off as a result, because they would have spent a high proportion of their income on food and wage goods from China. However, this does not mean that they would have suffered an absolute decline in well-being. Even if the wage rates had not changed over this period, as suggested by official wage statistics, the average household income of working families must have increased in the course of rapid growth in industrial employment. Such an increase could have been brought about through changes in the industrial and occupational composition of the labour force, through an increase in the average number of hours worked per week, or by an increase in the number of earners per household.[25] A creeping inflation in the cost of living, at any realistic rate, would have reduced rather than eliminated their welfare gain over this period.

1959–68

For this period more reliable information on employment, wages and output is available. Employment was increasing rapidly. It went up by 33 per cent between the two census years of 1961 and 1971. By comparison, the population of prime age (20–64) rose by only 25 per cent

Table 5.5 INDUSTRIAL WAGES AND THE COST OF LIVING

Year	Wages of Manufacturing Workers			Retail Price Index (March 1947 = 100)		Consumer Price Index for Low-income Households (1963–4 = 100)	
	Average Daily Wages (HK dollars)		Index of Average Daily Nominal Wages (March 1964 = 100)				
	Unskilled	Semi-skilled		All Items Index	Food Index	All Items	Foodstuffs
	(1)	(2)	(3)	(4)	(5)	(6)	(7)
1953	4.25	5.75		121	132		
1954	4.00	5.75		118	126		
1955	4.00	5.75		114	119		
1956	4.00	5.75		118	126		
1957	4.50	6.50		119	127		
1958	4.25	6.00	60	117	123		
1959	4.25	6.00	64	126	140		
1960	5.00	6.75	73	121	129		
1961	5.00	6.75	78	122	132		
1962	5.00	6.75	82	120	127		
1963	7.15	8.40	87	123	132		
1964	7.15	11.05	100	127	136		

1965	8.42	11.05	110	127	136	102.3	103.5
1966	8.20	13.25	116	132	143	105.6	108.3
1967	9.50	13.80	125	144	164	112.8	120.6
1968	10.15	15.10	133			116.0	125.1
1969	10.30	15.25	142			120.3	132.5
1970	11.30	16.10	165			129.8	146.6
1971	11.85	17.65	195			133.9	151.7
1972			215			142.8	162.6
1973			245			170.1	203.2
1974			265			195.3	235.8
1975			265			196.5	230.4
1976			301			202.0	234.6
1977			338			213.8	250.5
1978			385			226.5	267.7
1979			462			252.9	296.4
1980			525			292.1	340.1

Sources: (1) and (2) Riedel, J. (1974), *The Industrialization of Hong Kong*, p. 97.
(3) Riedel, p. 99; and *Hong Kong Monthly Digest of Statistics*, various issues.
(4) and (5) *Hong Kong Statistics 1947-1967*, p. 144.
(6) and (7) 1965–76 from 'Modified Consumer Price Indexes'; and 1977–80 by extending the above series using the inflation rates in 'Consumer Price Index (A).' Data from *Hong Kong Annual Digest of Statistics* (1978), p. 86, and various issues of *Monthly Digest of Statistics*.

over the same period. The increase in employment was, therefore, accomplished through a more intensive use of the labour force. The most notable development here was a sharp increase in the labour force participation rate of females. The cause of this growth is to be found in the export-oriented manufacturing industries.[26] Employment in manufacturing as a whole went up by 47 per cent. Indications are that the slack in the labour market was largely worked off by the end of the 1950's. At the time of the 1961 Census, unemployment, including job seekers, was only 1.7 per cent of the labour force, and the labour force participation rate was already very high. The limitations of the concept of and data for unemployment for developing economies are well recognized. But many other indicators of a tightening labour market were reported in the early 1960's: increased participation by secondary workers, a labour shortage in certain localities or for certain types of employment (such as domestic help), and the ratio of vacancies to job seekers at employment bureaux. The most convincing indicator is, of course, wage rates.

As shown in both sets of wage statistics presented in Table 5.5, wage rates took a big jump in 1960. Thereafter, average nominal wages in manufacturing went up steadily, by 5 per cent or more per year. For the period 1959–68, the average rate of annual increase was 8.5 per cent, so that wage rates more than doubled over the period. In comparison, the cost of living was relatively stable over that time. Food prices went up by only 21 per cent between 1959 and 1968, and the cost of living for low-budget households by about 17 per cent. Consequently, real wages increased by about 78 per cent over this period.

Wages in the 1960's could no longer be tied directly to the cost of subsistence, because they were substantially above it. Under these circumstances, the most direct way for a change in the cost of living to affect wage rates is through collective bargaining. But the role of trade unions and collective bargaining was much weaker in the 1960's, compared with the previous decade. In the most dynamic manufacturing industries, which created all the new jobs at the time, unions were 'virtually non-existent'.[27] It would have had to have been these rapidly expanding industries which set the pace for wage increases. Atomistic competition existed for this segment of the labour market. Skills were not specific and were relatively easy to acquire. The industries were often newly developed — at least for Hong Kong, with little established practice or vested interest. Workers were mostly employed on a short-term basis, with a high mobility of workers between firms and between industries. In such a competitive labour market the impact of a change in the cost of living had to work through demand and supply. On the demand side, it is clear that there was little connection between export markets and the cost of living. On the supply side, the labour supply of prime males and heads of households is known to be wage-inelastic. For secondary workers, who formed a majority of the new recruits to manufacturing industries, the utility of their wage incomes would not have been much affected by a moderate increase in the cost of food and daily necessities (in as much as the latter did not precipitate an inflationary spiral). Their wages, or that part of their wages which they kept for themselves, were not spent on food and necessities from China, but on services and on consumer durables imported from other sources. Thus an increase in prices of foodstuffs would have had little effect on their willingness to work. Moreover, the system of cost-of-living allowances, which linked food prices to wages for those employed by the government and large employers in the 1950's, was abandoned in 1960.[28]

On theoretical grounds, therefore, we would not expect a moderate increase in the cost of foodstuffs imported from China, as hypothesized in the previous section, to effect significantly money wages in Hong Kong between 1959–68. Wage offers from the export-led industrial sector were largely determined by international demand. The observed increases in wages and employment opportunities resulted in an unprecedented improvement in the standard of living of the working class. A moderately higher rate of inflation in food prices should not have affected, in this circumstance, the overall supply of labour. A cursory comparison between the year-to-year changes in food prices or cost-of-living index and the wage index for industrial workers lends support to our deduction (a statistical analysis will be attempted later with a longer series).

1969–81

This was a most eventful epoch in the world economic scene. With the energy crisis, the long period of prosperity in Western industrialized countries came to an end. It was followed by double-digit inflation, the deepest post-war recession, and stagflation. Politically, China emerged from its isolation after 1972; and the drastic re-orientation of economic policy (the 'four modernizations') took place in the late 1970's. Each of these developments had a profound impact on Hong Kong. The industrialized Western countries are major markets for its exports. Hong Kong is completely dependent on imports for its energy consumption. And any major development in China has repercussions for Hong Kong. As a result of a general relaxation of socialist discipline, for example, 350,000 illegal immigrants entered Hong Kong in 1979–80. In view of such dependency, Hong Kong fared surprisingly well in this turmoil. Over the decade 1971–80 it achieved an average GDP growth of 9.6 per cent per annum, and a 7.0 per cent growth in per capita income, which are very similar figures to the 9.1 per cent and 7.0 per cent achieved between 1962–70.

For our purposes, the most significant development of this period was the acceleration of the rate of inflation. Between 1969–81 the annual increase in the cost of living for low-income households averaged 8.8 per cent, compared with 2.1 per cent for the decade of 1959–68. The dominant sources of this rising cost were food prices (which rose at an average rate of 9.3 per cent per annum) and energy-related expenditure (fuel and transport). As can be seen from Table 5.5, the rates of change fluctuated widely from year to year. At the same time, exports of manufactured products, and with them the demand for labour by industries, were also volatile. And the two did not always move together. This therefore provides an excellent opportunity to examine the relationship between the cost of living, wages and labour demand. The most notable development in this respect was the downward flexibility of industrial wages — not only real wages, but money wages as well. From the table, we note that there was no change in average wages in 1975. As it is not possible for all wages to stay unchanged, the wages in some industries must have fallen absolutely. Real wages fell sharply in both 1974 and 1975. These results suggest that demand factors played a dominant role in wage determination.

We employ regression analysis to evaluate the influence of the cost of living and labour market demand on money wages. The money wage of manufacturing workers, as presented in Table 5.5, is the dependent variable. To measure living costs for working class families, we use, alternatively, the consumer price index for low-income households and food prices (also presented in Table 5.5). Labour demand is represented, alternatively, by employment in manufacturing industries and real domestic exports. All variables are expressed as annual rates of change and linear regressions are fitted. The relationships are estimated over the period 1962–80. The results are presented in Table 5.6. Consider first the impact of the cost of living. As expected, there is a very high correlation between food prices and cost of living indexes in our data (a correlation coefficient of 0.96), so the use of one or other variable as regressor produces little change in the results (compare (1) and (2), or (1a) and (2a)). Both variables in their current or lagged form turn out to be statistically insignificant at the 5 per cent level. Theoretically, we would expect wages to respond to changes in living costs with a lag. This is particularly so in the present case, as the wage statistics pertain to the month of March. So equation (1a) or (2a) should be the appropriate formulation for testing the effect of changes in living costs on wages. Both relationships are, however, statistically highly insignificant. Regression coefficients for both cost variables are estimated with the wrong sign and are smaller than their standard errors. On the other hand, both variables used as proxies for change in labour demand, namely manufacturing employment and domestic exports, also fail to explain changes in the wage level. The coefficient for the employment variable is estimated with the wrong sign in both equations. And the value of exports is uncorrelated with wages.[29]

We argue, a priori, that in a highly competitive labour market, where wage rates are substantially above subsistence level, and demand for the finished products is likely to be price elastic, money wages will not be sensitive to moderate changes in the cost of living. The results of our empirical study lend support to this conclusion. Over the period 1962–80, when there were sharp fluctuations in both the inflation rate

Table 5.6 REGRESSION EQUATIONS OF WAGE DETERMINATION, 1962–80

Equation	Intercept	Regression Coefficients						R^2	D.W. Stats.
		CPI	CPI Lagged	Food Prices	Food Prices Lagged	Manufacturing Employment	Domestic Exports at Constant Prices		
(1)	8.34 (5.0)	0.376 (1.8)						0.163	1.47
(1a)	11.63 (6.3)		−0.120 (0.49)					0.015	1.51
(2)	8.58 (5.4)			0.300 (1.79)				0.159	1.42
(2a)	11.50 (6.7)				−0.086 (0.46)			0.013	1.53
(3)	12.84 (7.2)					−0.284 (1.6)		0.129	1.80
(4)	10.31 (4.4)						0.028 (0.16)	0.002	1.40
(5)	14.78 (5.4)		−0.268 (1.1)			−0.326 (1.52)		0.147	1.86
(6)	14.49 (5.6)				−0.195 (1.0)	−0.320 (1.5)		0.141	1.91

Notes: Numbers in parentheses are t-statistics (in absolute value). All variables are rates of growth.

and wage changes, there is no evidence that the magnitude of wage increases responded to preceding changes in the cost of living.

IV. The General Impact on Hong Kong's Growth Performance

A gradual but persistent increase in the cost of living due to higher prices for food imports from China would have a far-reaching effect on the growth performance of the Hong Kong economy. There are two channels of influence. The change in the cost of living would be accompanied by a transfer of income from Hong Kong to China. The size and incidence of such a transfer can be assessed by means of a comparative static analysis. Secondly, rising food prices would contribute to a higher rate of inflation, which has its own dynamic influence on economic growth.

Exports, Employment and Growth

Export-oriented manufacturing has long been the engine of growth in Hong Kong. Our analysis of the general impact on production and income of an acceleration of inflation and higher food prices would start with repercussions in this segment of the economy. As analysed above, industrial wage rates would not be appreciably affected by the hypothetical upward drift of living costs during any of the phases of development since the early 1950's. This being the case, there should be no short-run, direct impact on manufacturing exports. Faced with an unchanged wage structure, the composition and direction of exports would have stayed on its observed course of development over any given period.[30]

Alongside this export sector is the sheltered sector producing exclusively for the domestic market — services, food-processing, utilities, building and construction. The relationship between these two sectors can be explained in term of the Aukrust model developed for the open economy of Scandinavian countries.[31] Wage levels are determined by the open sector. Given wage rates, prices in the sheltered sector will be determined by labour productivity and normal profits. Of course, wage rates and multiplier effects of income growth from the open sector also determine the relative size of these two sectors, as well as the output and employment combination within the sheltered sector. In as much as the wage signal and income effect emitted from the open sector will not be significantly different, the impact on the sheltered sector will also be small. There is also an intermediate sector of truck farmers and producers of traditional consumer goods in direct competition with imports from China. But the size of this sector is exceptionally small in Hong Kong, and many of the workers belong to a non-competing group, so that the overall impact on the rest of the economy is likely also to be small.

In the long run, however, the higher rate of inflation and the resulting fall of real income will affect the supply of savings and hence capital formation. The cumulative effect can be significant, though its magnitude will be impossible to estimate for lack of data. The change is not of the Kaldor type resulting from redistribution of income between wages and profits. In our case, the functional distribution of income is left unchanged. Instead, the real income of all classes is depleted by rising costs of living. The impact on the working class would be especially heavy. Relatively large households not only spend a high proportion of their budget on purchasing foodstuffs, but the import content of their food bill is likely to be high. Rising import prices would effectively erode their discretionary income and hence their ability to save. In spite of their relatively low income, working class households have been observed to have a very high saving propensity.[32] There is also an effective institutional set-up for channelling such savings into productive investment. The industrial scene in Hong Kong is characterized by a large number of small enterprises. In most of these cases, the business was started by someone who was formerly a foreman, technician or salesman in the same line of work. To start their businesses, these entrepreneurs had to draw on their own savings, and to borrow from relatives, friends, or clansmen. According to a 1968 survey, 75 per cent of small factories were first established by entrepreneurs relying entirely on their own resources.[33]

In the long run, therefore, higher costs of living will lead to a decline in the supply of industrial capital in general, and the supply of capital to small enterprises in particular. This, in turn, would hamper the supply of entrepreneurship. The prospect of starting one's own business, of rising from rags to riches, is a strong stimulant for Hong Kong people to work hard, to pick up new skills, and to look out for opportunities. The result is an abundance of highly motivated Schumpeterian entrepreneurs who are quick to seize an opening in the market. This aggressiveness and adaptability has contributed directly to some of the spectacular successes in Hong Kong's export drive. The same outlook promotes an economy-wide dynamism, efficiency and single-minded economic motivation which has so amazed observers. This 'gung ho' spirit could have been a crucial factor in sustaining Hong Kong's high rate of growth. According to Robinson 'The state of the "animal spirits," which is largely a function of the energy and competitiveness of groups of firms, is the most important factor in capitalist development.'[34]

As a long-run effect, higher costs of living would undoubtedly slow down the momentum of Hong Kong's economic growth by curtailing the supply of capital, enterprise and general industriousness. The degree, and to some extent the nature, of the end result of such an impact depends on how far the hypothetical changes would erode the well-being and prospects of the working class. At the extreme, if upward mobility were effectively blocked, a new behaviourial norm of wage earners might evolve. Workers might turn to collective bargaining as a means of improving their economic well-being, and the government might be compelled to intervene in various ways to arbitrate conflicts between various segments of the economy. It is necessary, therefore, to assess the magnitude of the distributional consequences.

The Impact on the Distribution of Income and Welfare

Direct Effects

In accordance with Engel's Law, lower-income households spend a higher proportion of their income on foodstuffs. The burden of higher food prices must therefore fall disproportionately on low-income households, resulting in more inequality. The magnitude of such an effect and its overall impact on the size distribution of household income can be evaluated. We assess first the impact of the hypothetical change in China's pricing strategy on food costs. From results of the 1973–4 Household Expenditure Survey we note that about 24 per cent of food expenditure was spent on commodities for which China was not the dominant source of supply.[35] In addition, 'meals bought away from home' accounted for another 26 per cent of the food budget. Assuming that the cross elasticity of prices of restaurant meals with respect to prices of foodstuffs from China was 0.5, a 1 per cent increase in prices of foodstuffs from China will lead to an increase of food bills by about 0.66 per cent. And the hypothetical 3 per cent price increase will lead to an additional 2 per cent increase in food costs per annum. The cumulative effects of food costs depend, of course, on the initial year of the change in pricing. By 1957, the end of China's First Five-Year Plan, the transformation to collective ownership was completed, both in towns and in the countryside.[36] The hypothetical pricing strategy could conceivably have been initiated in 1958. The cumulative effect on food costs for various terminal years is calculated in Table 5.7. Another year of possible initiation, 1961, is included for purposes of comparison.

To calculate the distributional impact of such increases in food costs we need to know the propensity of food consumption by various income groups. We use the average propensity to consume estimated

Table 5.7 THE CUMULATIVE INFLATIONARY IMPACT ON FOOD COSTS IN HONG KONG OF HIGHER PRICES FOR FOODSTUFFS FROM CHINA

Initial Year	Resulting Increase in Food Costs in Selected Terminal Years (percentage)			
	1961	1971	1976	1981
1958	8.24	31.95	45.68	60.84
1961		21.90	34.59	48.59

for six different income groups by the National Income Branch of the Census and Statistics Department with data from the 1979–80 Household Expenditure Survey.[37] The proportion of expenditure spent on food can be readily obtained from results of household expenditure surveys.

We have estimated the distributional impacts on the two census years 1971 and 1981, for which income distribution data are available. In Table 5.8, results obtained for 1981 are presented in full. Statistics for observed size distribution of household income pertaining to February 1981 appear in Columns 1 to 4. Impacts of the higher cost of food derived above are worked out as in Columns 5 to 8. Using the consumption propensity shown in Column 5, along with the relevant weight of food expenditures obtained by the 1979–80 Household Expenditure Survey[38], we obtain total food expenditure for each income class. As a result of higher food prices, less food could be obtained with the given expenditure. This loss, evaluated at actual 1981 prices, is shown in Column 6. The incidence of this loss is shown in Column 7. We note that the incidence of this income loss is highly regressive. For the two lowest income groups, the erosion of their purchasing power amounts to more than 20 per cent of their income, but to only 6 per cent for the richest 5 per cent of households. The overall income inequality goes up by 4 per cent in terms of the Gini coefficient of concentration, or 4.5 per cent in terms of the Kuznets ratio.[39]

Similar calculations were made about the impact on the size distribution of income for 1971. The results are, generally, comparable. The burden of higher food costs falls disproportionately on lower-income households, eroding about 15 per cent of total income for the three bottom income groups, compared with a 4 per cent loss for the top income class. Overall, the Gini coefficient rises from 0.419 to 0.435, and the Kuznets ratio, from 60.64 to 62.93, a 3.8 per cent increase in the degree of inequality in both cases.

In all, we may say that the acceleration in food cost inflation resulting from the hypothetical changes of import prices would have brought about an appreciable increase in the inequality of income distribution. The magnitude, however, appears to be quite tolerable, given the social climate. It is much smaller than the actual increase in inequality between 1971 and 1981. More important, the cost represents a small part of the absolute gain in income and welfare over the period under consideration. The low-income groups would have suffered a 20 per cent loss in income in 1981 (Table 5.8). But that would be a cumulative effect of a change dating from 1958. Over the same period, real daily wages of manufacturing workers went up by 200 per cent.

On the other hand, it should also be noted that our calculation represents only part of the undesirable distributional impact of rising food costs, and an underestimation at that. The result is biased downward, because it is calculated on the assumption that food expenditure remained unchanged, in spite of much higher food prices. But the demand for food is inelastic. More would have been spent on it, and the actual impact would surely have been larger. Additionally, the income distribution itself would have been affected by the higher rate of inflation, lower growth and reduced scope for upward mobility analysed earlier. We shall turn to consider briefly such long-term effects.

Long-term Effects

A more rapidly rising level of food prices would have added to the rate of inflation, which started to accelerate after the mid-1960's. By and large, inflation itself has a detrimental impact on income distribution. This is effected through three channels: expenditure effects, functional distribution of income and asset structure. The poor will suffer more from inflation if the prices of goods and services that they buy go up more rapidly than the prices of those bought by the rich. This impact is accounted for in the direct effects just discussed. A classical hypothesis on the redistributive effect of inflation is that money wages tend to lag behind prices, resulting in a fall in the share of wage income. Finally, low-income households are less able to protect their net worth against the erosion of inflation, because a higher proportion of their assets are fixed in monetary terms: cash, deposits, bonds and insurance savings.

We have already noted the weak correlation between wage changes and the rate of inflation in our discussion on wage determination. To decide whether a wage lag existed we shall compare growth rates of wages, prices and income over two periods: 1960–70, characterized by

Table 5.8 THE IMPACT OF HIGHER FOOD COSTS ON THE SIZE DISTRIBUTION OF HOUSEHOLD INCOME, 1981 (land households)

Household Income (HK dollars)	Number of Households	Total Income (thousand HK dollars)	Percentage Share of Households	Percentage Share of Income	Average Consumption Propensity	Loss of Income due to Higher Food Prices (thousand HK dollars)	Percentage Income Loss	Revised Income Share
	(1)	(2)	(3)	(4)	(5)	(6)	(7)	(8)
Under 600	66,959	26,784	5.41	0.51	1.00	5,674	21.2	0.45
600–999	50,763	35,534	4.10	0.68	1.00	7,125	20.1	0.60
1,000–1,499	112,683	101,415	9.10	1.95	1.00	18,799	18.5	1.75
1,500–1,999	123,231	154,084	9.96	2.96	1.00	25,648	16.6	2.73
2,000–2,499	156,481	352,082	12.64	6.76	0.87	49,827	14.2	6.42
2,500–2,999	119,935	329,821	9.69	6.33	0.87	46,677	14.2	6.01
3,000–3,999	199,242	697,347	16.10	13.39	0.78	80,250	11.5	13.10
4,000–4,999	123,889	557,501	10.01	10.71	0.77	60,086	10.8	10.56
5,000–5,999	84,157	462,863	6.80	8.89	0.70	40,448	8.7	8.97
6,000–7,999	90,992	636,944	7.35	12.23	0.61	48,504	7.6	12.49
8,000–9,999	42,439	381,951	3.43	7.33	0.61	24,679	6.5	7.58
10,000 and over	66,872	1,471,184	5.40	28.25	0.61	88,269	6.0	29.35
All land households	1,237,643	5,207,510	100.00	100.00		495,986	9.5	100.00
Gini coefficient				0.481				0.500
Kuznets ratio				68.84				71.90

Sources: Census and Statistics Department (1982), *Hong Kong 1981 Census, Basic Tables*, pp. 42–3; and Census and Statistics Department (1981), *Report of the Household Expenditure Survey, 1979-80 and the New Consumer Price Index System*, pp. 176–93.

high income growth and a low rate of inflation, and 1971–81, characterized by high income growth and a high rate of inflation. The relevant information is presented in Table 5.9.

In the 1960's, when the rate of inflation was low, the rapid growth in money wages resulted in a growth in real wages comparable to that of per capita GDP. Therefore, even if there were no change in the labour force participation rate of low-income, wage-earner households, they would have managed to maintain their relative income position. In the 1970's, the outcome was quite different. While the growth of money wages managed to overtake the high rate of inflation, it left a growth in real wages much smaller than the growth of per capita real income. The relative income of working-class households deteriorated sharply over the decade. This conclusion is borne out by statistics on the size distribution of household incomes. The Gini coefficient of income concentration fell sharply from 0.487 to 0.411 between 1966 and 1971, and we have reason to believe that the improvement started in the early 1960's.[40] The situation reversed itself during the 1970's. The Gini coefficient went up sharply from 0.417 to 0.487 between 1971 and 1981. In sum, experiences in Hong Kong support the wage-lag hypothesis.

Systematic information on the asset structure of various income

Table 5.9 THE RATE OF GROWTH IN CONSUMER PRICES, WAGES AND INCOME (percentage)

Period (inclusive)	General Consumer Price Index[a]	Wages for Workers in Manufacturing Industry (March)		Per Capita GDP (constant market prices)[c]
		Nominal[a]	Real[c]	
A. 1959–69	2.3	–	–	–
1960–70	–	8.6	6.7	7.0*
B. 1970–80	8.7	–	–	–
1971–81	–	12.5	2.7	7.5

[a] Average annual growth rate.

[c] Compounded annual rate of growth between the two terminal years.

* For 1961–70.

classes is not available for Hong Kong. But given the conspicuous movements of asset prices over the past two decades, the direction and significance of the distributional impact of inflation-induced appreciation of certain assets is unequivocal. For over two decades, real estate prices sustained an almost uninterrupted double-digit growth in Hong Kong. Between 1959 and 1970, the average price per square foot of industrial land in the metropolitan areas (excluding the New Territories) went up from HK$9.70 to HK$102.90.[41] Comparable gains were probably achieved by residential land, while prime commercial sites appreciated even more. Between 1968 and 1981, the index for domestic rents of large flats went up from a base of 100 to 1,111! For flats of smaller sizes, the gain was from 100 to about 760. Between 1976 and 1981, the average purchase price of small flats went up from $2,723 per square metre to $10,450 per square metre, a 3.8-fold increase over five years! This appreciation of real assets was, of course, a world-wide phenomenon in the 1970's. People everywhere were snatching up precious metals, rare coins, antiques, pieces of art, as well as real properties, as a hedge against inflation. In Hong Kong, the overwhelming preference was for real estate. Land has always been a favoured store of value for the Chinese. And the absolute scarcity of land in Hong Kong added to its appeal. The distributional consequences of this development should be obvious. The distribution of real estate properties is much more unequal than that of income. Mostly reacting to the property boom, prices of common stocks also registered spectacular gains between 1969 and 1973, and again between 1978 and 1981. Only the rich and the upper-middle-income class had access to such capital gains. Gold provided, perhaps, a countervailing development. Gold is a favourite store of value for low-income households, and the price of gold held out quite well over this period. But there is little question that, for the period under consideration, its influence on income distribution was swamped by that of the property boom.

A reduction in the ability to save referred to earlier affects equity over the long term in two ways. Directly, it reduces the opportunities for upward mobility. Aspiring entrepreneurs of working-class origin find it more difficult to assemble the initial investment by pooling their own savings with those of their relatives and friends. The motivation to hard work is also undermined for the same reason. Moreover, parents have less to invest in their children's education. Children of the poor, in particular, may be compelled to leave school at an early age in order to augment the family income. With a minimum of education, they are destined to unskilled jobs, and poverty is transmitted to the next generation. Indirectly, a slowing down of growth tends to hurt the poor relatively more. They are more likely to be unskilled, or semi-skilled workers, employed on a casual basis at piece-rates or daily rates.[42] With a reduction in labour demand, they are the first to lose their jobs. The poor are likely to suffer in yet another way. A less buoyant economy would result in a fall in government revenue. Given the balanced budget policy of the government, this would be matched by a reduction in public expenditure. It is almost certain that social expenditure, which expanded rapidly during the 1970's, would be the prime target for trimming.

V. Conclusion

A standard query in discussing Hong Kong's remarkable economic performance in recent decades is the replicability of this experience elsewhere, in view of Hong Kong's many specific circumstances. One of the historically special factors alleged was the supply of foodstuffs, consumer goods and raw materials from China at concessionary prices. In this paper we have examined first the nature and extent of cost advantages derived by Hong Kong from imports of foodstuffs and wage goods from China. And secondly, we have assessed the effect of such an advantage on Hong Kong's overall economic performance.

It was indeed a special advantage for Hong Kong to be provided with a dependable supply of foodstuffs and certain wage goods from China at stable prices. This elastic supply of primary products to an urban conglomerate resulted from political considerations, a special blessing for Hong Kong that we referred to as its 'special China connection'. Prices of foodstuffs imported from China have certainly been lower than could have been obtained from other sources. But the magnitude of such price advantages, and hence the size of the benefits enjoyed by Hong Kong from its food imports, cannot be determined objectively. Market forces were not operative on the supply side. Many of the products sold to Hong Kong could not have been exported to other markets — such as live animals, fresh vegetables, fruit and fish. On the demand side, alternative sources of supply might not have been feasible for many of these products. One can only postulate some alternative pricing behaviour and deduce how and how much it would have affected the course of Hong Kong's economic development. On the basis of comparative movements between prices charged by China for its food exports to Hong Kong and prices of food exports in the world market in the 1970's, we concluded that China could have marked up the prices of its food exports by an average of an extra 3 per cent per year over this period to keep up with world inflation. Considering the market power enjoyed by China, and the supply constraints of agricultural products that market economies had to contend with in the process of industrialization, such a mark-up could have been initiated much earlier. So we assume that China started to mark up the prices of those foodstuffs and wage goods, for which it was the leading supplier, after it had completed its collectivization in 1957. Our prime interest is in deducing how the growth process would have responded to such a change.

Our attempt to unhinge the direct link between money wages and a moderate rise in the cost of living represents a crucial postulate of the paper. It is based on the following considerations: an initial standard of living for industrial workers considerably above the subsistence level in the early 1950's, sustained increases in real wages and a rapid rise in living standards for two decades, much of the labour demand originating from export-oriented manufacturing built up largely with imported capital, and a highly competitive labour market conspicuous for its lack of collective bargaining. Our conclusion is supported by the results of regression analysis of wage movements between 1962–80. In particular, wage behaviour over the 1974–5 recession provides strong support for our view. Responding to falling labour demand, both money and real wages were flexible downward.

In the long run, higher prices for imported foodstuffs would slow down the economic growth of Hong Kong. This is an obvious conclusion. The hypothesized change represents a transfer of income from Hong Kong to China. Part of this must be at the expense of domestic savings, resulting in a lower rate of capital formation. We also noted that the impact would be more far-reaching than this. Because of the regressive nature of the impact, not only investible funds but also the spirit of enterprise and hard work would be depleted.

More tangible results are obtained for the impact on income distribution. As is well known, the incidence of rising food prices tends to be highly regressive. The partial effect of the postulated upward adjustment of prices of imported foodstuffs from China would have led to a 4.5 per cent increase in inequality in the size distribution of household income. As more would be spent on food at higher prices by each income class, the actual impact would be larger. Even so, the degree of deterioration in income equality brought about by this change would have been smaller than the one actually observed between 1971 and 1981, brought about by recession and inflation. As such, the specific distribution effect would not have upset the social equilibrium.

In sum, the cost advantages enjoyed by Hong Kong from the supply of foodstuffs and wage goods from China have been an important contributing factor to Hong Kong's rapid growth. But they were not a crucial factor. A realistic upward revision of the prices of such imports, either to keep pace with prices in the international market, or as a means to siphon off part of the increase in income to China, would not have jeopardized Hong Kong's rapid growth and full employment, given the vigour and resiliency of its economic machinery. A deterioration in its terms of trade similar to the cumulated effect of the postulated price changes materialized overnight from the quadrupling of oil prices in the 1973 energy crisis, which also touched off the deepest post-war recession. The rapid recovery of the Hong Kong economy since 1976 is a convincing testimony to its economic strength.

Notes

[1] Results from a couple of unpublished studies on the subject will be discussed in the text.

[2] The land area under food production fell by 30 per cent between 1958 and 1977. Between 1961 and 1981 the working population in agriculture and fishing fell by 49 per cent; its share of the total working population went down from 7.3 per cent to 2.1 per cent.

[3] The average daily wage for skilled and semi-skilled manufacturing workers in 1963–4 was HK$12.8, see Riedel (1974), p. 97. The corresponding monthly earnings, for 26 working days, would be HK$333.

[4] The point was emphasized by K.R. Chou (1966), p. 7; reiterated by Turner *et al.* (1980), p. 158; and referred to by almost everyone writing about the economic growth of Hong Kong.

[5] Hsueh and Woo (1981), p. 10.

[6] Hang Seng Bank Research Department (1975), p. 12.

[7] Hang Seng Bank Research Department (1975), pp. 6–7 and 43–5.

[8] Woo made an extensive comparison of unit values between imports from China and imports from other sources, see Woo (1977), p. 166–86. Interestingly, price differentials were small for such standardized items as eggs and peanut oil.

[9] Woo (1977), p. 40.

[10] Food items included are: rice, fresh vegetables, live cattle, live pigs, meat and meat preparations, fish and fish preparations, fruit and eggs. They were weighted according to values of imports (from China) over 1968–70.

[11] Kaldor (1960), pp. 239–42; and Robinson (1956), pp. 48–9.

[12] Kirkpatrick *et al.* (1976), pp. 132–3.

[13] S.H. Chou (1966), pp. 653–63.

[14] Kim (1976), pp. 27 and 29.

[15] Using 1954–64 data, Tang found that the price elasticity of food consumption was statistically insignificant, see Tang (1969), p. 51. Hsueh and Woo found that the price elasticity of demand for foodstuff imports from China was about 0.6, see Hsueh and Woo (1981), p. 17.

[16] K.R. Chou (1966), pp. 40 and 51.

[17] Chau (1976), p. 87.

[18] Riedel (1974), pp. 93 and 97.

[19] Lewis (1954), p. 409.

[20] Robinson (1956), p. 49.

[21] Szczepanik (1958), pp. 71–2.

[22] Riedel (1974), pp. 82–3.

[23] It was clearly so specified with the presentation of these wage statistics in the *Annual Reports* for the early 1950's. The coverage was broadened after 1955, complicating the comparability of the series.

[24] In 1953, for example, the reported daily wages for unskilled workers ranged from HK$3.50 to HK$5.00, but it was noted that daily wages in Chinese firms could be as low as HK$2 (HK$1.50 in certain unskilled jobs for women), see *Hong Kong Annual Report* (1953), pp. 26–7. Similar observations were made for other years.

[25] In as much as 'efficiency wage' should be defined in terms of take-home pay rather than wage rate, and in terms of household income rather than income of the primary earner, the connection between wage rates and the cost of living is weakened in a rapidly growing economy.

[26] Chau (1976), pp. 103–6.

[27] England and Rear (1975), p. 88.

[28] England and Rear (1975), p. 284.

[29] In this connection we should note the limitations of the data. Data on employment are much less accurate than those on the cost of living. Before 1974, data pertains to employment in establishments registered or recorded by the Labour Department (establishments using power-driven machines or employing more than five persons); since 1974, all manufacturing establishments are covered. For the export variable, the correlation between real exports and labour demand is complicated by changes in product mix and 'trading up', both of which were quite important for Hong Kong.

[30] We abstract from our discussion the effect of any change in the costs of raw materials and intermediate products imported from China concomitant to the hypothetical change in China's pricing strategy.

[31] Our analysis parallels the version developed by Edgren *et al.*, based on the experience of Sweden, see Edgren *et al.* (1969), pp. 145–52.

[32] Topley (1969), p. 208.

[33] Owen (1971), p. 192.

[34] Robinson (1971), p. 108.

[35] Supply of the following foodstuffs was not dominated by China: rice, fresh salt-water fish, fresh fruits, milk and milk powder, coffee, fruit juices and other soft drinks, butter and cheese, sugar and confectionery.

[36] King (1968), pp. 184–5.

[37] Census and Statistics Department, National Income Branch (1981), pp. 64–7.

[38] Census and Statistics Department (1981), pp. 176–93.

[39] The Kuznets ratio is the sum of absolute differences between the shares of total income and the shares of income recipients over all income classes. Its calculation does not involve any approximation, as is the case with the Gini coefficient. As such it is useful for assessing the change in the degree of inequality.

[40] Hsia and Chau (1978), pp. 142–3 and 147.

[41] Jao (1976), p. 301.

[42] 'Hong Kong employment contracts are notable for a distinction among three types of workers — ... permanent employees, ... long-term casual workers, and short-term casuals. This distinction is reflected in very different degrees of security ...' Turner (1980), p. 47.

References

Caves, R.E. (1976), 'Looking at Inflation in the Open Economy,' in D.A. Belsley *et al.* (eds.), *Inflation Trade and Taxes, Essays in Honour of Alice Bourneuf* (Columbia, Ohio State University Press), pp. 75–95.

Census and Statistics Department (1975), *The Household Expenditure Survey 1973-74 and the Consumer Prices Indexes* (Hong Kong, Government Printer).

—— (1981), *Report of the Household Expenditure Survey, 1979-80 and the New Consumer Price Index System* (Hong Kong, Government Printer).

Census and Statistics Department, National Income Branch (1981), *Household Consumption Analysis of Hong Kong* (unpublished).

Chau, L.C. (1976), 'Industrial Growth and Employment in Hong Kong,' *Philippine Economic Journal*, 15(1 and 2), pp. 82–138.

Chou, K.R. (1966), *The Hong Kong Economy, A Miracle of Growth* (Hong Kong, Academic Publications).

Chou, S.H. (1966), 'Prices in Communist China,' *Journal of Asian Studies*, 25(4), pp. 645–63.

Commerce and Industry Department, Statistics Branch (1965), *The Household Expenditure Survey, 1963/64 and the Consumer Price Index* (Hong Kong, Government Printer).

Edgren, G., *et al.* (1969), 'Wages, Growth and the Distribution of Income,' *Swedish Journal of Economics*, 71, September, pp. 133–60.

England, J., and Rear, J. (1975), *Chinese Labour under British Rule* (Hong Kong, Oxford University Press).

Hang Seng Bank Research Department (1975), 'China's Support of the Hong Kong Economy', mimeograph.

Hang Seng Economic Quarterly (1982), 'Hong Kong–China Trade,' January, 8–17.

Hopkins, K. (ed.) (1971), *Hong Kong: the Industrial Colony* (Hong Kong, Oxford University Press).

Hsia, R., and Chau, L. (1978), *Industrialization, Employment and Income Distribution* (London, Croom Helm).

Hsueh, T.T., and Woo, T.O. (1981), 'Trade between Hong Kong and China,' University of Hong Kong, Centre of Asian Studies working paper, No. CC 12.

Jao, Y.C. (1976), 'Land-Use Policy and Land Taxation in Hong Kong,' in J. Wong (ed.), *The Cities of Asia: A Study of Urban Solutions and Urban Finance* (Singapore, University of Singapore Press), pp. 277–303.

Jarvie, I.C. (ed.) (1969), *Hong Kong: A Society in Transition* (London, Routledge & Kegan Paul).

Kaldor, N. (1960), *Essays on Economic Stability and Growth* (London, Duckworth).

Kim, Y.W. (1976), 'Evaluation of Economic Growth in 1960's,' in Institute of Development Economies, *Performance and Perspective of the Korean Economy* (Tokyo).

King, F.H.H. (1968), *A Concise Economic History of Modern China* (Bombay, Vora & Co).

Kirkpatrick, C.H., and Nixson, F.I. (1976), 'The Origins of Inflation in Less Developed Countries,' in M. Parkin and G. Zis (eds.), *Inflation in Less Developed Countries* (Manchester, Manchester University Press), pp. 126–74.

Lewis, W.A. (1954), 'Economic Development with Unlimited Supplies of Labour,' in A.N. Agarwala and S.P. Singh (eds.), *The Economics of Underdevelopment* (London, Oxford University Press, 1958), pp. 400–49.

Lewis, W.A. (1964), 'Closing Remark,' in W. Baer and I. Kerstenetzky (eds.), *Inflation and Growth in Latin America* (New Haven, Yale University Press), pp. 21–53.

Lupton, C.M. (1972), 'Hong Kong's Role in Sino-Western Trade,' in A.A. Stahnke (ed.), *China's Trade with the West* (London, Praeger), pp. 175–208.

Mah, Feng-hwa (1971), *The Foreign Trade of Mainland China* (Chicago, Aldine Atherton).

Owen, N. (1971), 'Economic Policy in Hong Kong,' in K. Hopkins (ed.), *Hong Kong: the Industrial Colony* (Hong Kong, Oxford University Press), pp. 141–206.

Riedel, J. (1974), *The Industrialization of Hong Kong* (Tubingen, J.C.B. Mohr (Paul Siebeck)).

Robinson, J. (1956), *The Accumulation of Capital* (London, Macmillan).

—— (1971), *Economic Heresies* (London, Macmillan).

Szczepanik, E. (1958), *The Economic Growth of Hong Kong* (London, Oxford University Press).

Tang, A.M. (1969), *Long-term Economic and Agricultural Commodity Projections for Hong Kong, 1970, 1975, and 1980* (Hong Kong, Chinese University, Economic Research Centre).

Topley, M. (1969), 'The Role of Savings and Wealth among Hong Kong Chinese,' in I.C. Jarvie (ed.), *Hong Kong: A Society in Transition* (London, Routledge & Kegan Paul, 1969), pp. 167–227.

Turner, H.A. (1980), *The Last Colony: but Whose?* (Cambridge, Cambridge University Press).

Warren, B. (1977), *Inflation and Wages in Underdeveloped Countries* (London, Cass).

Woo, T.O. (1977), 'Imports from China: Its Impact on Hong Kong's Manufactured Export Performance' (Unpublished M. Phil thesis, The Chinese University of Hong Kong).

Yeung, P. (1970), 'Trade ties between Hong Kong and Mainland China,' *Asian Survey*, September, X(9), 820–39.

—— (1974), 'Patterns of Trade between Mainland China and Hong Kong,' *Hong Kong Economic Papers*, March, 46–64.

6. On Some Problems of Modelling Chinese Economic Growth

FU-SEN CHEN and TOW CHEUNG*

I. Introduction

This chapter discusses the application of some standard models to the analysis of Chinese economic growth. We will suppose that the following two conditions are essential characteristics of the economic system of China:

(a) a fixed quantity of land suitable for economic activity, which is fully utilized; and

(b) a large population growing at an appreciable rate over time.

We make no defence for putting emphasis on these two factors, except to say that perhaps even the most casual observation would suggest that they are rather crucial aspects of the problem of economic development in China.[1]

Section II of this chapter contains a discussion of agricultural development in China. Agriculture has always played an important role in the Chinese economic system, and its development is one of the objectives of the 'Four Modernizations' programme. In Section II, a simple macromodel of the agricultural sector is used to study some problems associated with rent and income distribution suggested by the work of L.V. Kantorovich on efficient allocation and growth in a socialist economy.[2]

* The authors are much indebted to C.H. Chai for many helpful comments and suggestions.

In Section III the discussion is extended to the Chinese economy as a whole, by means of a closed linear growth model. The possibility of balanced growth is studied, even with the limitations imposed by a fixed quantity of land.

II. A Ricardian Model of Chinese Agriculture

This section owes its origin to some questions arising from the efficient use of land, rent and land taxation in socialist agriculture, which are associated with the work of Kantorovich. He has shown, in a model of short-term planning of crop allocation, how it is possible to calculate rent in terms of the shadow prices ('objectively determined valuations') of a linear programming problem. Rent is imputed as a cost for the use of more productive plots of land as compared with 'marginal' land, which carries no rent. Kantorovich then argues that it is essential for the efficient use of land that rent should be taken into account as a factor price in costing. He writes:

> In solving problems of the use of natural resources which are more efficient but in short supply, their use must be determined by allowing for differential rent. If rent is included in expenditure, then the principle of least cost is observed in the optimal plan.[3]

This analysis has important implications for the development of agriculture in a socialist economy. As Kantorovich points out:

> The correct accounting of rent holds especially great importance for agriculture. Such accounting would lead to significant changes in prices on agricultural products and in financial relationships between agricultural enterprises and the government.[4]

However, the problems of rent and land scarcity, and their relationship with agricultural development, are not discussed in Kantorovich's works on growth models, which are generally one sector models with constant returns to scale technology.[5] In this section we will try to incorporate Kantorovich's observations into a growth model of

Chinese agriculture. In particular, we are interested in the consequences of the imputation of rent on income distribution and growth. We will work with a simple model of the agricultural sector, considered as an independent sub-economy of a multi-sector system. We will first describe the model, and then try to find some reasonable assumptions under which the approach is justified.[6]

From the discussion in Section I it seems clear that a model of Chinese agriculture must be based on an assumption of the scarcity of arable land in what Marshall called an 'old country',[7] where farming has been an occupation for a long period of time. This requirement immediately suggests Ricardo, for as Hicks has shown, Ricardo's one sector ('corn') model treats the economy as if it were a giant farm operating in more or less the conditions that we require.[8] It seems useful, therefore, to use Ricardo's corn model as the starting point of the discussion.

A fundamental characteristic of Ricardo's corn model is that there is a fixed quantity of land, with continuously declining fertility.[9] We will initially suppose, for simplicity, that inputs to agriculture consist of labour alone, which produces a single crop, 'corn'. Machinery inputs will be introduced later, after the properties of the simple model have been established.

If we write X as the output of corn per 'year' (period of production), the agricultural production function can be written:[10]

$$\text{(II.1)} \quad X = f(N).$$

Ricardo's assumption of diminishing returns is then represented by the conditions:

$$\text{(II.2)} \quad f'(N) > 0, \quad f''(N) < 0.$$

We add the Pasinetti viability condition:

$$\text{(II.3)} \quad f'(0) > \bar{x}$$

where $\bar{x}$ is Ricardo's natural wage, which will be given a different interpretation in our model.

The most important consequence of the assumption of diminishing returns is the existence of a producer's surplus in agricultural production. Under Ricardo's assumptions, land is leased out to competitive capitalist farmers by its owners. In this case, the producer's surplus is paid to the landlord class as rent.[11] In the standard treatments of Ricardo, for example, that of Kaldor (1960) and Pasinetti (1960, 1977), this is shown (together with the other income shares of profits and wages) in Fig. 6.1 below.

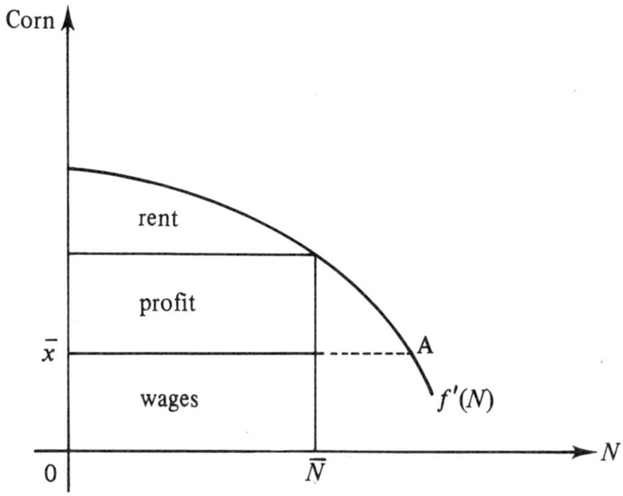

Fig. 6.1 Pasinetti's Ricardo diagram.

There is, however, one difficulty, as noted for example by Hicks and Hollander (1977). The diagram refers to some point on the equilibrium growth path which is not the stationary state. As Pasinetti writes:

> Ricardo investigates the properties of his system at a very particular stage of the whole movement, which he considers to be the relevant one. Most of his analysis is carried on as if the demographic mechanism has already fully worked through, while the capital accumulation process has not yet been completed.[12]

In Fig. 6.1, then, the natural wage $\bar{x}$ is that wage at which the population is constant. However, profits are positive, so by assumption there is an accumulation of capital (wage fund). But if the wage fund increases, the population and the real wage cannot remain at the natural level. The diagram therefore shows at any given moment of time both a fixed real wage and a tendency for it to increase.[13]

However, it seems possible to interpret the Ricardo diagram as a model of socialist agriculture, without the difficulty noted above. It is an essential feature of a socialist economy that everybody is employed. Applying this principle to agriculture, at any moment of time the margin of cultivation is determined by the number of farm workers.[14] Given the margin, the amount of producer's surplus is found by the Pasinetti equation:[15]

$$\text{(II.4)}\quad PS = f(0) + \int_0^N [f'(z) - f'(N)]\,dz$$
$$= f(N) - Nf'(N),$$

where PS is producer's surplus measured in terms of corn, and N is the number of agricultural workers, which is given at any moment of time.

In a socialist system, property rights over land are held by the farmers themselves. (We can perhaps imagine the agricultural sector to be a giant co-operative, or a giant commune.) In this case, the producer's surplus becomes an imputed rent R, which is Kantorovich's result.

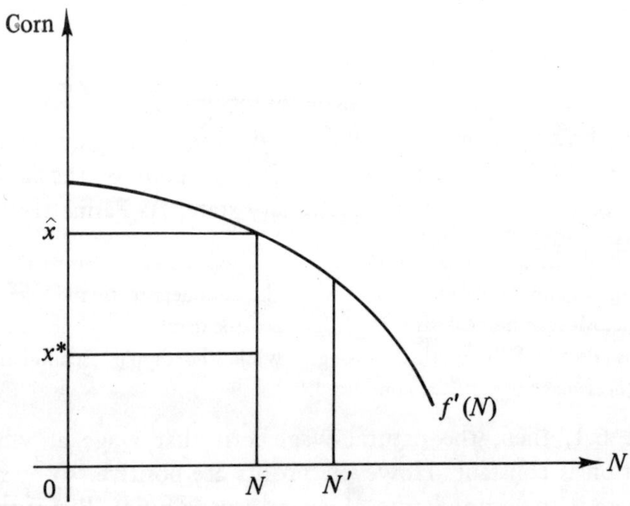

Fig. 6.2 Ricardo diagram for socialist agriculture.

The distribution of the output of corn net of rent can also be determined by the socialist principle of total employment. We can look at two instances. In the first case, the maximum wage at which total employment is possible is equal to $\hat{x}$ in Fig. 6.2. (Note $\hat{x}$ is equal to the marginal product of labour.) In this case, the wage bill is equal to the whole of output net of rent, or $W = X - R$. Accumulation is still possible because there is a surplus available in the form of imputed rent. However, the level of consumption $\hat{x}$ is not sustainable; if there is population growth so that the work force next year is N', the maximum real wage would fall.

The next case is one in which the real wage is constant over time. By the socialist principle, at any point of time the demand and supply of farm workers are required to be equal. The demand for labour, or more correctly, the relationship between the real wage and the number of workers supportable by a given wage fund at any moment of time, can be expressed as:

$$\text{(II.5)} \quad N^D = \frac{W}{x},$$

while supply is given by the agricultural population, say N. The condition of total employment then requires that:

$$\text{(II.6)} \quad \frac{W}{x} = N$$

in which case, the real wage should be set a certain level, say x^*, such that the given wage fund is equal to the wage bill for total employment.[16]

Let us suppose that population grows at some positive rate $n = n(t)$. Then, a continuous equality between the demand and supply of agricultural labour can be maintained at a constant real wage, if the following condition holds:

$$\text{(II.7)} \quad \frac{\dot{W}}{W} = \frac{\dot{N}}{N} = n, \text{ for all } t.$$

As we shall see, equations (II.7) require that the rate of growth of population n should be an endogenous variable, unlike the case in neo-classical models.

So we can see that, unlike Ricardo's case, in our socialist model it is possible to have a constant real wage with a growing population. This constant wage we can define as a natural wage, in the sense that it is the wage at which the labour force grows at the same rate as the wage fund, such that the socialist principle of total employment is satisfied at all points of time. If we imagine that (II.5) and (II.6) refer to the initial conditions of the model (so that, $W = W(0)$ and $N = N(0)$ at '$t = 0$'), then the natural wage is the maximum sustainable consumption per head which is consistent with the given initial conditions and the socialist principle of total employment. If we wish, we can therefore interpret x^* as a measure of permanent consumption in the socialist agricultural model.

Let us call the natural wage defined by (II.5) to (II.7) the socialist natural wage, to distinguish it from the Ricardian natural wage. In Fig. 6.2 this is given as x^*; and with the real wage equal to x^*, corn output net of imputed rent is divided into a wage bill (wage fund) and a surplus S.[17] We can write, using (II.1), (II.4) and (II.6),

$$\text{(II.8)} \quad S = X - R - W = N[f'(N) - x^*] \geqq 0.$$

S is a surplus in the classical sense (such that its dual is profits), as explained, for example, in Walsh and Gram (1980).

To complete the model, we need a relationship describing capital accumulation. Let us try the simple assumption that the commune authorities follow a directive to invest the entire surplus from agriculture. On our assumption at any point of time, agricultural capital is equal to the wage fund; so we have:

$$\text{(II.9)} \quad W = K,$$

and

$$\text{(II.10)} \quad \dot{K} = R + S.$$

Let us study the case in which the real wage is equal to the socialist natural wage. The properties of the model at any point of time can then be summarized by the following eight equations:

$$\text{(II.1)} \quad X = f(N)$$

$$\text{(II.4)} \quad R = f(N) - Nf'(N)$$

(II.6) $W = Nx$

(II.8) $S = N[f'(N) - x]$

(II.9) $W = K$

(II.10) $\dot{K} = R + S$

(II.7) $\frac{\dot{W}}{W} = \frac{\dot{N}}{N} = n.$

The endogenous variables of the model are: X, N, R, W, K, S, n and x. Since (II.6) and (II.7) describe what may be called equilibrium conditions, we may say that the eight equations depict a momentary equilibrium of the system.

We must now pause to ask: does the model make any sense? In particular, is it valid to construct a model of the agricultural sector, independent of the other sectors of the economy? A similar problem confronted Ricardo with his corn model, and we know how he was forced to extend it to include an industrial sector ('gold') and to develop a theory of relative prices (the labour theory of value). However, it appears that this problem can be avoided here. The reason is that, as Robinson has shown,[18] in a socialist system the relative price between agricultural products as a whole and industrial products as a whole is in general a distributive and not an allocative variable. That is, the government uses this relative price to tax the agricultural sector, so that it is an exogenous policy variable, not as in Ricardo's case.[19] Further, because of our assumption that labour is the only input, consumption and investment are all in terms of corn, so that the model is self-contained with respect to demand conditions.

Thus in our model the only link between the agricultural sector and the rest of the economy is its relationship with the government, as part of an overall development plan, especially with respect to taxation. As far as central directives on output/investment decisions are concerned, we have made the assumption represented by (II.10); for the moment, we will rely on the exogenous nature of taxation to assume it away until a later stage of the discussion.

We have seen that (II.1), (II.4), and (II.6) to (II.10) describe a momentary equilibrium of the system. Let us now examine its dynamic properties. We can reduce the model to:

$$\text{(II.1)} \quad X = f(N)$$

$$\text{(II.11)} \quad K = Nx$$

$$\text{(II.12)} \quad \dot{K} = f(N) - Nx$$

$$\text{(II.13)} \quad \frac{\dot{K}}{K} = \frac{\dot{N}}{N}.$$

As we have seen, (II.13) implies that the real wage is constant at a level x^* (the socialist natural wage). It follows that:

$$\text{(II.14)} \quad \frac{\dot{N}}{N} = \frac{\dot{K}}{K} = \frac{f(N)}{Nx^*} - 1,$$

so that the growth rate of capital depends on the number of natural wage units contained in output per man. The differential equation (II.14) determines the time path of the model. As an illustration, suppose $f(N)$ has the simplest form for which (II.2) is satisfied:

$$\text{(II.15)} \quad X = N^{\alpha}, \; 0 < \alpha < 1.$$

Then (II.14) can be written:

$$\text{(II.16)} \quad \frac{\dot{N}}{N} = \frac{N^{\alpha - 1}}{x^*} - 1,$$

or

$$\text{(II.17)} \quad \dot{N} = \left(\frac{1}{x^*}\right)N^{\alpha} - N = \beta N^{\alpha} - N, \; \beta \equiv \frac{1}{x^*}.$$

(II.17) is a Bernoulli equation with the solution:

$$\text{(II.18)} \quad N = \{[N(0)^{1 - \alpha} - \beta]e^{-(1 - \alpha)t} + \beta\}^{\frac{1}{1 - \alpha}}.$$

In this case, since $0 < \alpha < 1$,

$$\text{(II.19)} \quad \lim_{t \to \infty} N = \beta^{\frac{1}{1 - \alpha}} = \left(\frac{1}{x^*}\right)^{\frac{1}{1 - \alpha}}$$

so that the stationary value of N depends on the level of the socialist natural wage x^*.

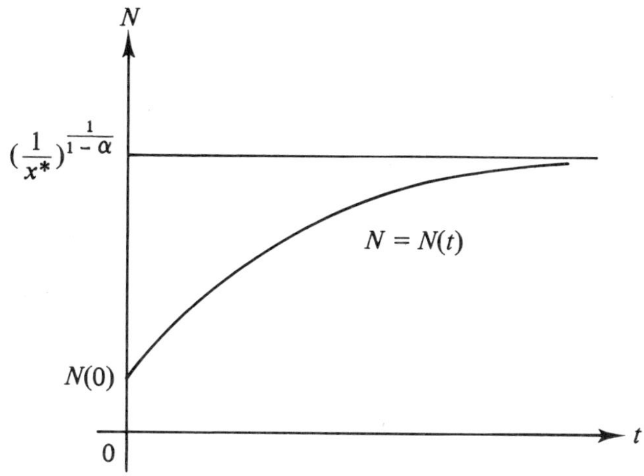

Fig. 6.3 The time path of N with $X = N^\alpha$.

Once the function $N = N(t)$ is known, the dynamic behaviour of the other variables can be found by substitution. Coming back to the general case. From (II.14), the growth rate of capital is:

$$\frac{\dot{K}}{K} = \frac{f(N)/N}{x^*} - 1.$$

It follows that the stationary value of N is given by the equation:

$$\text{(II.20)} \quad \frac{f(N)}{N} = x^*.$$

This value is denoted $\bar{N}$ in Fig. 6.4.

The growth rate of corn output can also be found. For $X = N^\alpha$, we have:

$$\text{(II.21)} \quad \frac{\dot{X}}{X} = \alpha\frac{\dot{N}}{N},$$

so that corn output grows at a smaller rate than that of capital. (It

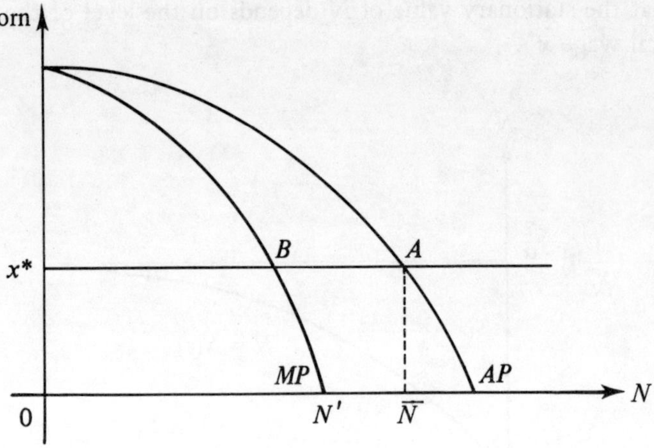

Fig. 6.4 Growth in the socialist Ricardo model.

should be noted that here α is only a technical elasticity of X with respect to N, and it has no distributive interpretation.) In the general case, the relationship is:

$$\text{(II.22)} \quad \frac{\dot{X}}{X} = \frac{Nf'(N)}{f(N)} \frac{\dot{K}}{K},$$

which is also smaller than $\frac{\dot{K}}{K}$, since $Nf'(N) < f(N)$ when there are diminishing returns.

The above results show that if rent is properly accounted for as suggested by Kantorovich, it is possible to work out a consistent theory of income distribution in a model of socialist agriculture. In Hicksian terminology,[20] this is a fix-wage model, with the wage being equal to the socialist natural wage (permanent consumption). We can, if we like, then interpret (II.14) and (II.22) as the maximum rates of growth of capital and output which are consistent with permanent consumption. We can also see that agricultural output can continue to grow even for values of $N(N' \leqq N \leqq \bar{N})$ for which the marginal product of labour is negative. Thus, even when part of the agricultural work force is 'surplus' in this sense, the continual increase in imputed rent makes it possible for agricultural output to support permanent consumption per head as well as providing a surplus for accumulation. It follows that, in the stationary state, the size of rent net of the negative contribution of the surplus work force is just enough to 'renew' the wage fund each year for a stationary population.

It may be an interesting exercise in 'comparative economic systems' to study the relationship between our socialist Ricardian model and Ricardo's corn model of capitalist agriculture, as interpreted for example by Pasinetti. For a meaningful comparison, we will suppose the same technology for the two models, and that Ricardo's natural wage $\bar{x}$ is equal to the socialist natural wage x^*. The growth rate of the Ricardo corn model is given by Pasinetti as:[21]

$$\text{(II.23)} \quad \frac{\dot{K}}{K} = \frac{f'(N)}{\bar{x}} - 1.$$

We can see that this growth rate is smaller than that given by (II.14), by virtue of diminishing returns. For the same reason, the stationary state level of N is also smaller for Ricardo's model, because this is the value of N for which $MP = \bar{x} = x^*$, in other words, at point B in Fig. 6.4. These results are really what one should intuitively expect. In Ricardo's model, capitalist farmers seek a maximum growth rate of agriculture, and so invest their entire income share (profits), while landlords consume all of their rent. On our assumptions, profits in the capitalist model are equal to surplus S in the socialist model, if measured in terms of corn. The same motive of maximum accumulation applies in both cases, but since in the socialist model there is no landlord class, imputed rent can also be invested, which gives a higher level of investment at any moment of time.

We now turn to the simplifying assumptions made earlier; here, we hope to replace them by assumptions which are simple and which make economic sense. The first simplifying assumption concerns the use of machinery in agriculture. Let us suppose there is only one kind of machine, say, a tractor. We may also suppose that in the present case of a large agricultural work force, the machine is of the intermediate technology type proposed by Schumacher.[22]

Following standard practice,[23] we can introduce machine services into corn production by supposing that there are fixed proportions between tractors and labour and variable proportions between labour and land. Then the diminishing returns property (II.2) would still hold, with a production function which is formally written in the same way as (II.1), though the interpretation is now different. That is, we have:

(II.24) $X = F(N)$, with

(II.25) $F'(N) > 0,\ F''(N) < 0,\ F'(0) > x^*$.

We may also point out that the wage fund must now be imagined to be equal to circulating capital; with this interpretation, (II.9) still holds.

A more interesting consequence of the assumption of the fixed tractor : labour ratio is that as agricultural population increases, the input requirement of tractors increases at the same rate. Let us suppose that investment in tractors is made by the central authorities, so that the agricultural sector hires the necessary machinery from the government. This assumption derives from Polanyi's observation (Polanyi, 1969): the essential property of a socialist system, whether planned or 'market', is that investment decisions are always made by the government. (To this observation we may add another: only the central authorities possess the economy-wide data and computational power which are necessary for co-ordinated investment planning.)[24]

Therefore, we can suppose that the central authorities determine, on the basis of a plan (which includes data on machine : labour ratios and the trend of population growth), the type and quantity of machinery to be produced and assigned to agriculture. As to the time span of this plan, we have a choice of assumptions. We can suppose the authorities plan in stages, for example, one short-term plan after another, with specified targets for terminal capital in each plan. Or one can suppose longer-term planning on the basis of a full inter-temporal model. As Kantorovich has shown, logically it is possible to imagine a long-term plan and sequence of short-term plans to have the same properties and give the same results.[25] In this case, we may suppose that, for operational purposes, a long-term plan is decomposed into a set of short-term plans. This is probably what we should assume for the case of Chinese economic development.

Given that the agricultural sector hires machinery from the central authorities, the next question is: what determines the rental? Would this price have any efficiency basis or would it just be of an administrative nature? For an answer, we turn once again to Kantorovich, who shows that, in a typical short-term plan of the kind we suppose to apply here, efficiency requires that machine services should carry a 'hire valuation' equal to their shadow price. It follows that the efficient user cost of any machine would be equal to its hire valuation plus depreciation.[26]

We can apply the Kantorovich theorem to our model by assuming, as a reasonable administrative procedure, that the agricultural authorities apply for the rental of the required quantity of tractors once every short-term planning period, paying a charge per tractor equal to its hire valuation. We will defer discussion of the form in which total rental charges are paid for the moment.[27]

The second of our simplifying assumptions concerns the absence of taxation. In a capitalist model such as assumption may carry us a long way, but in a socialist model this cannot be done. For as Robinson has shown, in a socialist system, apart from direct taxes, many prices are really instruments of 'indirect' taxation. In a more relevant context, she has argued that in a socialist system a land taxation scheme is the most efficient way for the government to bring about a desired distribution of income between agriculture and industry. Compared to a price taxation policy, land taxation possesses all the theoretical advantages of lump sum taxation, and it also reduces the likelihood of black market transactions.[28] It is also proposed that the government should enter into a long-term supply contract with the agricultural authorities, so as to act as a buffer to stabilize food prices.[29]

We can incorporate a land taxation scheme of this type into our model by supposing a tax on total agricultural surplus $R + S$ at a constant rate τ, $0 < \tau < 1$. It would seem simplest to imagine that the government receives the taxation in terms of corn, which it then sells to consumers in the industrial sector at a stabilized price, absorbing any excess supply into stocks, and meeting excess demand from stocks. The tax rate and the price of corn then together form a 'policy package' which is adjusted so that the food component of industrial real wages conforms with desired income distribution over time. Since the relative price of corn remains a (distributive) policy variable with respect to the agricultural sector, the model is still self-contained.

We now come back to the problem of the payment of total rental charges for tractors. Since the price of corn and the user cost of tractors are given, it seems simplest to suppose that the cost of machine services is paid for in terms of corn. In this case, we can imagine a value of τ to be chosen such that corn deliveries to the government include both taxation and rental payments.

As we have seen, the number of machines required increases with population growth in the agricultural sector. Whether the total hire cost would also increase depends on what happens to hire valuation over time. As Kantorovich has shown,[30] other things being equal, the shadow prices of a plan generally fall over time, so it is likely that the total cost of machine services increases at a lower rate than that of machine requirements.

The growth properties of the agricultural model under the present assumptions can be found by noting that now:

$$\text{(II.26)} \quad \dot{K} = (1 - \tau)(R + S)$$

so that

$$\text{(II.27)} \quad \frac{\dot{K}}{K} = (1 - \tau)\,\frac{F(N)/N}{x^*} - 1$$

where the socialist natural wage has the same value as before, since the initial conditions have not changed. We can also find that:

$$\text{(II.28)} \quad \frac{\dot{X}}{X} = \frac{NF'(N)}{F(N)}\frac{\dot{K}}{K}$$

holds, as before.

It is not possible to compare these results with those obtained previously, because as we have seen, the production functions are not the same in the two cases. It is possible, however, to use equations (II.26) and (II.27) to say one or two things about the problem of increasing mechanization in agriculture. Suppose the authorities wish to introduce a newer, more productive kind of machine to agricultural production. If it is possible to charge the use of the new machine by its hire valuation, then we can see from (II.26) and (II.27) that the growth rate of output need not always rise even though the new machine is more productive, as τ may increase (due to higher rental charges) at the same time that the productivity functions shift upwards. This observation suggests a way by which an appropriate technology for the mechanization of agriculture can be chosen. A calculation like the one above can be made for each new kind of machine, and that machine is selected for which the resulting increase in the growth rate of output is highest. Of course, the method depends on the hire valuations assigned to the various machines. As we have seen, this is a matter of the shadow prices of a multi-sector system, interpreted as efficiency prices. Some crude steps towards the construction of such a model under Chinese conditions are made in the next section.

III. A Linear 'Kernel' Model of the Chinese Economy

In this section we will try to study the implications of land scarcity in a multi-sector linear growth model of the Chinese economy. Following the approach of the previous section, we will start with the general von Neumann–Kemeny–Morgenstern–Thompson (NKMT) model[31] and then introduce assumptions which reflect the special conditions of the Chinese economy.

The NKMT model is too familiar for a summary to be necessary here. We will just note that, in its most general version, it can be proved that at least one balanced growth path for the model exists, with a growth factor α = the interest factor β, and where the process intensity vector x and the price vector y are restricted to lie within given bounds.

The equations of the NKMT model do not explicitly take into account the limitations imposed by fixed resources on growth. However, without changing the formulation of the model, we can still deduce a general result about the effects of land scarcity. For we may imagine that the limitations imposed by a fixed quantity of land affect the parameter vector $\bar{x}$, the upper bound to the intensities vector x. That is, we suppose that over time the effects of land scarcity and diminishing returns lower the maximum level at which activities can be operated. Given this assumption, we can apply a theorem of the NKMT model, which states that, with a parametric decrease in $\bar{x}$, the system would shift over, in the comparative dynamics sense, to a balanced growth path characterized by a lower value of α.[32] In this way, with successive falls in $\bar{x}$, the system may end up on a balanced growth path with $\alpha = 1$, namely, the stationary state path.[33] This result is similar to the one obtained in the previous section for the one-sector model.

But before accepting this conclusion, we must find out more about the relationship between process intensities and land scarcity, since in the above discussion the effect of the latter on $\bar{x}$ is just an assumption between two exogenous variables. If this relationship can be incorporated into the analysis, we must then ask: would the theorem still apply in a NKMT model modified to take into account the special conditions of the Chinese economy?

Our first problem is to study the properties of the process intensities x_i. The NKMT model assumes an activity analysis technology. As Koopmans has noted, the activity analysis model of production is a 'pure' technical model, and is 'devoid of "institutional" assumption', that is, its description of production abstracts from all non-engineering aspects. Koopmans argues that this approach is justified 'with regard to the allocation problems of an entire economy,' for which 'it may help to start from models that formalize nothing but the range of technological alternatives open to a producing organization.'[34]

Though the activity analysis model in this 'pure' form is adequate for the static problems of efficient allocation of resources, for the analysis of growth it seems that we need a little more, since now changes in the institutional structure of the economy should also be considered. An important aspect of production not allowed for in the activity analysis model is the organizational structure of the production unit. Now production units are usually organized in the manner of hierarchies, and nowhere more so than in socialist economies.[35] With this kind of organizational structure, then, as Polanyi has shown, complex tasks may often be very difficult to handle.[36]

If the organizational aspect of production is also taken into account, the constant returns to scale property of the activity analysis model may not hold. For the increase in organizational complexity demanded by an increase in output may not be possible, given the institutional set-up and the administrative abilities of management personnel. That is, the 'span' (to use Polanyi's term) of direction in the hierarchy may not be enough to organize and co-ordinate the necessary number of input-output relations within the production unit. If, nonetheless, one goes ahead with an *ad hoc* (and hence, in general, inefficient) production plan, then it is not likely that doubling the quantity of inputs would double output.

An important implication of the above discussion seems to be this. In the analysis of production, it is often necessary to consider both the quantitative, technical aspect and the qualitative, organizational aspect. Planning for an increase in output requires planning for the appropriate qualitative as well as quantitative inputs.

Let us now consider a way in which the qualitative requirements of production can be measured. The major organizational problem, as far as we are concerned, is that of production planning. Let us suppose that, in problems of this nature, a certain level of output can be characterized by a quantity of input data proportional to it. (So that the linearity property of activity analysis still applies.) Then the organizational activity required by any level of output may be measured by the time complexity of the most efficient algorithm which solves the associated production planning problem.[37]

In general, the time complexity of an algorithm is non-linear, so that a doubling of output (and hence input data) requires a more than doubling of the solution time.[38] If such a measure of the organizational requirements of production is used, then it seems that the linearity property of 'pure' activity analysis need not hold, when production is considered more generally.

The time complexity measure is, of course, not the only one possible, but it does give us some idea of the time cost of organizing a certain level of production.[39] Hicks has recently reminded us that it is essential to take into consideration the fact that production takes time.[40] Here, we note that production, both in its engineering aspect and its organizational aspect, takes time. Moreover, the two kinds of time requirement may not be the same, so that it is possible in many cases that the 'longer' side of the problem exerts a limiting influence on the overall production process. As an example, we may imagine the following situation. Suppose, in some given plan based on the NKMT model, the time assigned to a production unit for the supply of a certain output is based only on the engineering data of activity analysis. In this case, the planning anthorities would expect constant returns to scale, and hence would allocate a certain quantity of inputs for a target output. But it may happen that the time required to organize the production plan and then to produce the target output efficiently according to the optimal solution exceeds the time allocated for supply. Consequently, either the target output has to be fulfilled by an arbitrary (and hence generally inefficient) production schedule,[41] in which case more inputs would be required, or the target output has to be reduced in order that production can be efficiently organized within the allotted time, in which case the plan would not be fulfilled, and it is likely that some of the inputs originally assigned would not be used.[42]

So we can see that economic growth in a socialist system, even in the abstract formulation of our linear model, cannot be taken just to mean a planned increase in physical outputs. The corresponding increase in the qualitative inputs must also be planned for, so that a co-ordinated accumulation of both physical and human capital, in terms of education organizational ability, and so on, is required.[43] In other words, a socialist plan aiming for balanced growth must ensure that there is co-ordinated expansion in both the quantitative and qualitative levels of production.

For the present discussion, we have the following problem: how to introduce the qualitative aspect of production into the 'pure' activity analysis technology of the NKMT model? A simple, and perhaps not unreasonable way is to suppose that:

$$\text{(III.1)} \quad x_i = \overset{*}{x}_i \hat{x}_i, \; i = 1, 2, \text{ for given } t,$$

where $\overset{*}{x}_i$ is an index of the intensity of engineering production activity and $\hat{x}_i$ is a measure of the corresponding qualitative level. (For example, $\hat{x}_i$ can be in terms of the time complexity measure discussed above.) We can define:

$$\text{(III.2)} \quad \frac{x_i^*(t+1)}{x_i^*(t)} = \xi_i^*(t), \; i = 1, 2,$$

as the quantitative coefficient of process i, and

$$\text{(III.3)} \quad \frac{\hat{x}_i(t+1)}{\hat{x}_i(t)} = \hat{\xi}_i(t), \; i = 1, 2.$$

as the qualitative coefficient of process i. The relative intensity of process i over two consecutive periods is then given by:

$$\text{(III.4)} \quad \frac{x_i(t+1)}{x_i(t)} = \frac{x_i^*(t+1)}{x_i^*(t)} \cdot \frac{\hat{x}_i(t+1)}{\hat{x}_i(t)} = \xi_i^*(t)\hat{\xi}_i(t), \; i = 1, 2.$$

The (proportional) rate of increase in the intensity of process i is:

$$\text{(III.5)} \quad \frac{x_i(t+1) - x_i(t)}{x_i(t)} = \xi_i^*(t)\hat{\xi}_i(t) - 1, \; i = 1, 2.$$

A constant rate of increase (balanced growth) in the intensity of process i then requires:

$$\text{(III.6)} \quad \xi_i^*(t)\hat{\xi}_i(t) - 1 = g_i, \; i = 1, 2,$$

where g_i is a constant. We can write:

$$\text{(III.7)} \quad \xi_i^*(t)\hat{\xi}_i(t) = 1 + g_i = \alpha_i, \; i = 1, 2.$$

Process i can be interpreted as 'expanding' if $g_i > 0$, 'stationary' if $g_i = 0$, and 'contracting' if $g_i < 0$.

At any point of time and for given g_i, the possibility of substitution between the quantitative and qualitative aspects of production exists. In our simple case, this takes the form:

$$\text{(III.8)} \quad \xi_i^* = \alpha_i/\hat{\xi}_i = \sigma(\hat{\xi}_i; \alpha_i, t), \; i = 1, 2;$$

so that:

$$\text{(III.9)} \quad \sigma' < 0 \text{ and } \sigma'' > 0.$$[44]

The substitution function (III.8) is sketched in Fig. 6.5.

We now consider the problem of modifying an NKMT linear model to incorporate the two essential assumptions of land scarcity

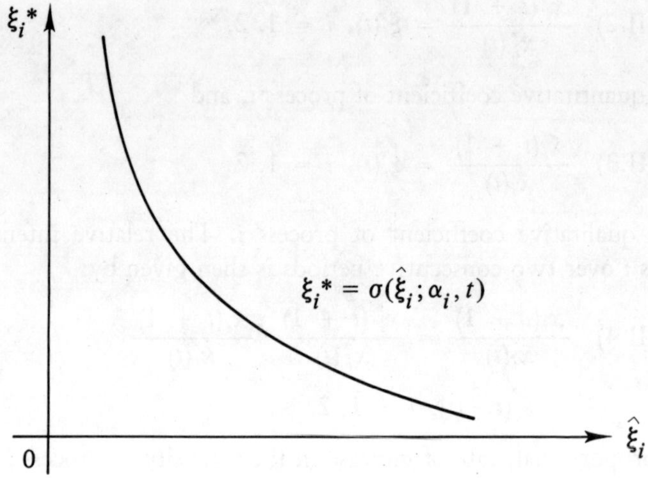

Fig. 6.5 Substitution possibilities between ξ_i^* and $\hat{\xi}_i$, at any point of time, given α_i.

and total employment. We will work with the simplest possible case, a 2 × 2 system. The justification for doing so is contained in what may be called the kernel economy theorem of Morgenstern and Thompson.[45] The kernel of an NKMT model is defined as follows:

> The kernel consists of a minimal set of industries and goods such that further deletions of industries and/or goods would result in the collapse of the economy.[46]

Given the kernel economy, then, as Morgenstern and Thompson have shown, it is possible to build a larger system from it, in a stepwise manner.[47] The kernel can therefore be interpreted as the smallest viable system for which a balanced growth path can be constructed. Extensions to larger systems would, in general, change the properties of the growth path, especially the value of the growth factor α. For example, in one of the cases considered by Morgenstern and Thompson,[48] a 2 × 2 kernel agricultural economy with $\alpha = 2$ is extended to a 8 × 9 'urban model' with $\alpha = 1.5$. In terms of the larger system, the kernel then becomes a subset of processes and commodities.[49]

Following Morgenstern and Thompson, we will start with a 2×2 kernel. Later on, we will identify the two commodities as land and labour, to apply it to Chinese conditions. But first we would like to summarize one or two useful properties of the kernel economy in the general case.

(a) In the formulation of the NKMT model, no institutional assumptions are made; therefore, we will call its kernel a pure kernel economy. If our two special assumptions are added on, this becomes a C-kernel economy. We suppose that the C-kernel economy is centrally planned, and pursues an objective of balanced growth.

(b) Since the kernel economy is an NKMT system, the existence theorem applies, so that we are assured that at least one balanced growth path for it exists.

(c) By definition, the processes and commodities in the kernel economy are essential to its viability. Therefore, it is reasonable to suppose that both processes operate at positive intensities and that both commodities have positive prices.

We will now write out the equations of the kernel model in the general case and then interpret them under the special conditions of the Chinese economy. From property (c), the (input–output) conservation conditions can be written.

$$\text{(III.10)} \quad x_1(t+1)a_{1j} + x_2(t+1)a_{2j} = x_1(t)b_{1j} + x_2(t)b_{2j},\ j = 1, 2.$$

In the Chinese economy, we can suppose that commodity (1), land, is fixed in quantity and fully used; the condition of land scarcity can then be expressed by the identity:

$$\text{(III.11)} \quad x_1(t+1)a_{11} + x_2(t+1)a_{21} \equiv x_1(t)b_{11} + x_2(t)b_{21}.$$

By the rule of free goods[50] then, land always earns a positive rent, which agrees with property (c) and the result obtained in the one-sector model. Though the intensity levels of both processes are positive, the values are constrained by (III.11), so that there is a kind of Say's Law for land. Substituting from (III.1) and (III.4), (III.11) can be written:

$$\text{(III.12)} \quad x_1(t)\xi_1^*(t)\hat{\xi}_1(t)a_{11} + x_2(t)\xi_2^*(t)\hat{\xi}_2(t)a_{21} \equiv x_1(t)b_{11} + x_2(t)b_{21},$$

which we can call the land equation.

As regards commodity (2), labour, we have from (III.10):

$$\text{(III.13)} \quad x_1(t+1)a_{12} + x_2(t+1)a_{22} = x_1(t)b_{12} + x_2(t)b_{22},$$

or, using (III.1) and (III.4),

$$\text{(III.14)} \quad x_1(t)\xi_1^*(t)\hat{\xi}_1(t)a_{12} + x_2(t)\xi_2^*(t)\hat{\xi}_2 a_{22} = x_1(t)b_{12} + x_2(t)b_{22}.$$

The socialist principle of total employment is then satisfied; moreover, we can see that the planning authorities have the option of adjusting $\xi_i^*(t)\hat{\xi}_i(t)$ (or one of them) so that (III.14) is satisfied. We can also see that, by the rule of free goods, labour receives a positive wage.[51]

From property (c), prices are positive, so that the financial conditions of the pure kernel economy can be written:

$$\text{(III.15)} \quad a_{i1}\gamma_1(t) + a_{i2}\gamma_2(t) = b_{i1}\gamma_1(t+1) + b_{i2}\gamma_2(t+1), \; i = 1, 2.$$

These equations express what Kantorovich calls the principle of profitability in socialist planning; that is, any process used with a positive intensity would exactly break even, in terms of efficiency prices.[52] However, as we have seen, the actual prices (accounting prices or quoted prices) in a socialist system need not correspond to efficiency prices. Let us suppose that the (parametric) bounds on the efficiency prices γ_j are in terms of accounting prices p_j, or $\min p_j \leqq \gamma_j \leqq \max p_j$, with $0 \leqq \min p_j \leqq \max p_j$. Then the actual quoted values for accounting prices can lie on both sides of γ_j. Therefore, we have:

$$\text{(III.16)} \quad p_j(t) = l_j(t)\gamma_j(t), \; j = 1, 2,$$

where $p_j(t)$ is the accounting price of the jth commodity, as quoted by the planning authorities. We can safely suppose that, since $\gamma_j > 0$, p_j and $l_j > 0$,

$$\text{(III.17)} \quad \frac{p_j(t+1)}{p_j(t)} = \frac{l_j(t+1)}{l_j(t)} \cdot \frac{\gamma_j(t+1)}{\gamma_j(t)}$$

$$= \lambda_j(t)\eta_j(t),\ j = 1, 2,$$

where $\lambda_j(t) \equiv l_j(t+1)/l_j(t) > 0$ and $\eta_j(t) \equiv y_j(t+1)/y_j(t) > 0$. We note that, for any balanced growth solution of the pure kernel economy, $y_j(t+1)/y_j(t) = \beta^{-1}$ for some balanced discount factor β, so that in this case:

$$\text{(III.18)} \quad \eta_j(t) = \beta^{-1},\ j = 1, 2.$$

As a matter of accounting, the cost of running the ith process at unit level for time t is:

$$\text{(III.19)} \quad a_{i1}p_1(t) + a_{i2}p_2(t),\ i = 1, 2,$$

which need not reflect efficiency costing. Similarly, one period later, the accounting revenue from operating process i at unit level is:

$$\text{(III.20)} \quad b_{i1}p_1(t+1) + b_{i2}p_2(t+1),\ i = 1, 2.$$

If $m_j(t)$ is the one period rate of time preference (rate of discount) assigned to commodity j in a given plan, the present value of the accounting revenue (III.20) is:

$$\text{(III.21)} \quad b_{i1}\frac{P_1(t+1)}{1+m_1(t)} + b_{i2}\frac{p_2(t+1)}{1+m_2(t)},\ i = 1, 2.$$

In a planned economy, differential rates of discount may be interpreted as indices of the priority assigned to a commodity in a plan. Suppose, for example, that at any moment of time a commodity is available in large quantities. Then, it would very likely be assigned a low priority. Given its present abundance, future quantities of this commodity would not be reckoned to be worth much; therefore, its future availability would be heavily discounted. It follows that a low priority for a commodity is associated with a high rate of discount, at any point of time.[53]

In terms of accounting values, the financial conditions of the C-kernel economy can be written:

$$\text{(III.22)} \quad a_{i1}p_1(t) + a_{i2}p_2(t)$$

$$\geqq b_{i1}\frac{p_1(t+1)}{1+m_1(t)} + b_{i2}\frac{p_2(t+1)}{1+m_2(t)},\ i = 1, 2.$$

A process would show an accounting loss if the strict inequality holds. (There is, of course, no reason for the principle of profitability to hold for accounting values.) But we have seen that both processes are operated at positive levels, so for accounting consistency,[54] the planning authorities would have to adjust the quoted prices p_j and/or the discount rates m_j so that the financial conditions hold as equations:

$$\text{(III.23)}\quad a_{i1}p_1(t) + a_{i2}p_2(t) = b_{i1}\frac{p_1(t+1)}{1+m_1(t)} + b_{i2}\frac{p_2(t+1)}{1+m_2(t)},\ i = 1, 2.$$

Substituting (III.16) and (III.17) into (III.23), we have:

$$\text{(III.24)}\quad a_{i1}p_1(t) + a_{i2}p_2(t) = b_{i1}\frac{\lambda_1(t)\eta_1(t)p_1(t)}{1+m_1(t)} + b_{i2}\frac{\lambda_2(t)\eta_2(t)p_2(t)}{1+m_2(t)},\ i = 1, 2,$$

in which case, by (III.18),

$$\text{(III.25)}\quad a_{i1}p_1(t) + a_{i2}p_2(t) = b_{i1}\frac{\lambda_1(t)\beta^{-1}p_1(t)}{1+m_1(t)} + b_{i2}\frac{\lambda_2(t)\beta^{-1}p_2(t)}{1+m_2(t)},\ i = 1, 2,$$

for any balanced growth solution of the pure kernel economy. From these equations, we can see that the efficiency prices of the plan are concealed in the financial relations of the accounting price system.

We can develop one or two implications of these equations, based on general observations of current conditions in China. Consider first the land equation (III.12); together with (III.6) we can write:

$$\text{(III.26)}\quad x_1(t)(\alpha_1 a_{11} - b_{11}) \equiv x_2(t)(b_{21} - \alpha_2 a_{21})$$

so that

$$\text{(III.27)}\quad (\alpha_1 a_{11} - b_{11}) \gtreqless 0 \text{ iff } -(\alpha_2 a_{21} - b_{21}) \gtreqless 0,$$

for $\alpha_1 \neq \alpha_2$.[55]

Suppose, for example, that $\alpha_1 > 1$ and $0 < \alpha_2 \leqq 1$. Then, from (III.6), $g_1 > 0$ and $g_2 < 0$, that is, $x_1(t+1) > x_1(t)$ and $x_2(t+1) < x_2(t)$. But the quantity of land is fixed, so that the expansion of process 1 does not increase it and the decline in process 2 does not decrease it.

Therefore, we can say that the existence of Say's Law for land requires that the expansion in productive method is used to compensate for the negative effect of the other process.

Taking the labour equation (III.14) with (III.6), we have:

$$\text{(III.28)} \quad x_1(t)(\alpha_1 a_{12} - b_{12}) = -x_2(t)(\alpha_2 a_{22} - b_{22}).$$

The total employment principle expressed in (III.14) would then hold under two situations. Either:

$$\text{(III.28}'\text{)} \quad x_1(t)(\alpha_1 a_{12} - b_{12}) = -x_2(t)(\alpha_2 a_{22} - b_{22}) > 0,$$

or

$$\text{(III.28}''\text{)} \quad x_1(t)(\alpha_1 a_{12} - b_{12}) = -x_2(t)(\alpha_2 a_{22} - b_{22}) = 0.$$

Let us suppose, for present purposes, that process 1 is based mainly on technical operations, while process 2 is a more 'organizational' type of production method. (For example, it may depend quite a lot on exhortations and ideological learning.) The first condition of (III.28′) gives:

$$x_1(t + 1)a_{12} > x_1(t)b_{12}.$$

That is, process 1, considered by itself, generates an excess demand for labour, due to its relatively high technological nature. An empirical example often found in China is the highly labour-intensive way in which water control projects such as dams are built. With such techniques, the number of workers (especially of the more unskilled types) that can be absorbed is quite flexible. The second condition of (III.28′) yields in a similar manner:

$$x_2(t + 1)a_{22} < x_2(t)b_{22}.$$

Taken by itself, this condition demonstrates that the 'organizational' method of production would permit a labour surplus with a zero wage rate.

If both conditions are taken together, we can say that there is a redistribution of income from those workers who have gained from process 1 to those who are involved in process 2. For example, many of the intellectuals transferred to the communes would be classified as 'surplus labour' if measured by their productivity alone. But the socialist principle of total employment is not based so much on productivity; therefore, these persons would also receive a positive wage, in which case there is a redistribution of income.[56]

Now consider (III.28″). Here, both methods of production seem capable of absorbing large amounts of labour. The intensities $x_i(t)$ might differ, of course; if $x_2(t) > x_1(t)$, then the economy relies more on the 'organizational' method of production. Furthermore, since $x_i(t) > 0$ in (III.28″), then,

$$\text{(III.28‴)} \quad \alpha_1 = b_{12}/a_{12} \text{ and } \alpha_2 = b_{22}/a_{22},$$

so that $\alpha_1 \neq \alpha_2$, and it is likely that $\alpha_1 > \alpha_2$, if this equation is taken by itself.

A rearrangement of the financial condition (III.23) gives:

$$\text{(III.29)} \quad p_1(t)\left[a_{i1} - b_{i1}\frac{p_1(t+1)}{1+m_1(t)}\right] = -p_2(t)\left[a_{i2} - b_{i2}\frac{p_2(t+1)}{1+m_2(t)}\right], \quad i = 1, 2.$$

Since commodity 1 is land and commodity 2 is labour, we may imagine that in a land-scarce and labour-abundant economy like China, the planning authorities would choose the differential rates of time preference such that:

$$\text{(III.30)} \quad m_1(t) < m_2(t),$$

and that the accounting prices are likely to be such that

$$\text{(III.31)} \quad p_1(t) > p_2(t).$$

The recent policy of birth control in China can be expressed by (III.30), in which the high rate of discount for labour reflects the policy for containing the growth of the labour force. It is also likely that:

$$\text{(III.32)} \quad \frac{b_{i1}p_1(t+1)}{1+m_1(t)} > \frac{b_{i2}p_2(t+1)}{1+m_2(t)},$$

in view of (III.30) and (III.31), so that the present value of earnings from a relatively scarce factor is higher.

The accounting prices in the C-kernel economy are, of course, set by the planning authorities. We do not know the criteria by which this is done, but in general we would expect the accounting prices p_j and the differential rates of discount m_j to be set with reference to one another. We can show this by means of an example. Suppose the planning authorities set a price norm in terms of the proportional rate of change in accounting prices. Then we may express the relationship between the price norm and the rate of discount as:

$$\text{(III.33)} \quad b_j(m_j) = \frac{\Delta p_j(t)}{p_j(t)} = \frac{p_j(t+1)}{p_j(t)} - 1 \geqq 0,$$ [57]

with $b_j(0) = 0, j = 1, 2$.

There are, in general, four possibilities.

(i) $b_j(m_j) = b_j = 0$. Then, $\Delta p_j/p_j = 0$, so that accounting prices are planned to follow a constant path over time, independent of the rate of time preference.

(ii) $b_j(m_j) = b_j > 0$, with $b_j'(m_j) \equiv 0$. Here, accounting prices are planned to increase over time, independent of m_j.

(iii) $b_j(m_j) > 0$, and $b_j'(m_j) < 0$. Once again there is planned inflation over time, but now the rate of increase of accounting prices varies inversely with the rate of discount. The reason is as follows. The purpose of a high rate of time preference is to discount the future heavily, so that all income streams would have relatively small present values. But if prices are planned to increase rapidly in the future, all nominal income streams would shift upwards, so that present values would increase, contrary to the purpose of a high discount rate. Therefore, we would expect that, with rational planning, $b_j'(m_j) < 0$.

(iv) $b_j(m_j) > 0$ and $b_j'(m_j) > 0$. This is the opposite case to (iii), so that it is not likely that the planning authorities would adopt such a scheme.

In anticipation of later results, we may note here that if there is a common discount rate $m = m_1 = m_2$, the relationships $b_1(m)$ and $b_2(m)$ (taken by themselves) would no longer distinguish between the two commodities, so that we can suppose $b_1(m) = b_2(m) = b(m)$.

Having set out the equations of our 2×2 C-kernel economy, we must now show that it satisfies the essential property of a kernel, namely that there is at least one balanced growth path for it. On the technological side, this requires that the two processes expand by the same factor $\alpha = 1 + g$. But so far, we have allowed the two processes in our model to show different growth rates: $\alpha_1 \neq \alpha_2$ (or $g_1 \neq g_2$). We must therefore show that the condition $\alpha_1 = \alpha_2 = \alpha$ is possible in the C-kernel economy.

From the land equation (III.26) and the labour equation (III.28), we obtain:

$$\text{(III.34)} \quad \frac{\alpha_1 a_{11} - b_{11}}{b_{21} - \alpha_2 a_{21}} = \frac{x_2(t)}{x_1(t)} = \frac{\alpha_1 a_{12} - b_{12}}{b_{22} - \alpha_2 a_{22}},$$

which can be re-arranged to give:

$$\text{(III.35)} \quad A_1\alpha_1 + A_2\alpha_1\alpha_2 + A_3\alpha_2 + A_4 = 0,$$

where

$$\begin{aligned} A_1 &= a_{11}b_{22} - a_{12}b_{21}, \\ A_2 &= a_{12}a_{21} - a_{11}a_{22}, \\ A_3 &= b_{11}a_{22} - b_{12}a_{21}, \text{ and} \\ A_4 &= b_{12}b_{21} - b_{11}b_{22}. \end{aligned}$$

We require the conditions for the existence of a non-trivial solution $\alpha_1 = \alpha_2 = \alpha$ for (III.35). Obviously, we must have

$$\text{(III.36)} \quad A_1, A_3 \text{ and } A_4 \not\equiv 0.$$

Since $\alpha_i = 1 + g_i$, (III.35) defines an implicit function of the form $g_2 = \phi(g_1)$. Let us look for its endpoints in the non-negative quadrant, where economically meaningful cases would lie. If we set $g_1 = 0$ ($\alpha_1 = 1$), then for the economically meaningful case of $g_2 > 0$ ($\alpha_2 > 1$), we have from (III.35)

$$\text{(III.37)} \quad \alpha_2 = 1 + g_2 = \frac{-(A_1 + A_4)}{A_2 + A_3}$$

$$g_2 = \frac{-(A_1 + A_4)}{A_2 + A_3} - 1 = \frac{-\Sigma A_k}{A_2 + A_3}.$$

This implies that:

$$\begin{aligned} \text{(III.37}'\text{)} \quad \text{sign}[-(A_1 + A_4)] &= \text{sign}(A_2 + A_3) \\ &= \text{sign}(-\Sigma A_k). \end{aligned}$$

Similarly, for $g_2 = 0$ ($\alpha_2 = 1$), $g_1 > 0$ ($\alpha_1 > 1$), we can find

$$\text{(III.37'')} \quad \alpha_1 = 1 + g_1 = \frac{-(A_3 + A_4)}{A_1 + A_2}, \; g_1 = \frac{-\Sigma A_k}{A_1 + A_2},$$

and

$$\text{(III.37''')} \quad \operatorname{sign}[-(A_3 + A_4)] = \operatorname{sign}(A_1 + A_2) = \operatorname{sign}(-\Sigma A_k).$$

The values for g_2 and g_1 given by (III.37), (III.37″) are the required endpoints. Since the LHS of (III.35) is a polynomial and (III.36) is assumed to hold, we can suppose that the function $g_2 = \phi(g_1)$ is continuous. In this case, there is at least one point at which the graph of the function will intersect the 45° line, as depicted in Fig. 6.6.

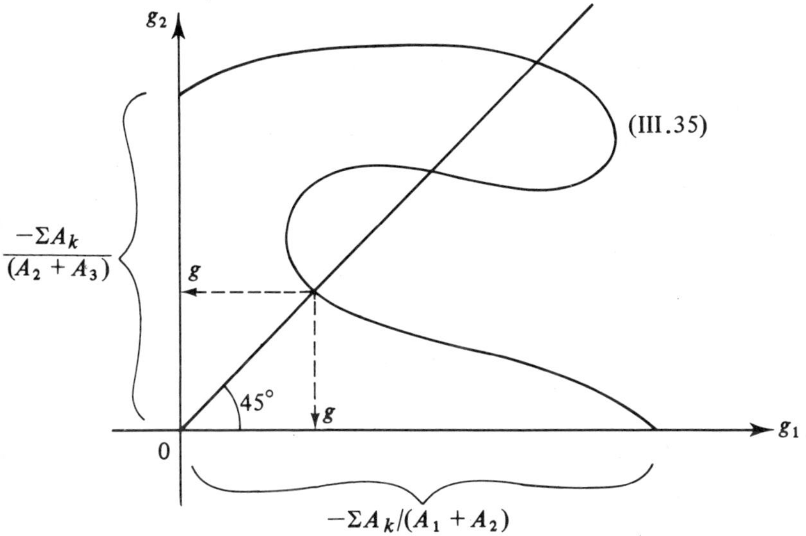

Fig. 6.6 The existence of a growth rate g, common to both processes.

Hence there exists at least one common growth rate g for the two processes. We have thus proved:

Proposition A

> *In the C-kernel economy, there exists a balanced growth rate g and balanced growth factor $\alpha = 1 + g$ which is common to both processes.*

We now test whether the common growth rate g is unique. From the fact that, in (III.35), $A_2 \gtreqless 0$, we have three cases:

(i) $A_2 = 0$, or

$$\text{(III.38)} \quad \frac{a_{12}}{a_{11}} = \frac{a_{22}}{a_{21}}$$

which means that the input requirement ratio for the two processes are equal. From (III.35) then, we have:

$$\text{(III.38}'\text{)} \quad g_2 = \frac{-\Sigma A_k}{A_2 + A_3} \bigg|_{A_2 = 0} - \frac{A_1}{A_3} g_1,$$

where $A_2 = 0$ and the first term on RHS of the equation is positive due to (III.37′). The balanced growth rate will be unique if $A_1/A_3 > 0$. This case is shown in Fig. 6.7. To see the economic meaning of the condition $A_1/A_3 > 0$, we can use (III.35) to obtain as an implication:

$$\text{(III.38}''\text{)} \quad \text{sign}(a_{11}b_{22} - a_{12}b_{21}) = \text{sign}(b_{11}a_{22} - b_{12}a_{21})$$

or

$$\frac{b_{22}}{b_{21}} \gtrless \frac{a_{12}}{a_{11}} \text{ iff } \frac{a_{22}}{a_{21}} \gtrless \frac{b_{12}}{b_{11}}.$$

But $\frac{a_{12}}{a_{11}} = \frac{a_{22}}{a_{21}}$ from (III.28); therefore

$$\text{(III.38}'''\text{)} \quad \frac{b_{22}}{b_{21}} \gtrless \frac{b_{12}}{b_{11}} \text{ or } \frac{b_{11}}{b_{21}} \gtrless \frac{b_{12}}{b_{22}},$$

which can be interpreted as a requirement for an unchanged relative effectiveness of the two processes in terms of land and labour.

(ii) $A_2 < 0$, or

$$\text{(III.39)} \quad \frac{a_{12}}{a_{11}} < \frac{a_{22}}{a_{21}}.$$

To deduce the implications of (III.39), let us put $\alpha_1 = \alpha_2 = \alpha$ in (III.35). Then, we obtain the quadratic equation:

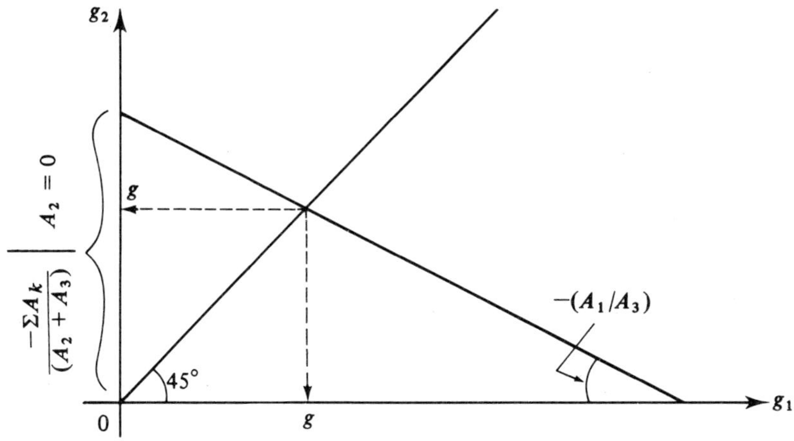

Fig. 6.7 The uniqueness of a balanced growth rate, $g = \alpha - 1$, of the productive methods when the inputs are proportionately released from the productive methods.

$$\text{(III.39}'\text{)} \quad A_2\alpha^2 + (A_1 + A_3)\alpha + A_4 = 0,$$

so that

$$\text{(III.39}''\text{)} \quad \alpha = 1 + g = \frac{-(A_1 + A_3) \pm \sqrt{(A_1 + A_3)^2 - 4A_2A_4}}{2A_2}.$$

The condition for equal real roots is then $(A_1 + A_3)^2 = 4A_2A_4$ or $A_4 < 0$ since $A_2 < 0$. Using (III.35), we have therefore:

$$\text{(III.39}'''\text{)} \quad \frac{b_{11}}{b_{21}} > \frac{b_{12}}{b_{22}}$$

which means that the relative effectiveness of process 1 is higher than that of process 2. From (III.39″), the condition for $g > 0$ is

$$\text{(III.39}^{\text{iv}}\text{)} \quad A_1 + A_3 > 2\,|A_2|.$$

We are unable to find any meaningful economic interpretation of this condition. So it seems to be purely a restriction on the technical coefficients of the model.

(iii) $A_2 > 0$, or

$$\text{(III.40)} \quad \frac{a_{12}}{a_{11}} > \frac{a_{22}}{a_{21}}$$

which has an interpretation the opposite of the previous case. Proceeding in the same way as before, we again obtain the quadratic equation (III.39′), from which the condition for equal real roots gives

$$\text{(III.40}'\text{)} \quad A_4 > 0 \text{ or } \frac{b_{11}}{b_{21}} < \frac{b_{12}}{b_{22}}$$

which again is the opposite of the previous case. For $g > 0$, we require

$$\text{(III.40}''\text{)} \quad -(A_1 + A_3) > 2A_2$$

which is once again a restriction on the technology of the problem. Putting together (III.38) through (III.40″), we have:

Proposition B

A unique growth rate for the two processes in the kernel economy can be found if the relative effectiveness of the processes remain unchanged over time.

We next tackle the problem of the discount rate in a balanced growth solution for the C-kernel model. First, we note that, from (III.17), (III.18) and (III.33),

$$\text{(III.41)} \quad 1 + b_j(m_j) = \lambda_j \eta_j = \lambda_j \beta^{-1}$$

for any balanced growth solution of the pure kernel economy. For any given m_j, we then have

$$\text{(III.42)} \quad \lambda_j = [1 + b_j(m_j)]\beta.$$

A rearrangement of the accounting financial condition (III.25) gives

$$\text{(III.43)} \quad \left[a_{i1} - \frac{b_{i1}\lambda_1(t)\beta^{-1}}{1 + m_1(t)} \right] p_1(t)$$

$$= -\left[a_{i2} - \frac{b_{i2}\lambda_2(t)\beta^{-1}}{1 + m_2(t)}\right] p_2(t), \quad i = 1, 2.$$

Setting $i = 1$ and 2 respectively, we obtain

$$\text{(III.44)} \quad \frac{a_{11} - \dfrac{b_{11}\lambda_1(t)\beta^{-1}}{1 + m_1(t)}}{\dfrac{b_{12}\lambda_2(t)\beta^{-1}}{1 + m_2(t)} - a_{12}} = \frac{p_2(t)}{p_1(t)} = \frac{a_{21} - \dfrac{b_{21}\lambda_1(t)\beta^{-1}}{1 + m_1(t)}}{\dfrac{b_{22}\lambda_2(t)\beta^{-1}}{1 + m_2(t)} - a_{22}}$$

which reduces to

$$\text{(III.45)} \quad \frac{[1 + m_1(t)]a_{11} - b_{11}\lambda_1(t)\beta^{-1}}{[1 + m_1(t)]a_{21} - b_{21}\lambda_1(t)\beta^{-1}} = \frac{[1 + m_2(t)]a_{12} - b_{12}\lambda_2(t)\beta^{-1}}{[1 + m_2(t)]a_{22} - b_{22}\lambda_2(t)\beta^{-1}}$$

where $\lambda_j\beta^{-1} = 1 + b_j(m_j) \geqq 1$, $j = 1, 2$, and the denominators and numerators are all positive, from (III.43) and the condition $p_j > 0$. The problem of the common discount rate can then be analysed in two cases: (1) the existence of an $m_1 = m_2 = m$ with constant accounting prices, and (2) the existence of an $m_1 = m_2 = m$ with variable accounting prices.

Case I

Since $b_j(m_j) = \Delta p_j/p_j = 0$, we have, from (III.33) and (III.41), $\lambda_j = \beta^{-1}$, $j = 1, 2$, so that (III.45) reduces to

$$\text{(III.46)} \quad \frac{[1 + m_1(t)]a_{11} - b_{11}}{[1 + m_1(t)]a_{21} - b_{21}} = \frac{[1 + m_2(t)]a_{12} - b_{12}}{[1 + m_2(t)]a_{22} - b_{22}},$$

or

$$\text{(III.46}'\text{)} \quad B_1M_1 + B_2M_1M_2 + B_3M_2 + B_4 = 0,$$

where

$$M_j = 1 + m_j, j = 1, 2,$$
$$B_1 = a_{11}b_{22} - b_{12}a_{21},$$
$$B_2 = a_{21}a_{12} - a_{11}a_{22},$$
$$B_3 = b_{11}a_{22} - b_{21}a_{12}, \text{ and}$$
$$B_4 = b_{21}b_{12} - b_{11}b_{22}.$$

(III.46′) has the same form as (III.35), so that, with the same reasoning as in the former case, we obtain the following conditions for a non-trivial solution $M_1 = M_2 = M$:

(III.46″) $B_1, B_3 \text{ and } B_4 \not\equiv 0,$

(III.46″′) $m_2 = \dfrac{-\Sigma B_k}{B_2 + B_3} > 0 \text{ for } m_1 = 0,$

(III.46^{iv}) $\text{sign}[-(B_4 + B_1)] = \text{sign}(B_2 + B_3) = \text{sign}(-\Sigma B_k),$

(III.46^{v}) $m_1 = \dfrac{-\Sigma B_k}{B_1 + B_2} > 0 \text{ for } m_2 \neq 0,$

(III.46^{vi}) $\text{sign}[-(B_3 + B_4)] = \text{sign}(B_1 + B_2) = \text{sign}(-\Sigma B_k).$

The endpoints of the implicit function $m_2 = \phi(m_1)$ defined by (III.46′) are given by (III.46″′) and (III.46^{v}). It follows that, as before, the graph of the continuous function $\phi(m_1)$ must intersect the 45° line at at least one point, as shown by Fig. 6.8. So we have:

Proposition C

If the planning authorities set a constant accounting price norm, then there exists at least one discount rate m common to both commodities.

As before, we must now investigate the conditions for the uniqueness of m in three cases, since $B_2 \gtreqless 0$. Since the development is the same, to save time and space we will just list the results and indicate the correspondence to the previous case.

(i) $B_2 = 0$

(III.47) $\dfrac{a_{12}}{a_{11}} = \dfrac{a_{22}}{a_{21}}$ [(III.38)]

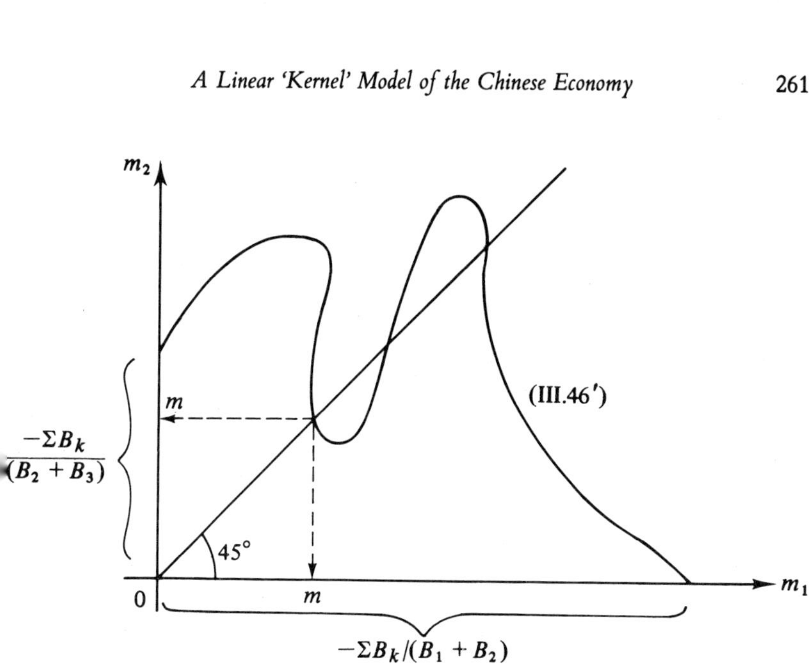

Fig. 6.8 The existence of a discount rate common to both commodities under a quoted constant price.

(III.47′) $m_2 = \left.\frac{-\Sigma B_k}{B_2 + B_3}\right|_{B_2 = 0} - \frac{B_1}{B_3} m_1$ [(III.38′)]

(See Fig. 6.9)

(III.47″) $\text{sign}(a_{11}b_{22} - b_{12}a_{21}) = \text{sign}(b_{11}a_{22} - b_{21}a_{12})$ [(III.38″)]

(III.47‴) $\frac{b_{11}}{b_{21}} \gtrless \frac{b_{12}}{b_{22}}$ [(III.38‴)]

(ii) $B_2 < 0$:

(III.48) $\frac{a_{12}}{a_{11}} < \frac{a_{22}}{a_{21}}$ [(III.39)]

(III.48′) $B_2M^2 + (B_1 + B_3)M + B_4 = 0$ [(III.39′)]

(III.48″) $M = 1 + m$

$$= \frac{-(B_1 + B_3) \pm \sqrt{(B_1 + B_3)^2 - 4B_2B_4}}{2B_2}$$

[(III.39″)]

$$\text{(III.48}'''\text{)} \quad B_4 < 0 \text{ or } \frac{b_{11}}{b_{21}} > \frac{b_{12}}{b_{22}} \qquad \text{[(III.39}'''\text{)]}$$

$$\text{(III.48}^{iv}\text{)} \quad B_1 + B_3 > 2\,|B_2| \qquad \text{[(III.39}^{iv}\text{)]}$$

(iii) $B_2 > 0$:

$$\text{(III.49)} \quad \frac{a_{12}}{a_{11}} > \frac{a_{22}}{a_{21}} \qquad \text{[(III.40)]}$$

$$\text{(III.49}'\text{)} \quad B_4 > 0 \text{ or } \frac{b_{11}}{b_{21}} < \frac{b_{12}}{b_{22}} \qquad \text{[(III.40}'\text{)]}$$

$$\text{(III.49}''\text{)} \quad -(B_1 + B_3) > 2B_2 \qquad \text{[(III.40}''\text{)]}$$

Proposition D [Proposition B]

A unique discount rate for the two commodities can be found for a constant accounting price policy, if the relative effectiveness of the two processes remains unchanged over time.

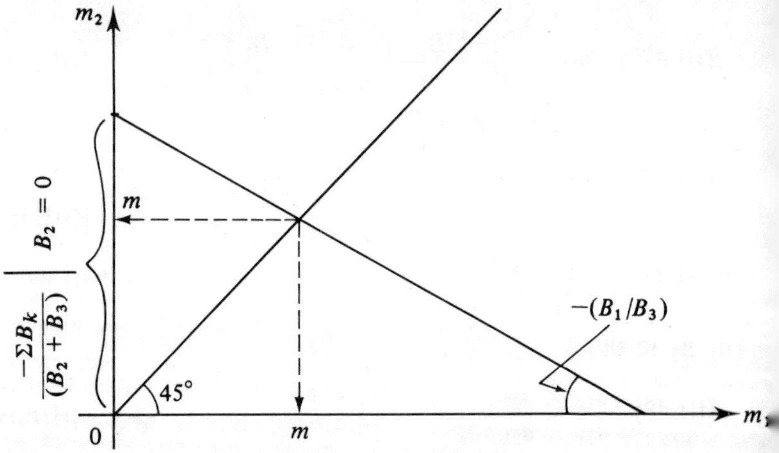

Fig. 6.9 The existence of a uniquely balanced discount rate when $a_{12}/a_{11} = a_{22}/a_{21}$.

Case II

We now assume $\lambda_j\beta^{-1} = 1 + b_j(m_j) \geqq 1$, with $b_j'(m_j) \neq 0$. In this case, (III.45) takes the form:

$$\text{(III.50)}\quad \frac{M_1a_{11} - b_{11}\lambda_1(t)\beta^{-1}}{M_2a_{21} - b_{21}\lambda_1(t)\beta^{-1}} = \frac{M_2a_{12} - b_{12}\lambda_2\beta^{-1}}{M_2a_{22} - b_{22}\lambda_2\beta^{-1}},$$

or

$$\text{(III.50}'\text{)}\quad B_1M_1\lambda_2\beta^{-1} + B_2M_1M_2 + B_3M_2\lambda_1\beta^{-1} + B_4\lambda_1\lambda_2\beta^{-2} = F(m_1, m_2) = 0,$$

in which B_k is defined as in (III.46′) and λ is given for some balanced growth solution of the pure kernel economy. For a non-trivial solution, we require

$$\text{(III.50}''\text{)}\quad B_1, B_3 \text{ and } B_4 \not\equiv 0.$$

Now, $b_j(0) = 0$ from (III.33). So, if we set $m_1 = 0$, $\lambda_1 = \beta$ and $M_1 = 1$, in which case (III.50′) reduces to

$$\text{(III.50}'''\text{)}\quad (B_2 + B_3)(1 + m_2) + (B_1 + B_4)[1 + b_2(m)]\beta^{-1} = 0.$$

For $m_2 = 0$ also, we have:

$$\text{(III.50}^{\text{iv}}\text{)}\quad \Sigma B_k\big|_{m_1,\, m_2 = 0} = 0.$$

Using (III.50″), we have

$$(B_2 + B_3) + \beta^{-1}(B_1 + B_4)b_2'(m_2) = 0 \text{ or}$$

$$\beta^{-1}(B_1 + B_4)b_2'(m_2) = -(B_2 + B_3), \text{ that is,}$$

$$\text{(III.50}^{\text{v}}\text{)}\quad b_2'(m_2)\big|_{m_1 = 0} = \frac{-(B_2 + B_3)\beta}{B_1 + B_4} \gtrless 0,$$

so that the sign of $b_2'(m_2)$ does not change. In this case, the function $b_2(m_2)$ can be inverted; therefore, for $m_1 = 0$, m_2 would have a unique value from the inverse function, say,

$$\text{(III.50}^{\text{vi}}\text{)}\quad m_2\big|_{m_1 = 0} = \overset{*}{m_2} > 0$$

for the meaningful case. Similarly, for $m_2 = 0$, namely, $b_2(0) = 0$, $\lambda_2 = \beta$ and $M_2 = 1$, we have, from (III.50′),

$$\text{(III.50}^{\text{vii}}\text{)} \quad (B_1 + B_2)(1 + m_1) + (B_3 + B_4)[1 + b_1(m_1)]\beta^{-1} = 0.$$

Using the same reasoning, we can show that, since

$$\text{(III.50}^{\text{viii}}\text{)} \quad b_1'(m_1) = \frac{-(B_1 + B_2)\beta}{B_3 + B_4} \gtrless 0,$$

we can derive:

$$\text{(III.50}^{\text{ix}}\text{)} \quad m_1 \big|_{m_2 = 0} = m_1^* > 0.$$

If we suppose that (III.50′) defines an implicit function of the form $m_2 = f(m_1)$, then (III.50^{v}) and (III.50^{ix}) give the end points of its graph, with reference to the first quadrant. Since (III.50′) is a polynomial, then we can suppose the function f(m_1) to be continuous, so that its graph will intersect the 45° line at least once (Fig. 6.10). So we have proved:

Proposition E

A common discount rate m also exists in the case of a variable accounting prices policy.

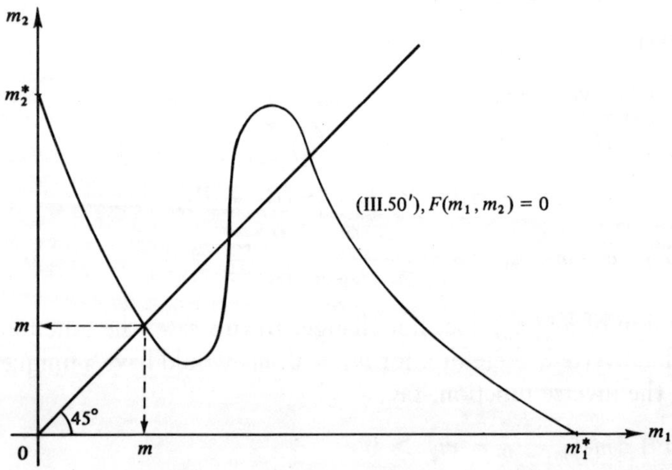

Fig. 6.10 The existence of a common discount rate under the system of variable quoted prices over time.

From (III.50′), we have, as before, three possibilities.

(i) $B_2 = 0$, that is,

$$\text{(III.51)} \quad \frac{a_{12}}{a_{11}} = \frac{a_{22}}{a_{21}}.$$

In this case, (III.50′) reduces to

$$\text{(III.51′)} \quad B_1(M_1\beta/\lambda_1) + B_3(M_2\beta/\lambda_2) + B_4 = 0.$$

Note that $M_j\beta/\lambda_j = 1$ implies $m_j = b(m_j)$, an identity function, which is a special case. For $M_j\beta/\lambda_j > 0$ and $\neq 1$, we can proceed as follows. We have:

$$\text{(III.51″)} \quad \left.\frac{M_2\beta}{\lambda}\right|_{\frac{M_1\beta}{\lambda}=1} = -\frac{(B_1 + B_4)}{B_3} > 0$$

and

$$\text{(III.51‴)} \quad \left.\frac{M_1\beta}{\lambda}\right|_{\frac{M_2\beta}{\lambda}=1} = -\frac{(B_3 + B_4)}{B_1} > 0.$$

The condition for a unique $M\beta/\lambda$ can be summarized in Fig. 6.11.

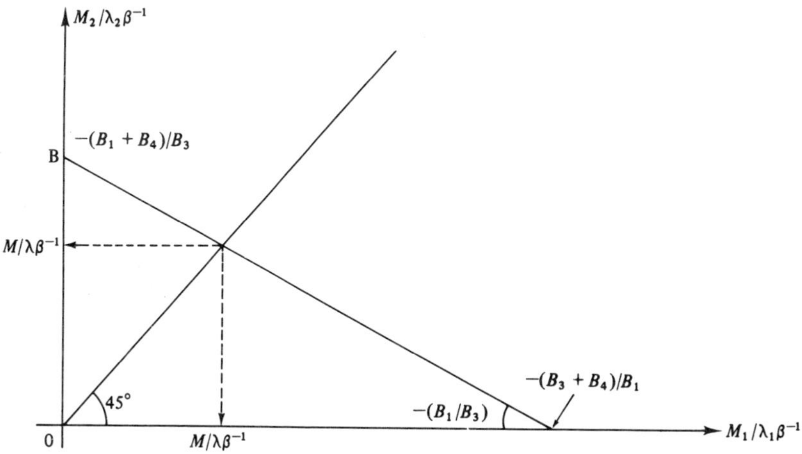

Fig. 6.11 The uniqueness of a common $M/\lambda\beta^{-1}$ under the system of variable quoted prices over time.

We require that the curve *BB* is downward sloping, or

(III.51[iv]) $\text{sign } B_1 = \text{sign } B_3$

which is, from (III.46′)

(III.51[v]) $\frac{b_{22}}{b_{12}} \gtrless \frac{a_{21}}{a_{11}} \text{ iff } \frac{a_{22}}{a_{12}} \gtrless \frac{b_{21}}{b_{11}},$

so that, using (III.51), we have

(III.51[vi]) $\frac{b_{11}}{b_{21}} \gtrless \frac{b_{12}}{b_{22}}$

which is the same as (III.38″′) and (III.47″′).

(ii) $B_2 < 0$, or

(III.52) $\frac{a_{21}}{a_{11}} < \frac{a_{22}}{a_{12}}.$

Putting $M_1 = M_2 = M$ and hence $\lambda_1 = \lambda_2 = \lambda$, then (III.50′) gives

(III.52′) $B_2\left(\frac{M\beta}{\lambda}\right)^2 + (B_1 + B_3)\left(\frac{M\beta}{\lambda}\right) + B_4 = 0.$

So that the condition for a unique real root is

(III.52″) $(B_1 + B_3)^2 = 4B_2B_4,$

or since $B_2 < 0$,

(III.52″′) $B_4 < 0 \text{ or } \frac{b_{12}}{b_{11}} < \frac{b_{22}}{b_{21}},$

which is identical to (III.39″′) or (III.48″′).

(iii) $B_2 > 0$, that is,

(III.53) $\frac{a_{12}}{a_{11}} > \frac{a_{22}}{a_{21}}.$

Again, putting $M_1 = M_2 = M$ and $\lambda_1 = \lambda_2 = \lambda$, we can derive from (III.50′) the same quadratic equation as (III.52′), so that the condition for a unique root $M\beta/\lambda$ is:

(III.53′) $B_4 > 0$, or $\dfrac{b_{12}}{b_{11}} > \dfrac{b_{22}}{b_{21}}$,

the same as (III.40′) or (III.49′).
Hence, we can state:

Proposition F

With variable accounting prices, the ratio $(1 + m_1)/[1 + b_1(m_1)] = (1 + m_2)/[1 + b_2(m_2)]$ *is uniquely determined, if the relative effectiveness of the two processes remains unchanged.*

We now proceed to examine the possibility of a unique m under Proposition F. Now

$$\text{(III.54)} \quad \frac{M\beta}{\lambda} = \frac{1 + m_1}{1 + b_1(m_1)}.$$

For a given LHS, we have

$$\text{(III.54}'\text{)} \quad b_1'(m_1) = \frac{\lambda}{M\beta} > 0.$$

Similarly, for

$$\text{(III.54}''\text{)} \quad \frac{M\beta}{\lambda} = \frac{1 + m_2}{1 + b_2(m_2)},$$

$$\text{(III.54}'''\text{)} \quad b_2'(m_2) = \frac{\lambda}{M\beta} > 0.$$

Hence the functions $b_j(m_j)$ are invertible, with $b_j(0) = 0$. The possibility of a unique m can then be shown in Fig. 6.12. We choose a value $\bar{b}$ such that $\bar{b} = b_1(m_1) = b_2(m_2)$; then $0\overline{m_1} = 0\overline{m_2}$, because $\lambda/M\beta = \overline{b_1 m_1}/0\overline{m_1} = \overline{b_2 m_2}/0\overline{m_2}$, or $0\bar{b}/0\overline{m_1} = 0\bar{b}/0\overline{m_2}$. Hence, the unique value for m is $\overline{m_1} = \overline{m_2} = \overline{m}$. So we can prove:

Proposition G

For a policy of variable accounting prices, a unique value for the common discount rate can be found if the relative effectiveness of the two processes remains unchanged.

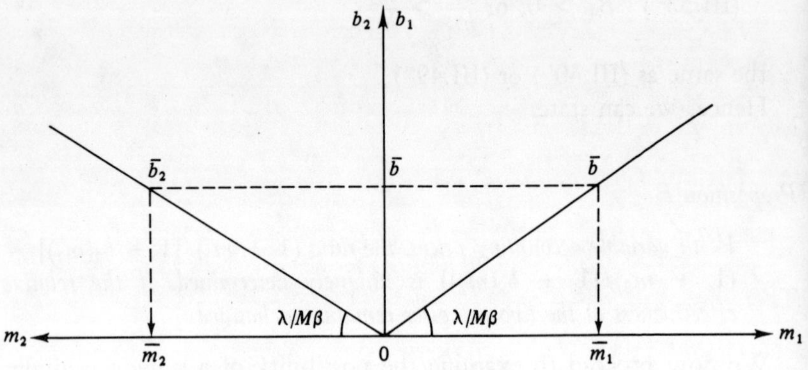

Fig. 6.12 Geometrical proof of a unique discount rate, m.

We can now examine the conditions under which a (planned) balanced growth rate exists for the C-kernel economy. From (III.12) and (III.14), and using (III.6), we have:

$$\text{(III.12}'\text{)}\quad \sum_i x_i(t)(1 + g_i)a_{i1} = \sum_i x_i(t)b_{i1}$$

$$\text{(III.14}'\text{)}\quad \sum_i x_i(t)(1 + g_i)a_{i2} = \sum_i x_i(t)b_{i2}.$$

From Propositions A and B, (III.12′) and (III.14′) can be written

$$\text{(III.55)}\quad (1 + g)\sum_i x_i(t)a_{ij} = \sum_i x_i(t)b_{ij},\ j = 1, 2.$$

Similarly, from (III.28) and (III.45), we have

$$\text{(III.56)}\quad \sum_j a_{ij}p_j(t) = \sum_j b_{ij}\frac{\lambda_j(t)\beta^{-1}P_j(t)}{1 + m_j(t)}$$

$$= \sum_j b_{ij}\frac{[1 + b_j(m_j)]\ P_j(t)}{1 + m_j(t)},\ i = 1, 2.$$

In view of Propositions C to G, (III.60) can be written:

$$\text{(III.57)}\quad (1 + m)\sum_j a_{ij}p_j(t) = [1 + b(m)]\sum_j b_{ij}p_j(t),\ i = 1, 2.$$

We multiply (III.59) by $[1 + b(m)]p_j(t)$ and sum over j:

$$\text{(III.58)} \quad [1 + b(m)](1 + g)\sum_i \sum_j x_i(t) a_{ij} p_j(t) = [1 + b(m)]\sum_i \sum_j x_i(t) b_{ij} p_j(t).$$

Multiplying (III.57) by $x_i(t)$ and summing over i:

$$\text{(III.59)} \quad (1 + m)\sum_i \sum_j a_{ij} p_j(t) x_i(t) = [1 + b(m)]\sum_i \sum_j b_{ij} p_j(t) x_i(t).$$

Therefore, from (III.58) and (III.59), we have

$$\text{(III.60)} \quad [1 + b(m)](1 + g) = 1 + m,$$

so that

$$\text{(III.61)} \quad g = \frac{m - b(m)}{1 + b(m)}, \text{ for } b(m) \geqq 0.$$

This relationship between the rate of expansion of the process intensities and the rate of discount holds for a balanced growth path. Therefore, we can call (III.61) the quasi-turnpike condition. The proper balanced growth (turnpike) condition

$$\text{(III.62)} \quad g = m$$

holds, if and only if

$$\text{(III.63)} \quad b(m) = 0.$$

Equations (III.61) to (III.63) have some interesting implications for central planning in a C-kernel economy. Consider (III.61), the quasi-turnpike condition. If there is balanced expansion in the process intensities, $g \geqq 0$; then, using (III.33) and (III.41), we have

$$\text{(III.64)} \quad m - b(m) = m - \frac{\Delta p}{p} \geqq 0.$$

This relationship shows that, on a balanced growth path, the discount rate and the planned rate of inflation set bounds on one another. The authorities should either take the discount rate as the ceiling for planned inflation, or the rate of inflation should be taken as the lower bound for the range of discount rates that can be selected.

Notice that, for any given rate of expansion $g = \bar{g}$, we can obtain from (III.61)

$$\text{(III.65)} \quad b'(m) = 1/(1 + \bar{g}).$$

This relationship is shown in Fig. 6.13.

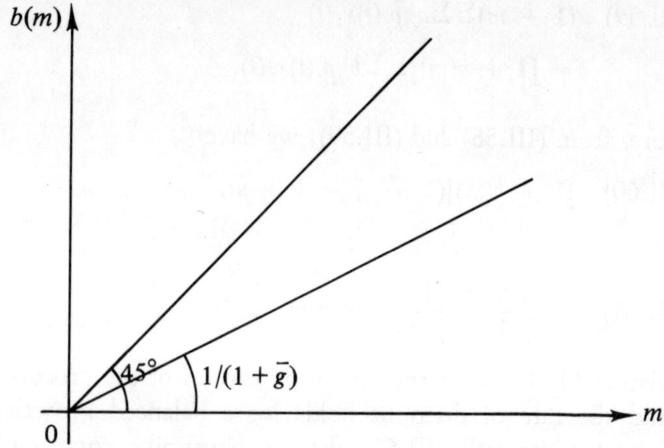

Fig. 6.13 The indeterminancy of the discount rate in the turnpike.

Only the slope of $b(m)$ is uniquely determined by the choice of g, but not the level of m and $b(m) = \Delta p/p$. That is, planning for balanced growth at a rate g only defines the technological side of the model, but not the financial side. A financial plan would also have to be selected, in order for m and $b(m)$ to be determined. This is a consequence of the fact that the quasi-turnpike condition (III.61) involves two independent sides of the model.

Next we consider (III.62) and (III.63), the conditions for a planned turnpike proper. These conditions can be fulfilled if, and only if, the planning authorities adopt a policy of constant accounting prices. We do not think that, even in a socialist planned economy like China, prices can be kept constant indefinitely. However, empirically it appears that they are stable for much longer periods of time than in capitalist systems. There is scope, therefore, for the authorities in the C-kernel economy to pursue an overall balanced growth policy on the basis of (III.62) and (III.63), provided that from time to time pragmatic measures are introduced to change the absolute levels of the accounting prices. As a result, the system would, in a comparative dynamics sense, shift through a series of balanced growth paths, each characterized by a different but constant level of accounting prices. The C-kernel economy therefore could be imagined to follow a zigzag path. This zigzag balanced growth path offers an alternative to the quasi-turnpike in socialist planning, if the authorities can, or wish to implement a policy of constant accounting prices for appreciable lengths of time.

An important question associated with the planned balanced growth condition (III.62) is how high a discount rate the planning authorities can choose. For if too high a rate is chosen, it may not be possible for the process expansion rate g to attain this level. But if m is set at a reasonable level, it seems that (III.62) can hold through a substitution between the qualitative and quantitative aspects of productive methods. Let m be set as $\bar{m}$; then (III.62) requires that $g = \bar{m} = \bar{g}$. From (III.6), we have:

$$\text{(III.66)} \quad \bar{g} = g_1 = g_2 = \xi_1^* \hat{\xi}_1 - 1 = \xi_2^* \hat{\xi}_2 - 1,$$

where, as we have seen, ξ_i^* denotes the quantity coefficient of the ith process intensity over two periods and $\hat{\xi}_i$ is the quality coefficient. That is to say, ξ_i^* stands for quantitative expansion, and ξ_i for qualitative expansion of process i. The last equation in (III.66) can be written

$$\text{(III.67)} \quad \xi_1^* / \xi_2^* = (\hat{\xi}_1 / \hat{\xi}_2)^{-1},$$

so that the relative expansion in quality is the reciprocal of the relative expansion in quantity. Clearly,

$$\text{(III.68)} \quad d(\xi_1^* / \xi_2^*)/d(\hat{\xi}_1 / \hat{\xi}_2) < 0,$$

$$d^2(\xi_1^* / \xi_2^*)/d(\hat{\xi}_1 / \hat{\xi}_2)^2 > 0.$$

Equations (III.67) and (III.68) are summarized in Fig. 6.14.[58] Any point on the substitution frontier *SS* can satisfy the technological requirement for balanced growth (III.62). If we suppose (as in some previous examples) that process 1 is of a more 'technical' nature and process 2 is of a more 'organizational' nature, a balanced growth rate $\bar{g} = \bar{m}$ can be found if it is possible to move along the frontier sufficiently to the

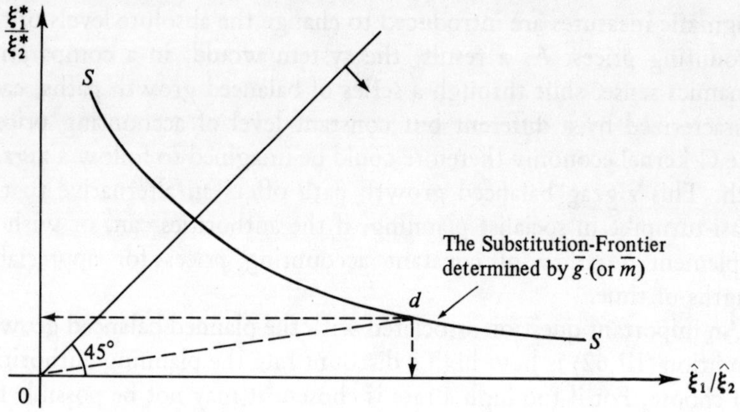

Fig. 6.14 The substitution-frontier of the relative expansion of process intensities (productive methods).

right of the 45° line, say, to a point like '*d*' in Fig. 6.14. At such a point, process 1 becomes more qualitatively augmented and process 2 more quantitatively augmented. In this sense, the scarce land is made more available than its fixed quantity permits, and the abundant labour is absorbed by a relatively higher level of quantitative activity. So we can say that planning for balanced growth in the C-kernel economy is feasible if there exists enough substitutability between the quantity and quality aspects of production. It would be up to the planning authorities to issue directives and implement measures to bring about the required movements along the substitution frontier.

Finally, we have argued previously that different commodities may be assigned different discount rates, with the suggestion that it is likely that $m_2 > m_1$, since labour is more abundant than land. Yet, for a planned balance growth path, we require a discount rate common to both commodities. Then how is it possible to reconcile the objective of balanced growth with $g = m$ with the differential rates of time preference $m_2 > m_1$?

As an answer, we can imagine institutional measures which are designed to bring about the effects of a differential discount rate ($m_2 > m_1$) policy, even though the system is on a growth path with $g = m = m_1 = m_2$. It is reasonable to impose the condition:

(III.69) $\min m_1 \leqq m \leqq \max m_2$.

Suppose that m is chosen such that $\acute{m}$ = min m_1. Then the discount rate for the abundant labour (m_2) must be reduced to the level of m for balanced growth. But this would mean that future labour would be overvalued at present, which might encourage a further increase in an already high birth rate, though it is likely that a fall in m_2 would lead to a rise in p_2, the accounting wage, other things being equal. The planning authorities would then have to introduce countermeasures of an institutional nature, for example, administrative control of the birth rate, penalties for having large families, and so on.

To illustrate the problem, let us work out one possibility. Let us suppose that there is a negative relationship between, say, the penalty for having too many children and the birth rate, given the social environment. For example, social convention may demand a son both for the sake of inheritance and contribution to production, and for social prestige.[59] This relationship may be called a birth control frontier (Fig. 6.15). The frontier will shift outwards as the desire for having a son increases; inwards as the desire decreases. The diagram summarizes the fact that the public is facing an opportunity cost for an increase in the birth rate. It is then up to the people to decide how great a penalty they intend to accept for the chance of having a son. The level of penalties is thus a policy variable for the planning authorities. A constant rate of deterrence would be represented by the straight line trade-off curve in Fig. 6.15. The authorities could also introduce a progressive rate of deterrence, as represented by the other curve in the

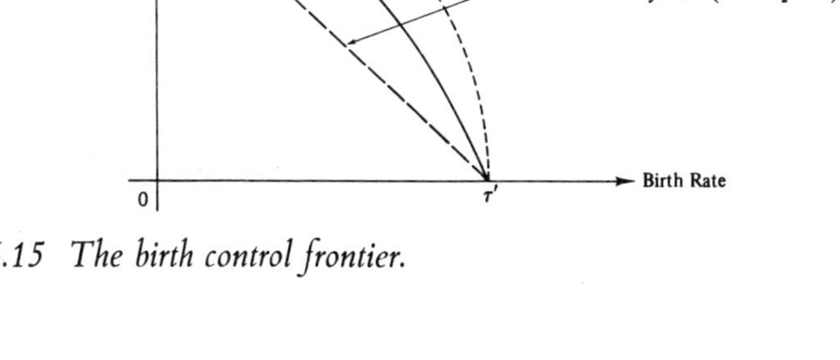

Fig. 6.15 The birth control frontier.

diagram. From the previous discussion, it is perhaps reasonable to suppose that the level of penalties imposed is influenced by the valuation of future labour (m_2) in comparison with the general valuation of the future represented by the common discount rate m. This is shown by the shape of the birth control frontier, which depends on the difference max $m_2 - m$. Thus, we can say that an institutional policy can be chosen to reconcile the choice of a common m required by balanced growth planning with the different valuation of land and labour represented by the differential rates of discount m_1 and m_2.

Notes

[1] For a survey of the general economic conditions in China, see, for example Eckstein (1977) and Myers (1980).

[2] We will be especially concerned with developing some of the ideas contained in Kantorovich's famous works; *The Best Use of Economic Resources*, and the later *Essays in Optimal Planning*. An excellent account of the contributions of Kantorovich can be found in Johansen (1976).

[3] Kantorovich (1965).

[4] Kantorovich (1976).

[5] There is a formal discussion of land scarcity in terms of a multi-period planning model. But Kantorovich is interested only in the properties of inter-temporal efficiency prices, and the effects of a fixed quantity of land on the time path of the system are not discussed. On this, see Kantorovich (1976), Ch. 4.

[6] Our approach follows that of Kantorovich's original contribution in *The Best Use of Economic Resources*, in which agricultural planning is studied as an independent sub-problem in a general short-term plan.

[7] See Marshall (1977), Bk IV, Ch. III.

[8] See Hicks (1965), Ch. IV. The same point was made by Marshall, see Marshall (1977), Bk IV, Ch. III, p. 130. We may also point out here that Ricardo's theory is explicitly growth-oriented, while Kantorovich's linear-programming approach

in *The Best Use of Economic Resources* is more suited to analysing allocative efficiency, and it also takes income distribution as given.

[9] There are quite a few problems connected with this assumption, especially that of defining 'fertility', which in general depends on the crop. Marshall has given a very thorough discussion of these problems in Marshall (1977), Bk IV, Ch. II and III. Here, we will just take the assumption as it stands, and suppose there is only one kind of crop, 'corn'.

[10] The notation here follows Pasinetti (1960, 1977).

[11] As Marshall was at pains to show, the existence of a producer's surplus is a technical consequence of diminishing returns, while the existence of rent as an income category is a separate issue which depends on the assumptions made about property rights over land and the nature of the tenancy agreement. See Marshall (1977) Bk IV, Ch. IX and X.

[12] Pasinetti (1960), p. 130.

[13] Hicks and Hollander (1977) suggest a solution to the problem by abandoning the constant natural wage condition. In the neo-classical theory, for example that of Marshall (1977), Bk IV, Ch. II and III, and Bk VI, Ch. IX, this problem does not arise because the analysis is confined to a point equivalent to Ricardo's stationary state.

[14] As Schumacher has shown, the principle of total employment in agriculture makes quite a lot of sense in many developing countries, regardless of the political structure. See Schumacher (1976), Ch. 11 and 12.

[15] See Pasinetti (1977), eq. (6) and (6a).

[16] As Robinson (1978, p. 157) has written: 'In a socialist economy there are, strictly speaking, no wages. The means of production are owned in common and everybody works, not for a particular employer, but for his fellow citizens. The payment which individuals receive is their share of the total proceeds of the economy.' This is the meaning of the real wages $\hat{x}$ and x^* discussed here.

[17] We should point out here that the viability condition (II.3) ensures that there is some positive range of N for which the situation summarized in Fig. 6.2 is possible.

[18] See Robinson (1978).

[19] We will have something more to say on the general relationship between the different kinds of prices in the next section.

[20] See Hicks (1965), Ch. VII.

[21] See Pasinetti (1977), p. 15.

[22] See Schumacher (1976), Ch. 11–13.

[23] See Marshall (1977), Bk IV, Ch. III; Kaldor (1960), p. 212; and Pasinetti (1977), p. 10.

[24] This is especially true for the allocation of resources to research and development. As Kantorovich and Makarov have shown, it is only within a planned growth model that this problem can be formulated on an optimization basis, and the likely results of such activities evaluated in terms of comparative dynamics. See Kantorovich and Makarov (1976), pp. 54, 64.

[25] See Kantorovich (1976), Ch. 4, section 3.

[26] See Kantorovich (1965), Ch. 2, section 5. On the problem of allowing for depreciation in a socialist economy, see Kantorovich (1976), Ch. 13. For simplicity, we will take depreciation as a constant.

[27] For further discussion of the problem of hire valuation for machinery, see Kantorovich (1965), Ch. II, especially sections 5 and 8.

[28] It may be interesting to quote here Kantorovich's comments on the Soviet scheme of price taxation in agriculture.

> At the present time differences in the natural fertility of land are allowed for through prices: the level of purchase prices is differentiated according to agricultural zones, and differential rent is collected in proportion to the volume of production. If procurement prices are made approximately uniform throughout the nation, and if fixed rent payments for natural resources are established, this will promote the fuller and more effective use of the land.

See Kantorovich (1976), Ch. 15, p. 214.

[29] It may be interesting to note that, even in as capitalistic and free market a system as Hong Kong, the government also operates a stabilization scheme for the price of rice. We are indebted to C.L. Wu for drawing our attention to this fact.

[30] See Kantorovich (1976), Ch. 4.

[31] For a detailed analysis of this model, see von Neumann (1945–6), Kemeny *et al.* (1956), Dorfman *et al.* (1955) and Morgenstern and Thompson (1976).

[32] For a proof of this result, see Morgenstern and Thompson (1976), Ch. 4, Theorem 4.6.

[33] See Morgenstern and Thompson (1976), Ch. 10, for a brief discussion of this possibility.

[34] Koopmans (1957).

[35] Kantorovich has argued that it is this characteristic that makes mathematical programming methods especially applicable to socialist systems. See, for example, Kantorovich (1965), Introduction, and (1976), Ch. 2 and 3; also Polanyi (1958a, 1969).

[36] See Polanyi (1958a, 1958b).

[37] The time needed for an algorithm to solve a certain problem, expressed as a function of its size as measured by the quantity of input data n, is defined as its time complexity. For example, the QUICKSORT algorithm for sorting problems has a time complexity of $c\, n \log_2 n$, $c > 0$. See, for example, Aho *et al.* (1974), Ch. 1 and 3.

[38] Take as an example the classic Kantorovich case of linear programming. In this case, the objective function, technology, constraints, and so on, are all linear, but the time complexity of the best algorithm is a polynominal, so that the time required for a solution may be as much as :

$$c(m + n)n^3\left[\sum_{i=1}^{m}\sum_{j=1}^{n}\log_2(|a_{ij}| + 1) + \sum_{i=1}^{m}\log_2(|b_i| + 1) + \log_2 mn + 2\right]$$

units of time, where c is some constant > 0, n the number of instruments and m the number of constraints, and assuming that one arithmetical operation takes one unit of time in a computer. See, for example, Brand (1981) for a more detailed discussion.

[39] Kantorovich and his team have formulated by linear programming a production scheduling and product distribution problem for rolled metal and tubing for the Soviet steel industry. In its most general form, the constraint coefficients matrix is of the order 3×10^6 by 3×10^4. It took about eight years to programme and solve this problem, using first a Minsk-20 and then a Minsk-22 computer. We are not told how much computation time was required for the solution, but this example serves to show that actual computation time really measures in many cases only a fraction of the total time cost of production planning. On all of this, see Kantorovich (1976), Ch. 18.

[40] See Hicks (1976).

[41] Kantorovich has studied the consequence of one particular case, that of 'rush work', see Kantorovich (1965), Introduction.

[42] We can note here an essay by Kantorovich which discusses the difficulties with the use of mathematical methods in socialist production planning. He refers in particular to the problems caused by 'rigid deadlines for obtaining solutions,' and 'the receipt of information in good time,' see Kantorovich (1976), Ch. 3.

[43] Perhaps in this way the crucial insights of such writers as Schultz (1981), and Schumacher (1976) — or indeed Marshall (1977), Bk IV, Ch. 1. — can be incorporated into the linear growth model.

[44] The reader is reminded that our formulation (III.1) $x_i = x_i^* \hat{x}_i$ is only intended as a simple example.

[45] See Morgenstern and Thompson (1976), Ch. 8 and 10.

[46] Morgenstern and Thompson, (1976), p. 170.

[47] See Morgenstern and Thompson (1976), which is denoted to this kind of construction, starting from a 2 × 2 kernel agricultural economy.

[48] See Morgenstern and Thompson (1976), Ch. 8.

[49] We should point out here that, in this case, the kernel is not a 'sub-economy' in the sense of KMT, because this latter concept is defined as: 'a subset of goods and processes of the original economy which has the same solution and the same growth rate as the original economy' (Morgenstern and Thompson, 1976, p. 87). Since the kernel need not have the same growth rate as a larger system constructed from it, it does not satisfy the definition for a sub-economy.

[50] In terms of an NKMT model, the rule of free goods states that overproduced goods carry a zero price.

[51] The reader is reminded of the nature of wages in a socialist system; see Section II above, note 19.

[52] By a well-known theorem, the solution of an NKMT model can be interpreted in terms of linear programming. See Morgenstern and Thompson (1976), Ch. 2 and 3. It follows that the prices y_j are the dual variables to the intensities x_i, so that the y_j are efficiency prices.

[53] Kantorovich has shown that, in investment planning, different projects can also be assigned differential discount rates ('norms of effectiveness'). Such a case may arise if the authorities believe that the probabilities of future returns vary from project to project, so that a lower norm for a given scheme would represent an allowance for the higher probability of payoff. See Kantorovich (1976), Ch. 14. Our $m_j(t)$ and the Kantorovich differential discount rates E_k can be related; for if a commodity has a high priority and if it is not a fixed factor, then there would also

be a high priority for investment in it, in which case a lower norm would be assigned to such projects.

[54] In our simple model we have no taxation so that there are no funds for direct subsidies to balance any losses, except in the case where the accounting profits of one process equal the accounting losses of the other. Since the activity levels are already determined, these sums are a matter of accounting prices only. We would therefore prefer to treat this case as just one example of indirect subsidies given through adjustments in accounting prices. After such adjustments are made, then both processes would show zero profits.

[55] As we will see below, it is likely that $\alpha_1 > \alpha_2$, if (III.26) is considered by itself.

[56] See the discussion of the socialist principle of total employment in Section II above, especially the remarks of Robinson on the nature of socialist wages.

[57] The relationship between $\Delta p_j/p_j$ and m_j with $\Delta p_j/p_j < 0$ is trivial because in this case the two concepts have the same meaning. It is like analysing the relationship between the rate of deflation and the interest rate on a balanced growth path of the NKMT model.

[58] The reader is reminded that the relationship (III.1) $x_i = x_i^* \hat{x}_i$ is just one particular case which we study because of its simplicity.

[59] This is probably true in many rural areas of China.

References

Aho, A.V., Hopcroft, J.E., and Ullman, J.D. (1974), *The Design and Analysis of Computer Algorithms* (Reading, Mass., Addison–Wesley).

Brand, R.G. (1981), 'The Ellipsoid Method, A Survey', *Operations Research*, vol. 29.

Dorfman, R., Samuelson, P.A., and Solow, R.M. (1958), *Linear Programming and Economic Analysis* (New York, McGraw-Hill).

Eckstein, A. (1977), *China's Economic Revolution* (Cambridge, Cambridge University Press).

Ellman, M. (1973), *Planning Problems in the USSR* (Cambridge, Cambridge University Press).

Hicks, J.R. (1965), *Capital and Growth* (Oxford, Oxford University Press).

—— (1976), 'Some Questions of Time in Economics', in A.M. Tang, *et al.* (eds.), *Evolution, Welfare and Time in Economics* (Lexington, Mass., D.C. Heath & Co.).

Hicks, J.R., and Hollander, S. (1977), 'Mr. Ricardo and the Moderns', *Quarterly Journal of Economics,* vol. XCI.

Johansen, L. (1976), 'L.V. Kantorovich's Contribution to Economics', *Scandinavian Journal of Economics*, vol. 78.

Kaldor, N. (1960), 'Alternative Theories of Distribution', in *Essays on Value and Distribution* (London, G. Duckworth & Co.).

Kantorovich, L.V. (1965), *The Best Use of Economic Resources* (Oxford, Pergamon Press).

—— (1976), *Essays in Optimal Planning* (New York, International Arts and Sciences Press Inc.).

Kantorovich, L.V., and Makarov, V.L. (1976), 'Growth Models and Their Application to Long-Term Planning and Forecasting', in T.S. Khachaturov (ed.), *Methods of Long-Term Planning and Forecasting* (London, Macmillan).

Kemeny, J.G., Morgenstern, O., and Thompson, G.L. (1956), 'A Generalization of the von Neumann Model of an Expanding Economy', *Econometica,* vol. 24.

Koopmans, T.C. (1957), *Three Essays on the State of Economic Science* (New York, McGraw-Hill).

Marshall, A. (1977), *Principles of Economics* (London, Macmillan), 8th ed.

Morgenstern, O., and Thompson, G.L. (1976), *Mathematical Theory of Expanding and Contracting Economies* (Lexington, Mass., D.C. Heath & Co.).

Myers, R.H. (1980), *The Chinese Economy Past and Present* (Balmont, Calif., Wadsworth, Inc.).

Pasinetti, L.L. (1960), 'A Mathematical Formulation of the Ricardian System', *Review of Economic Studies*, vol. 27; reprinted in P.K. Newman (ed.), *Readings in Mathematical Economics* (Baltimore, Johns Hopkins Press, 1968), vol II.

—— (1977), *Lectures on the Theory of Production* (London, Macmillan).

Polanyi, M. (1958a), 'The Span of Central Direction', in *The Logic of Liberty* (Chicago, University of Chicago Press).

—— (1958b), 'The Manageability of Social Tasks', in *The Logic of Liberty* (Chicago, University of Chicago Press).

—— (1969), 'The Determinants of Social Action', in E. Streissler (ed.), *Roads to Freedom* (London, Routledge and Kegan Paul).

Robinson, J. (1978), 'The Philosophy of Prices', in *Contributions to Modern Economics* (Oxford, Blackwell).

Schultz, T.W. (1981), 'The Economics of Being Poor', *Journal of Political Economy*, vol. 89.

Schumacher, E.F. (1973), *Small is Beautiful* (London, Abacus Books).

von Neumann, J. (1945–6), 'A Model of General Economic Equilibrium', *Review of Economic Studies*, vol. 13.

Walsh, V.C., and Gram, H. (1980), *Classical and Neoclassical Theories of General Equilibrium* (New York, Oxford University Press).

Wilcznski, J. (1969), 'Towards Rationality in Land Economics Under Central Planning', *Economic Journal*, vol. 79.

7. Hong Kong as an Economic Model for the Great Cities of China

AUDREY DONNITHORNE

Introduction

In Marxist ideology, the developed metropolis plays an imperialistic role and practises exploitation by exporting capital to its satellite regions from which it draws labour and raw materials. Such a notion was congenial to the Chinese Communists in the early days of their regime. The great cities of the coast, and especially Shanghai, had been centres of foreign economic interests which from there had penetrated the hinterland. While the Chinese Communist Party in its origins was not entirely rural — it was indeed founded in Shanghai and Liu Shaoqi worked among the Shanghai proletariat — its dominant trend as exemplified by Mao carried with it a deep peasant distrust of city life. On the one hand, it never entirely cast off the European Marxist view of the urban proletariat as the spearhead of revolution; on the other hand, the cities were felt to carry a certain contamination.

If this was the attitude towards Shanghai and Tianjin, much deeper was the suspicion and dislike of Hong Kong during the first quarter century of the People's Republic. Hong Kong exemplified so much that was execrated by China's leaders — colonialism, capitalism, cosmopolitanism — and to make matters worse, it prospered exceedingly. The attraction exerted by Hong Kong on the inhabitants of south-east China could not be denied but was sternly denounced. 'Hong Kongism' became a recognized term of abuse levied against those who hankered after its economic fruits.

All this was changed following the post-Mao coup against the 'Gang of Four'. As part of the great reversal of policy which occurred, emphasis was placed on the positive role not only of the great cities of the mainland (their virtues had already begun to be recognized from the late 1950's onwards), but even on that of Hong Kong. The metropolises of China came to be praised as growth centres and people have been urged to learn from the example of the most successful Chinese metropolis of them all — Hong Kong.

The topic of this chapter is Hong Kong as an economic model, but this will necessarily involve consideration of non-economic factors which have a close bearing on the economy and which indeed provide its essential infrastructure.

The Role of Government

The role of government is basic to the whole theme. The proper functioning of government, at any rate to some minimum level, is a necessary although not a sufficient condition of economic prosperity. This applies to what a government does and equally to what it refrains from doing. The Hong Kong Government is perhaps best known for what it refrains from doing. It is widely believed to practice *laissez-faire* in a classic manner. This, however, is not wholly accurate. The Hong Kong authorities themselves claim to have moved from *laissez-faire* to 'discreet guidance' of the economy.

The most significant contribution made by the government of Hong Kong to economic and social life is the provision of the legal framework. The law and its operation may not be ideal — human law is not — but it is there, it is predictable not arbitrary, it is known — or at least where it is in dispute there is a recognized public procedure for having it clarified. The judiciary which administers the law is independent of the executive government and is heir to the long British tradition of such independence. The rule of law does not yield its full benefits until it is taken for granted; indeed until then it can hardly be said to exist. It is not something which can suddenly be introduced by decree. The predictability and stability of the Hong Kong Government is in marked contrast to the violent swings that have characterized China in recent decades, with the stop/go policies these entail for the economy. In China, in the relatively liberal spell after the 1976 coup, much was said about the need for a rule of law which would override these swings. However, there seemed to be insufficient understanding of how tender and slow-maturing a plant this is, and how it needs the right environment for its nurture.

The law in Hong Kong has come to tackle the complexities of modern economic life, adopting and adapting provisions from overseas. Thus, laws and regulations dealing with modern banking, finance and commercial activities, with industrial health and safety measures, and with many other facets of an industrial and technologically-advanced society are now familiar in Hong Kong, not least to the staff of mainland-controlled concerns there. This does not mean that Hong Kong law in these spheres is adequate or above criticism, but it is much in advance of what exists in China. Debate in Hong Kong on legal adaptation to a growing economy must have an educational effect on those from the mainland involved in business in and with Hong Kong. Thus Hong Kong forms a shop window in which China can study these matters before selecting what it desires for its own needs.

The freedom of the press and of other media in Hong Kong confers economic as well as wider benefits. Public issues can be freely debated and the pros and cons of differing policies discussed. In China, on the contrary, the government chooses the issues to be aired and the opinions to be voiced. Thus it is much more difficult to assess the desirability and likely results of any policy and this must affect the quality of decision-making. Shanghai is one of the politically most intense places in China (the former centre of Cultural Revolution fervour) and these considerations are particularly significant there. Allied to this topic, the Hong Kong Government is often accused, with some basis, of being secretive. However, it is a practitioner of open government compared with officialdom across the border.

The Hong Kong Government does not plan, direct, protect or subsidize industry. Hong Kong is a free port; the few import duties are for revenue purposes only and are also charged on similar goods made locally. The procedure for setting up companies is simple both for local and overseas interests, and both are treated equally. The government evinces no 'soak the foreigner' mentality and foreign undertakings are faced with no requirement to take in local equity. Capital can be moved in and out of Hong Kong and profits remitted without restriction. Hong Kong has in the past been mercifully free of loss-making public enterprises; nor is there a protected import substitute sector. Corporate and personal taxes are low and are levied impartially. This means that the time, energy and ingenuity that is devoted to tax avoidance and its equivalents, in both advanced Western and socialist economies, is in Hong Kong spent on productive purposes.

The Exchange Fund, which provides backing for the currency, is managed by the government. The international value of the Hong Kong dollar fluctuates through the operation of a 'managed float', more or less according to market conditions. Thus, the exchange rate is not altered arbitrarily, nor are there differing exchange rates in operation at the same time. In China, 'internal accounting' exchange rates operate. These may differ from enterprise to enterprise and since they value the renminbi below its official parity, they have the effect of subsidizing exports and discouraging imports. The internal exchange rate applicable to individual undertakings can be subject to negotiation, which adds uncertainty and complexities to commercial dealings.

In Hong Kong, the price mechanism is permitted to operate unchecked, with certain important exceptions. These exceptions include control of the price of rice, a measure of rent control, strict regulation of the prices charged by public utility monopolies and a degree of government influence on rates of interest. For the rest, competitive prices formed by the interaction of supply and demand are allowed to allocate productive resources and to shape the direction of the economy, including the rise and decline of different sectors and industries. The price mechanism normally provides a more generally acceptable and effective discipline than do government controls. It brings about change in smaller steps because it comes about as a result of a great number of private decisions. In addition, without the operation of the price mechanism, there is no rational economic basis for investment decisions.

The positive role of the Hong Kong Government in the economy has evolved on an *ad hoc* basis. Whatever private enterprise can effectively do has in general been left to it, with the government stepping in to fill the gaps. Thus, in some sectors, such as housing, the government's role has been massive while in others it is minimal.

In the course of filling gaps, government departments in Hong Kong undertake some developmental tasks in relation to industry — but on the whole, as far as industry is concerned, they concentrate on regulatory activities. An important example of these regulatory activities is the allocation among manufacturers of Hong Kong's export quotas to various overseas markets. The procedures provide for flexibility and for a maximum utilization of quotas in a manner which might well be studied by China. After the initial allocation has been made by the Trade Industry and Customs Department, primarily on past performance, an open market for the trading of quotas is permitted. In this way quotas are channelled into the hands of those manufacturers who can make the most profitable use of them and this has had the effect of encouraging the export of products of a high per unit value. The transfer of quotas also gives individual producers the ability to switch between categories of goods. In general, the system prevents the stagnation that can arise from the use of a 'past performance' criterion alone. Applied to China, this system might tend to concentrate the manufacture of textile and garment exports even more than at present in Shanghai and Tianjin but without denying opportunities to enterprising and efficient producers elsewhere in the country.

The Hong Kong Government is spared the political pressures that occur in China for allocation of quotas to particular regions. Those pressures occur, of course, not in isolation but in the context of the whole network of negotiations and bargaining on political as well as economic matters that is constantly in progress between central and provincial level units (including the great cities) and between local units themselves.

The Hong Kong Productivity Council and Centre is an example of official initiative in the industrial field. The Council is a statutory organization, financed by annual government grants and by fees for services to individual clients. The Centre, the executive arm of the Council, acts as an industrial consultant and provides technical information and assistance, computer and technological services, as well as running training programmes in management, electronic data-processing and other forms of technology. It collaborates with the United Nations Development Programme in providing technical assistance to industry. As a result of link-ups with computer systems in the United States, the most recent technical information is available in Hong Kong almost instantaneously. This organization might usefully be studied by Shanghai and other Chinese industrial cities.

In the sphere of primary industries, the most notable government activities in Hong Kong are in the wholesaling of vegetables and fish through the Vegetable and Fish Marketing Organizations. The administration of both is vested in the Director of Marketing who is assisted by several senior officers of the Department of Agriculture and Fisheries. Each Organization has an advisory board on which sit representatives of the producers. In the large mainland cities, it is said that to get good-quality fresh produce it is necessary for customers to buy from stalls set up by peasants who bring in their own produce, rather than from the markets run by the state commercial departments. In Hong Kong, however, the official markets have apparently succeeded in ensuring high-quality supplies simultaneously with achieving the economies of scale, including the saving of producers' time, that result from centralized wholesaling. It would be interesting to make a comparative investigation of the agricultural and fishery wholesaling systems in Hong Kong and in the large mainland municipalities to see what lessons could be learned.

Some public utilities in Hong Kong are government-owned and operated. Most, however, are in private hands but are closely regulated by government, while joint government-private ownership is also to be found in this sector. The Post Office and the Hong Kong section of the Kowloon–Canton Railway operate as government departments and the water supply comes under the Water Supplies Department. The supply of electricity is divided on a geographical basis between two large and one small private enterprise companies. The two larger systems are now interconnected while one of them has an agreement to supply power to Guangdong. Gas supplies are also provided by a private enterprise company. Both electricity and gas undertakings are subject to government regulations which, among other things, cover tariffs and plans for capital expenditure, and set limits on profits.

General supervision of all telecommunications services in Hong Kong is exercised by the Postmaster General in his capacity as the officially denoted Telecommunications Authority. Most of the services themselves, however, are provided by private enterprise, notably the Hong Kong Telephone Co. Ltd. and (on the international side) Cable and Wireless Ltd. This ensures speedy introduction into Hong Kong of new telecommunications developments from overseas.

Similarly, the official Commissioner for Transport is the Statutory Authority with general responsibility for planning and regulating public transport. A Transport Advisory Committee, appointed by the government, advises on broad policy issues. Apart from the rail systems (the Hong Kong section of the Kowloon–Canton Railway and the Mass Transit Railway (MTR)) public transport is provided by non-government concerns. In the case of major public transport undertakings, schedules and routing as well as fares are controlled by the government.

Road traffic is the least efficient sector of Hong Kong's transport. Hong Kong people have the same eager desire for private cars found elsewhere in the world where this option is available. This has led to the clogging of the road system and frequent traffic jams. Higher taxes on private motoring might better reconcile private choice and public interest. This is not a problem which is likely to afflict the cities of China in the immediate future. However, it is one which should engage the Chinese authorities in advance. In the past, they have been inclined to brush it off with ideological statements that the Chinese would not want private cars. Now that it has begun to be acknowledged that the hopes and aspirations of Chinese on both sides of the border are not very different, it should be accepted that private motoring will increase in China and that it is desirable that it should do so, at least to a certain degree. It is not good for any society that political power should be the only path to affluent living. To extend car ownership to the wealthy as well as the powerful would provide a significant incentive to the entrepreneurs in China's growing private sector. It would also furnish openings for those services ancillary to private motoring. Nevertheless, there is no reason why private motoring should not be made to bear the social costs it imposes nor why it should not make an additional contribution to the revenue.

Hong Kong's port facilities and operations could with advantage be copied by Chinese ports. Turn-around times for ships in Hong Kong are much faster than in Chinese ports which have become notorious for delays. Hong Kong's container terminal is one of the most modern in the world. The port exhibits a similar mixture of government control and private enterprise found in many public utilities in Hong Kong. Most wharves and terminals are privately owned and operated. The port is administered by a government official who is advised by committees on which shipping and commercial interests are represented. It must be mentioned that China is currently undertaking an ambitious programme of expanding and modernizing its ports.

The choice on pragmatic grounds of public or private ownership and operation for public utilities, together with government regulation and supervision of private monopolies, seeks to combine a concern for the public interest with the flexibility and incentive to economical management which may be expected from private enterprise. Despite inevitable strains caused by a rapidly growing community, most of Hong Kong's public utilities have provided a quality of service which is high by the standards of developing countries.

The Hong Kong Government's achievement in housing over two million urban residents since 1954 is, like the comparable achievement of Singapore, an example to other parts of the developing world. If it had not been for the influx of immigrants from China in recent years, all Hong Kong's squatters would by now have been re-housed.

The Hong Kong Housing Authority is a statutory body with an overall responsibility for public housing which it plans, builds and manages. It is required to cover its recurrent expenditure from its income, which derives mainly from rent. The Authority's cash flow also covers much of the cost of new construction although it is authorized to borrow free of interest from the official Development Loan Fund. The government provides land free of charge and has on occasion remitted loans made to the Authority. The earlier blocks of flats constructed by the Authority were put up to meet an emergency and provided only very basic accommodation. These have been succeeded by constantly improved, newer versions, while the original blocks have been altered to achieve the higher standards now possible.

Much of the public housing being built in Hong Kong at the present time is in the new towns of the New Territories, where sites have also been made available for industry. These new towns, planned with the best advice available from overseas, are a model of their kind. Both in the redevelopment of old urban areas and in the design and construction of new towns, Hong Kong has much to offer by way of example.

The Municipality of Shanghai has built a number of new satellite towns to which over 400 factories and other units have moved. However, failure to provide adequate housing, schools and other facilities resulted in only some 15 per cent of the 300,000 workers in these factories living in the new towns in 1979. Shanghai's transport problems have therefore been aggravated by additional commuting.[1]

Both Hong Kong and Shanghai ban immigration from across their borders. In Hong Kong people are free to move their residence within these borders as they wish. This is not the case in Shanghai where household registration (which confers the right to live in the Municipality) is divided into three categories — city, satellite towns and rural. Moving from the city proper to a satellite town involves a change of registration. To leave the city entails a serious disadvantage for families in that children with city registrations are more likely, on leaving school, to be assigned work in enterprises or other units under municipal control which provide higher wages and fringe benefits than those units controlled by towns and counties, to which those with non-city registrations are assigned. The different forms of residential registration in Shanghai, and the different levels of remuneration, determined on institutional rather than economic grounds, bring about rigidities in the labour market which are absent in Hong Kong. Within the rural sector in the Chinese municipalities, as in the countryside at large, labour has been 'fixed' to particular agricultural units. Peasants have not been free to move from low to high productivity units or areas.

Owner-occupied housing is normal in the rural areas of both China and Hong Kong, but less common in the cities. In China, while some old urban housing remains in private ownership, there has been little possibility for would-be owners to buy a dwelling. However, some interest is now being taken in Shanghai and other cities in home ownership as a means of improving the often desperate housing situation. It might be worthwhile for Chinese municipalities to investigate the Hong Kong Government's Home Ownership Scheme which was launched in 1976 to help low- and middle-income earners to buy flats especially built by the Housing Authority, with mortgages arranged by banks and other financial institutions on advantageous terms. To augment the supply of housing available to these income groups, the government has encouraged private enterprise to build similar flats, including some in the new towns. Private building activity, subject to government regulation, has been spectacularly active in building residential accommodation for higher-income earners as well as in the construction of business and commercial premises. There has been no difficulty in attracting capital for these projects.

There are said to be two ways of destroying the fabric of a city: one is by bombing and the other by rent control. In China, stringent rent control on both public and privately-owned housing has existed for some three decades. Pride has been taken in the small proportion of wages that workers have had to pay for their housing. Less pride, however, has been shown in the maintenance of that housing and it is often in great disrepair. Hong Kong, beset since 1949 by a chronic shortage of housing, has tried to tack a difficult course between protecting tenants on the one hand and, on the other, giving incentives and funds to landlords to maintain the existing stock of housing and to build more. The measures taken have been to enforce rent control, at times only on housing built before a set date or for tenancies below a certain rent, at other times more comprehensively. However, periodic increases in rents have been allowed, with the advantages and disadvantages of rent control being recognized, carefully weighed and subject to public discussion. Business premises built since the Second World War are not subject to rent control.

Education forms a major part of the economy, both as a consumer good in demand for its own sake, and as one of the most important categories of investment. The Cultural Revolution left China's education system in a state of deterioration and collapse from which it is still in the process of recovering. The crisis in education which Hong Kong faced after 1949, caused by the huge inflow of refugees, was different in kind but equally challenging. In China, the worst ravages of the Cultural Revolution were visited on the higher levels of education, with universities and many middle schools being closed for years; while in Hong Kong in the 1950's, the greatest need was for basic schooling.

The Hong Kong authorities met their crisis by enlisting the resources of the voluntary sector which throughout Hong Kong history has educated more children than have government schools. All non-profit-making private schools which are up to the required standards are now eligible for aided status and can have most of their costs met from public funds. In addition, profit-making private schools provide education for many children for whom places are not available in government or aided schools. Private schools rely entirely on fees and thus relieve the government of substantial expenditure, although the education they provide may fall below the quality of government and aided schools. Aided schools, for the most part, provide education of at least an equal standard to that in government schools but at a lower cost per place. The desire for economy has been a significant factor in government support for the voluntary sector, in education as in other spheres. This policy has enabled the Hong Kong Government to extend compulsory education to the age of 15, at minimum cost to public funds. Because of international participation in the education scene in Hong Kong, the process of adopting educational ideas from overseas is made easier. This participation takes place through the operations of international religious orders and missionary groups and, at the tertiary level, through the London-based Association of Commonwealth Universities.

These formal relationships are supplemented by, and have given rise to, a huge range of informal and personal links in education. All this, of course, would have been impossible without a legal system which ensures that Hong Kong residents may associate freely not only with each other but also with outsiders both in Hong Kong and elsewhere. The full benefits flowing from such contacts are denied to the mainland so long as Chinese there are restrained, unless officially authorized, from mixing freely with foreigners. In an increasingly cosmopolitan world, international contacts are of great importance and could be invaluable in lifting Chinese education from the abyss into which it was cast by the Cultural Revolution and by the decades of narrow nationalism which preceded it.

The participation of the voluntary sector in education in Hong Kong is weaker at the tertiary level than at primary and secondary levels. This is partly because three leading private colleges were brought together to form the Chinese University of Hong Kong, thus virtually passing into the public sector. The Hong Kong authorities, being British, have modelled their policies on higher education mainly on those pursued in the United Kingdom where, in the course of this century, independent foundations such as Oxford and Cambridge have become increasingly absorbed into the public sector while the establishment of new universities has taken place almost entirely under government auspices. In the United States, on the contrary, private foundations such as the Ivy League universities have retained their independent status and have been joined, in tertiary education, by a multitude of other private institutions. This helps to provide much greater variety and responsiveness to consumer demand, as well as many more tertiary places in proportion to population in the United States compared with the United Kingdom. Those looking for a system of higher education that attracts the maximum amount of resources at the minimum cost to the public exchequer and that provides flexibility in meeting changes in consumer demand (which in turn is likely to reflect changing demands in the economy) might prefer a system that leaves greater scope for private initiative than does the British model; Hong Kong's shortfall in technical and business education might be remedied more speedily under such a system. Within the last few years a group of Hong Kong businessmen have, in fact, founded an independent tertiary institution, the University of East Asia, but owing to the Hong Kong ban on private universities this has had to be established in Macau.

Chinese families, even the poor, have a deep-rooted tradition of willingness to pay for the education of their children. In China today, many schools charge fees. This leads to more resources being devoted to education than would be the case if public coffers were the only source of funds. Also, it is likely to result in more value being attached to education than if it were free. In Hong Kong, the authorities have been torn between these considerations and modern Western ideology which dictates that education, at least at lower levels, should be free, regardless of parental means. The outcome is that primary and junior secondary schooling in government and aided schools is free, while below-cost fees are charged at senior secondary and higher levels, subject to remissions, grants and loans on a means-tested basis. In this matter, China would be ill-advised to follow Hong Kong in abandoning fees for the lower stages of education for those who can afford to pay. There is a wide variation in quality in schools in China, even if comparison is confined to those in cities. 'Key' schools attract a disproportionate share of resources. The pupils at these schools are mostly children of higher cadres and other privileged groups. A per capita or voucher system of funding education, by which each child at any given level of education, at least within any one city, was allotted the same amount of public funds, would ensure that the extra costs of the 'elite' schools were covered by the families of their pupils, instead of by taxes levied largely on poorer people. Rural schools are funded in a manner different to those in cities, and their administration is very localized, so that it might be impracticable to organize such a system over an area wider than a single municipality. Nevertheless, within a municipality it would seem to have much to commend it.

Since the Cultural Revolution, university entrants in China have come predominantly from urban upper class families. This may be economically rational, because both family background and environment may well result in these students yielding higher returns than others to any given educational investment. However, this is no reason why they should be subsidized by those poorer, less privileged and less gifted than themselves. In China, the present small number of places in higher education is more likely to be filled by those from the top echelons of society than the proportionately more numerous (but still inadequate) tertiary education places in Hong Kong. Therefore the case for university fees (with scholarships or loans for the needy) is even stronger in China than in Hong Kong.

The threefold system of government, assisted and private institutions that is found in Hong Kong's schooling system also operates in health services in Hong Kong. In this field the government sector bulks larger than in education, accounting for 46 per cent of hospital beds in 1979–80 (compared with 42 per cent in government-assisted, and 12 per cent in private hospitals) while for hospital outpatients, 88 per cent of attendances were at government institutions.

The financial benefits to the government from the involvement of voluntary bodies in health services are greater than the part of health costs that these bodies meet directly. If a government institution overruns its budget, the excess has to be met by the government; with a voluntary, assisted organization, the government can lay down a figure for the subvention it is to receive whether by way of a deficiency grant or as a lump sum, after which the responsibility rests with the organization's management.

Voluntary agencies in Hong Kong have also been prominent in other social services as well as in education and health. The first homes for abandoned babies, for the blind and for the aged were established by religious organizations with links abroad which were also prominent in meeting the needs of refugees from 1949 onwards. Other major voluntary welfare institutions, such as the Tung Wah Group of Hospitals, are wholly Chinese in origin and control. When new activity is required by changing situations, voluntary societies can switch rapidly, while government bodies move more ponderously. The operation of a vigorous voluntary sector harnesses the creative efforts of numerous individuals and groups whose energies would otherwise remain untapped, with resulting frustration to themselves and loss to the community. The willingness and ability of the Hong Kong authorities to make use of voluntary effort both from within Hong Kong and from abroad has been immensely beneficial and has been a necessary corollary of the Hong Kong Government's determination not to overstretch its own direct activities.

In certain circles in Hong Kong the opinion is expressed that the prominent role of voluntary agencies in running social services should be only a temporary phenomenon, yielding in time to more complete provision by the government itself. This would seem to indicate an over-confidence in the ability of government to extend its sphere without a loss of effectiveness and without diminishing the sum total of creative efforts in the welfare field. If government is to do well the massive tasks which no one else can do, it must leave to non-government agencies everything that can possibly be done by them. In a mature community the role of non-government agencies should be growing rather than declining. Voluntary agencies, in turn, should limit their demands, not expecting to have both complete control and full government funding of their activities. Indeed, the need to obtain financial support from the public can be a healthy inducement to keeping in touch with what is really needed and with the manner in which it should be provided.

The prominence of the voluntary sector in the provision of social services encourages private donations for these purposes. For the wealthy, this avenue of expenditure, with the public esteem it brings, can provide a spur to generating further wealth when the prospect of additional material consumption palls. In this way, the provision of social services provides incentive to entrepreneurial activity, not a disincentive as when such services are funded by taxation.

In addition to government partnership with voluntary agencies in social services and welfare, Hong Kong draws great advantage from the way in which private individuals, and representatives of non-government organizations, contribute to public life through membership of government-appointed advisory committees. These bodies are found in different sectors of economic and social affairs and in local government, and are especially significant in view of the small role that the constitutional limitations of Hong Kong place on the representation of interest groups through elections.

The degree of economic management attempted by the government of Hong Kong has been kept within the bounds of what can be implemented. In China, on the contrary, the government has attempted to control more than the capacity of its administrative structure can manage. Instead of pursuing a planned programme, the Chinese Government has lurched from one crisis to another, with successive violent shifts in economic policy. Therefore, in fact, the Hong Kong authorities may be said to have had more effective control in economic matters than their counterparts on the mainland.

Entrepreneurship, Capital and Labour

The great impetus to industrial growth in Hong Kong came with the exodus of industrialists from Shanghai and other Chinese cities at the time of the Communist victory in 1949. A simultaneous outflow of peasants and others from neighbouring Guangdong, as well as from further afield, provided willing and eager labour. While the initial attraction to both entrepreneurs and workers was the law and liberty available in Hong Kong, they also found other circumstances which enabled them to flourish.

The free movement of capital in and out of Hong Kong, and freedom to remit profits abroad, attracted funds from elsewhere which supplemented the capital (often in the form of equipment) which the Chinese refugee industrialists brought with them. A high rate of saving within Hong Kong was another source of capital. This saving was voluntary, unlike the saving under official pressure which has been common on the mainland, and thus it in no way acted as a deterrent to earning. Rather, the possibilities of profitable investment provided incentive both to earn and to save.

Once the post-1949 industrial development of Hong Kong had been initiated by refugee industrialists and by small local entrepreneurs, these were before long joined by factories established by American, Japanese and European firms which brought not only capital, but also technical and managerial skills and knowledge of foreign markets. The local stock exchanges have played a smaller role in raising finance for industry than for public utilities and for property development. Their complex and somewhat chequered history has been marked by feverish bouts of activity, with reluctant government intervention in such forms as the Securities Ordinance of 1974, which set up the Securities Commission, and by the decision in 1981 to establish a unified stock exchange. However, securities trading in Hong Kong has had a part in teaching the public the methods by which funds can be freely assembled for constructive as well as for speculative purposes. It has been one of the elements which has contributed to making Hong Kong a significant international financial centre. The closeness of contact with other centres is a striking feature of Hong Kong — there can be few places where branch offices of sharebroking firms of so many nationalities can be found and where the latest prices from so many overseas stock exchanges are eagerly followed. One result is that even moderately well-to-do Hong Kong families are apt to hold some of their capital overseas, in the form of real estate or shares. The willingness of the Hong Kong authorities to permit this makes Hong Kong attractive as a place for wealthy people to invest in and to live in. Otherwise, many rich Chinese, including talented entrepreneurs and professionals, who now live in Hong Kong (although sometimes with other passports in their pockets) would have gone to live elsewhere.

Hong Kong provides a congenial atmosphere for entrepreneurs. The examples of outstanding individual success that have marked, and contributed to, Hong Kong's recent development, together with an air of well-being brought about by a rapid general rise in living standards, results in an appreciation of economic creativity and an absence of envy at seeing it rewarded. There is not the desire to 'cut down the tall poppies' found in slower-growing economies. This feeling that opportunity exists for the able and lucky to rise in wealth and status goes a long way to allay discontent at unequal distribution of income, which, in any case, has probably not been increased in the course of Hong Kong's economic growth.[2]

Entrepreneurship is a scarce resource, invaluable to economic development. It is not the same as management and cannot be replaced by a diffusion of managerial techniques as the Chinese authorities have seemed in recent years to imagine. Rather, entrepreneurship presupposes a completely different outlook on life and on power to that officially fostered in China since 1949, which postulates that the Party or Government should be the source of initiative in all spheres. That is not to say that entrepreneurs have been absent in China, even in Maoist days. The frequent denunciation over the years of spontaneous capitalists, particularly in Shanghai, provides evidence to the contrary.[3]

In the last few years China has proclaimed a new policy towards small private enterprises. Whereas hitherto these had been denounced, they are now to be permitted. However, they are still circumscribed by severe limitations. For example, apart from family members, only a handful of employees are allowed.[4] Hong Kong provides an example of how, in a good environment and with the right supporting institutions, small industrial undertakings can contribute to export-oriented industrial development, and of how this can accord harmoniously with traditional and instinctive Chinese modes of social organization. In 1977, enterprises with fewer that 50 workers constituted 92 per cent of Hong Kong's total manufacturing establishments, provided 40 per cent of total employment in manufacturing industry and accounted for 29 per cent of the value added by manufacturing. These small enterprises exported around 37 per cent of their gross value in 1976. Between 1971–7 they increased their employment by 50 per cent; in these years total employment in all manufacturing rose by 34 per cent. Most Hong Kong small enterprises are family or individual businesses, with the original capital coming from personal and family savings and private borrowing.[5]

Many of the original small entrepreneurs were Cantonese refugees. Few had any technical education but most had experience as industrial operatives. They tended to set up in business in lines in which they had had experience, uninfluenced in their choice by any government advice. A high proportion of their profits was ploughed back in their businesses.[6]

Two very significant factors in the development of small industry in Hong Kong, and especially in its entry into export markets, were, first, the marketing mechanism which already existed in Hong Kong at the time of the initial growth and, second, the availability of finance. Substantial Western merchant houses had engaged in entrepôt trade in Hong Kong since the nineteenth century. When this activity was cut off at the time of the Communist victory in China in 1949, they looked for other lines of business. They took the initiative in giving orders to the small industrial establishments that were springing up in Hong Kong. The merchant houses had long experience of the markets in Europe and North America and they gave their suppliers the designs and specifications, and operated the quality controls, to meet the demands of those markets. This meant that the small enterprises could concentrate on production under a type of arrangement, working on commission for merchants, which was traditional in the Chinese economy. The multiplicity of merchant houses in Hong Kong (in 1962 there were thought to be at least 1,000 engaged in the export trade)[7] provided competition and made it unlikely that any manufacturer would become dependent on a single merchant.

Orders from merchants were accepted by banks in Hong Kong as security for loans for working capital. The availability of finance has been a vital factor in the growth of Hong Kong's small-scale industry.

Bank loans have been made not only for working capital but also for medium- and long-term purposes; so that whereas the initial capital for small manufacturing concerns usually came from the proprietors' own resources, funds for expansion — land, buildings and equipment — could be obtained from the banking system. The willingness and ability of banks to finance industry has been partly due to the profits obtained from the foreign exchange transactions of their clients. Competition between banks in Hong Kong, especially from the 1960's onwards, has meant that in finance, as in merchanting, local enterprises have had a choice with whom to deal.[8]

Certain characteristics of Hong Kong's small industrial undertakings are worthy of note. They are not cottage industries. Their machinery is normally modern and they have been swift in adopting new technology. Productivity in Hong Kong's small industries is not much below that in large factories while the return on capital is higher.[9] At the same time they have enjoyed the advantages of smallness, especially more flexibility in comparison with larger undertakings in which the greater amount of equipment per worker makes it more expensive to switch between processes and products. While economies of scale are important in the textile industry, this is much less significant in the garment industry — especially with fashion garments — where the ability to change quickly is essential.

In the case of flexibility between industries, Chinese family firms are often well placed, because they frequently have interests in a number of lines and can shift funds easily from one to another as changing profitability directs.[10]

The advantages enjoyed by small enterprises in Hong Kong, which have enabled them to make an immense contribution to economic growth, have depended on a restraint on the part of government which has been notably lacking in China. Large concerns can and do negotiate special terms with governments in many countries but small undertakings depend on the congeniality of the political and economic environment as a whole. In Hong Kong, entrepreneurs of all sizes and nationalities have been able to retain most of their profits and to choose freely their fields of activity. A private enterprise banking system has operated, with international links, as have also merchant houses from many lands. The great number of foreign contacts has facilitated the rapid introduction of new technology. Such technology is often initially introduced by transnational companies from which, however, local Hong Kong interests are quick to learn. Joint ventures between Chinese and foreign companies flourished in Hong Kong long before the idea of joint ventures was taken up by the Communist authorities in China. Businesses in Hong Kong are free to employ the number and type of workers they want. Chinese family structures have proved a good foundation for the growth of small enterprises, a circumstance which the Chinese Government is now seeking to harness to its economic policies.

The interdependence of the various sectors of the economy, for example, industry, merchanting and banking, is another area in which the Chinese cities can learn from Hong Kong's experience. If industrial development is sought, it is insufficient to give scope and encouragement just to industrial undertakings; to say, for example, that private enterprises, whether local or foreign, will be permitted in industry, if similar permission is not allowed for the complementary activities of commerce and finance. Freedom of contact between the different sectors must be permitted in order that the advantages of competition be realized. The benefits of free entry of foreign firms into all sectors of the economy, and of informal contacts and free association with foreigners, are also apparent.

Hong Kong illustrates that it is not necessary for the government to give active assistance to small enterprises, though in recent years the Hong Kong Government has in fact done so, as long as government measures do not actually harm the business environment, and as long as the government performs its essential functions of ensuring law and order, a sound currency and freedom from onerous imposts and regulations. No special assistance can compensate for the lack of these preconditions. Given these essentials, Chinese business ability would be as likely to flourish in Shanghai and Tianjin as it does in Hong Kong and Singapore. Opportunities are more important than subsidies.

One of the sharpest social divisions in present-day China is between those in regular jobs in state enterprises and organs on the one hand, and the urban unemployed on the other. In so far as state employees are often allowed to pass on their jobs to their children, or state enterprises set up ancillary undertakings especially to provide employment for workers' children, this division is becoming hereditary. The social contrast is particularly sharp in large cities, where wage rates tend to be higher than elsewhere and where the young are more likely to have grown up expecting employment in industry. Now that this expectation is not being fulfilled for many of them, they are having to content themselves with casual labour or with various forms of self-employment or co-operative work. This is similar to the situation in many Western economies. In both cases the existence of fixed, or at least sticky, wages has benefited those fortunate enough to be in secure employment at the expense of those, especially young entrants to the labour force, who are not. Hong Kong has in this respect avoided the mistakes of both Communism and of the West, at least until recently. In times of recession, Hong Kong workers have accepted wage cuts and work-sharing arrangements, thus equalizing the burden rather than heaping it on to some, who lose their jobs, while the others maintain their previous incomes. When demand increases there is willingness to work long hours of overtime.[11] Another manifestation of wage flexibility in Hong Kong is the widespread use of piece-rates. Together with this flexibility in the labour market, there also goes a measure of protection introduced by the government: health and safety regulations, minimum age of entrants, restriction on hours of work for women and young people, workers' compensation, a minimum number of rest days and holidays, and so on. In such matters the government has to tread a tightrope between giving the weak some protection, but not pricing them out of a job by making the least productive workers too expensive to employ.

The close connection between wages and productivity in Hong Kong arising from the relative flexibility of wages, the absence of the 'iron rice bowls' — the permanent tenure which in China (unlike in Japan) appears to have been a factor in making workers apathetic — and the belief that it is possible to better one's condition by hard work and intelligence — all these have led to Hong Kong having a highly motivated labour force. The first generation of workers in Hong Kong after 1949 were self-selected, consisting of those with the energy, initiative and desire to escape from Communist rule. Many of them came from a peasant background — that is, they had been self-employed and realized that a living had to be earned. In entering industrial employment they felt, like peasants in all developing countries, that they were rising in the world. They have also known all along, even in the early days when conditions in Hong Kong were grim, that their standard of living was well above that of their relatives across the border. Most, too, were glad to be free of the political campaigns and impositions to which those who remained in China were subject.

All this explains why the inequalities highly visible in Hong Kong have not caused the distress to most local workers that they do to some visitors from overseas. A feeling that one is upwardly mobile, a rapidly rising standard of living, opportunities for children to make their way, a sense of relief at having escaped: these circumstances allay jealousy of those who have done better in the world. As time goes by, and a new generation born and bred in Hong Kong takes over, some of these factors may become less significant.

In the Chinese cities, many, but not all, forms of inequality are less apparent; however, less visible inequalities in both living standards and power abound. Higher living standards are usually connected with official position, and are perks of office rather than the effect of personal wealth. The growth of private and collective enterprises and the more permissive attitude now adopted towards personal enrichment have, however, modified this situation. In any case, overt inequality arising from personal wealth, such as is found in Hong Kong, may well arouse less resentment than that coming from official position, especially in a society where general living standards are rising fast, where examples of rapid upward mobility abound and where inequality is not increasing.

Export Orientation

Hong Kong is one of the foremost examples of export-led growth. It forms a notable contrast to the many *dirigiste* economies which have concentrated on import substitution. The successful countries of the developing world are 'those which have resisted or overcome the temptation to adopt inward-looking trade policies and to delay transition to greater export orientation.'[12] Where the direction of development has been controlled by government, the planners' preference has usually been for import substitution rather than for export orientation. This is largely because import substitution is readily amenable to control. The factories which are to produce import substitutes are set up, the former imports are banned, and thereupon import substitution has occurred. The economic costs of this policy are no less onerous for being often difficult to quantify. The substitutes, produced by a plant which may well be a local monopolist, are very likely of inferior quality, though of equal or higher cost, compared with the displaced imports. The consumers no longer have a choice. Export orientation, on the contrary, provides a constant spur to efficiency, because foreign customers cannot be compelled to buy unsatisfactory goods but must be sold what they want, when they want it. This necessitates the pattern of production being frequently adjusted in response to changing demand. All these circumstances irk the practitioners of a planned, command economy.

Export orientation tends to lead to concentration on a fairly narrow range of industries for which the resource endowment of the economy concerned gives it a relative advantage. Thus Hong Kong has concentrated on textiles, garments, toys and, in recent years, electronic goods, photographic equipment, watches and clocks; tourism should also be included in the export sector of Hong Kong's economy. In Shanghai, the planners, perhaps more particularly the municipal planners, have grafted a heavy industry sector on to the city's original light industry base. On purely economic criteria, Shanghai should very likely have followed Hong Kong's path, which indeed would have been a continuation of Shanghai's own previous road, of concentrating first on the simpler types of consumer goods and then entering the field of more technical products for overseas markets. Shanghai could also supply cheaper goods of the same types for the domestic market in the interior and in the other cities of the China coast, in so far as these markets were not supplied by lower cost producers in other parts of the country or elsewhere.

In this way China would have benefited from regional specialization while at the same time boosting export earnings. As it was, each large municipality, and each province, strove for the maximum degree of self-sufficiency. The index of self-sufficiency (the percentage of consumer manufactures, and of agricultural produce, coming from within its own boundaries) became something to be maximized. This led to autarkic tendencies within territorial administrative units in China, which in this way became fragmented into a set of cellular economies.[13] An official Chinese commentator relates how

> leading administrative organs in some areas, in the name of protecting local industry and commerce and manufacturing complete sets of equipment locally, prohibited the purchasing of advanced products from other parts of the country. Some areas used means such as the bank refusing to pay for the products purchased and supplying no fuel for the buyers to force them to cancel the contracts and return the products already bought. Such artificially imposed barriers block the normal channels of circulation of commodities ... The quality of electrical machinery produced in Tianjin is not as good as that produced in Shanghai. In the past, Tianjin banned the purchase of electrical machinery from Shanghai in order to 'protect' local products. As a result, production units in Tianjin stood still and ... failed to improve the quality of their products for a long time.

Early in 1980 electrical machines from Shanghai were permitted to be sold in Tianjin with the result that the local products were soon improved.[14]

Tourism is an export industry which has flourished in Hong Kong and which China is now trying to boost. A competitive market economy, in which business has to strive to satisfy the consumer, provides a better environment for tourism than an economy which has not had to trouble too much about consumer tastes. The tourist, unlike the consumer in a planned economy, can take his patronage elsewhere if he dislikes what is offered in one place. Chinese service sectors catering for overseas tourists have had to undergo radical changes and learn new methods to cater for the new and critical customers. In hotel management, restaurants and retailing, and other facilities, Hong Kong has much experience and skill from which the Chinese metropolises could learn. Spin-offs for the internal market might also come about from, for example, improvements in retailing adopted first for tourists and later transferred to the domestic economy.

Agriculture and the Inter-Regional Division of Labour

In agriculture, Hong Kong's practice of free trade has meant that farming in the New Territories has become specialized in the production of those lines for which the benefit of proximity to the urban market outweighs Hong Kong's higher labour costs compared with neighbouring regions of China. Vegetables, poultry, eggs, pigs, flowers and pond fish are Hong Kong's chief farm products. The area under rice in Hong Kong fell from 9,450 hectares in 1954 to only 40 hectares in 1979, while between the same years land under vegetables and flowers rose from 910 hectares to 3,490 hectares.[15] The great municipalities of China, including Shanghai, Beijing and Tianjin, resemble Hong Kong in having considerable agricultural areas within their boundaries. In agriculture, as in industry, these Chinese municipalities are less specialized than Hong Kong and have deliberately aimed at attaining as high a degree of self-sufficiency as possible. Thus the Municipality of Shanghai's grain deficit was reduced from around one million tons in 1965 to about half that figure in 1974.[16] Beijing Municipality, too, through deliberate policy achieved something of the order of 75 per cent self-sufficiency in grain in 1978.[17] A high degree of self-sufficiency in vegetables has also existed in Beijing Municipality (in 1960 entire self-sufficiency was reported),[18] but this was at a level of supply which sometimes entailed severe shortages. In the Chinese context, in which no great reliance has at times been able to be placed on the certainty of getting interprovincial supplies, a policy of local self-sufficiency made some sense. However, had trade across provincial and municipal boundaries been freely conducted and determined by the market, a more economically efficient allocation of factors of production might have resulted. Although the outcome in any or all of the great Chinese municipalities might have diverged from the Hong Kong experience, it is likely that a product range more similar to that found in Hong Kong agriculture would have come about. If this was the case, the coastal cities would draw their easily transportable staples in greater measure than at present from abroad or from the interior of China. If comparative advantage had replaced local planners as the decisive factor, another difference would be that at least some of Shanghai's present heavy industry would have been developed elsewhere, probably in north-east China, the historic home of this sector. The north-east, in turn, would not have attempted the partial diversification into consumer goods industries which has come about, but would have continued to rely almost entirely on Shanghai and other areas for such products.

Since 1976 there has been much talk about greater division of labour between the different regions of China. Some progress in this direction has been achieved as a result of the greater scope now being allowed to market forces. However, substantial elements of a command economy still remain — deliberately so, since policy is that planning should be the dominant factor in the economy with the market as an auxiliary. Thus the dynamic possibilities for growth opened up by the free play of comparative advantage have not been realized.[19]

A scenario, which comparison with Hong Kong suggests, is of a China in which the great cities and favoured provinces — Shanghai, Tianjin and Guangdong, for example — bound ahead through export-led growth. Then, in their turn, the provinces of the interior would develop rapidly through internal 'exports' of foodstuffs, raw materials and simple manufactures to the coastal growth centres. Such a China would have discarded the cellular 'small but complete' fragmented economies of the 1960's and 1970's and would be pushing forward to join the company of the 'four tigers' of rapidly developing medium-income communities of East Asia — Hong Kong, Singapore, Taiwan and South Korea.

Certain obvious differences exist between a 'detached' unit such as Hong Kong on the one hand, and on the other the great Chinese municipalities which are embedded in a huge polity. Much of the revenues of Shanghai and the other cities are siphoned off for central use, which includes military expenditure, an item which weighs lightly on the Hong Kong budget. Doubt may be felt about the official claim that 90 per cent of Shanghai's revenue is remitted to the centre; Shanghai has many of the cleverest accountants in China and probably, by one means or another, more of Shanghai's revenues may remain at home than appears. However, be that as it may, large sums are remitted to the centre. Some claim that this is part of a nationwide equalization scheme, to lessen differences in living standards between wealthy coastal municipalities and impoverished inland provinces. Sceptics may rather consider that the expenditure from these revenues, including expenditure in the interior, is largely for the centre's political purposes rather than for local welfare. Even central subsidies to those provincial level units in chronic deficit — almost all being peripheral regions of strategic importance — can be argued to be little more than provision for expenditure on one form or other of defence-related costs. At the same time, the municipalities can be reminded that much of the profits of their consumer goods industries results from the state-enforced high prices obtained in the domestic market and that it is reasonable that such profits should be taxed away for national purposes. There can clearly be wide-ranging argument as to how far the lessons of Hong Kong's experience can be applied to the different circumstances of the Chinese municipalities.

It might be illuminating to examine the economic outreach of Hong Kong and, for example, Shanghai into their respective hinterlands and compare their roles in this respect. Unfortunately the basic research to enable such a comparison to be made is lacking. Both are major growth centres which have stimulated the regions near them and it is to be hoped that in future it will be possible to investigate this topic in a comparative manner.

Conclusion

The difference between the economies of Hong Kong and the great cities of China consists not just in the use of techniques which can be swiftly transplanted from one milieu to another. Rather it is one of fundamental philosophy and of a whole different outlook on life. Basic to Hong Kong's economic success has been the rule of law and all that is implied by it, including an acceptance by government that its power should not be arbitrary or absolute.

Notes

[1] *BBC Summary of World Broadcasts*, FE/6226/BII/15–16 New China News Agency, September 7, 1979.

[2] See S.C. Chow and G.F. Papanek (1981), 'Laissez-Faire, Growth and Equity — Hong Kong', *Economic Journal*, June, vol. 91, No. 362.

[3] In 1957 hundreds of 'clandestine industrial establishments' were said to exist in Shanghai. *People's Daily* (Renmin Ribao), October 13, 1957, p. 4. 'Several million' private industrial and commercial undertakings were believed to operate in China in 1959. *Finance (Caizheng)*, No. 18, September 24, 1959, p. 30. In September 1962 the Plenary Session of the Party Central Committee referred in its communique to the 'spontaneous tendency towards capitalism among part of the smaller producers.' New China News Agency, Beijing, September 28, 1962.

[4] 'In China, the manager of an individually run enterprise can, with the approval of the government, hire one or two assistants, or take on two or three (but not more than five) apprentices for a job that requires highly technical knowledge or special skills.' *Beijing Review*, No. 50, December 14, 1981, p. 26.

[5] V.F.S. Sit, S.L. Wong and T.S. Kiang (1979), *Small Scale Industry in a Laissez-Faire Economy: A Hong Kong Case Study* (Hong Kong, Centre for Asian Studies, University of Hong Kong), pp. 398, 405, and 21; and K. Hopkins (ed.), *Hong Kong: The Industrial Colony* (Hong Kong, Oxford University Press, 1971), p. 10.

[6] V.F.S. Sit, S.L. Wong and T.S. Kiang, pp. 402–4; and T.B Lin, R.P.L. Lee and U.E. Simonis (eds.), *Hong Kong: Economic, Social & Political Studies in Development* (New York, M.E. Sharpe, 1979), pp. 66–7.

[7] K. Hopkins (ed.), p. 12.

[8] Y.C. Jao (1982), 'Financial Structure and Monetary Policy in Hong Kong,' in S.Y. Lee and Y.C. Jao, *Financial Structures and Monetary Policies in Southeast Asia* (London, Macmillan), pp. 7–50. On the role of banks in the industrial development of Hong Kong, see also A.J. Youngson (1982), *Hong Kong Economic Growth and Policy* (Hong Kong, Oxford University Press), pp. 28–35.

[9] T.B. Lin, R.P.L. Lee and U.E. Simonis (eds.), pp. 56–7 and 61; and V.F.S. Sit, S.L. Wong and T.S. Kiang, pp. 398 and 406.

[10] K. Hopkins (ed.), p. 11.

[11] *Report of the Advisory Committee on Diversification* (Hong Kong, Government Printer, 1979), p. 25.

[12] World Bank, *World Development Report 1981* (New York, Oxford University Press), p. 25.

[13] See A. Donnithorne, 'China's Cellular Economy: Some Economic Trends since the Cultural Revolution', *China Quarterly*, No. 52, October–December 1972.

[14] *BBC Summary of World Broadcasts*, FE/6496/BII/5, August 13, 1980; and New China News Agency, August 7, 1980.

[15] *Hong Kong 1980* (Hong Kong, Government Printer, 1981), p. 58.

[16] R. Ash, 'The Quest for Food Self-Sufficiency', in C. Howe (ed.), *Shanghai — Revolution and Development in an Asian Metropolis* (Cambridge, Cambridge University Press, 1981), p. 202.

[17] E.E. Platte, *Farm Production and Rural Income in Beijing Municipality as a Case Study of Agricultural Development in China 1949-1979* (Unpublished Ph.D. thesis, Griffith University, Brisbane, 1982), p. 92.

[18] E.E. Platte, p. 84.

[19] In theory, of course, comparative advantage may be achieved by a rational planning system. In recent years some planned use of the comparative advantage principle has been made in China. However, politicians seldom permit planners much rationality.

Index